To   Mike Loxton

Wishing you a
speedy recovery

Tony Pawson

Chilcomb Nov 26th 1995

Flyfishing Around the World

Flyfishing Around the World

The International Guide for the Gamefisher

Tony Pawson

UNWIN HYMAN
London   Sydney

First published in Great Britain by Unwin Hyman, an imprint of Unwin
Hyman Limited, 1987

UNWIN HYMAN LIMITED
Denmark House, 37–39 Queen Elizabeth Street,
London SE1 2QB
and
40 Museum Street, London WC1A 1LU

Allen & Unwin Australia Pty Ltd
8 Napier Street, North Sydney, NSW 2060, Australia

Allen & Unwin New Zealand Ltd. with the Port Nicholson Press
60 Cambridge Terrace,
Wellington, New Zealand

British Library Cataloguing in Publication Data

Pawson, Tony
  Fly fishing around the world:
  the international guide for the gamefisher.
  1. Fly fishing – Handbooks, manuals, etc.
  I. Title
  799.1'2   SH456
  ISBN: 0–04–799033-3

Set in 10½ on 12 point Plantin by Computape (Pickering) Limited
and printed in Great Britain by Mackays of Chatham

To trout anglers worldwide and to the many who have helped me enjoy the sport and taught me more about it.

Contents

Illustrations

Acknowledgements

My thanks are due to the many who have helped with this book, especially to my brother Philip who has made such a major contribution, and to Hilarie and my children, Anthony, John and Sarah, who have tolerated or assisted my lifetime addiction to fishing, and to John for becoming a much better trout angler than I shall ever be. Particular thanks also to Marguerite Maynard for turning my illegible writing into perfectly typed copy, and to my nephew Richard for his contribution on the Falklands.

I owe special thanks to Dermot Wilson, Graham Swanson, Sidney Vines, Jonathan Niblett, Taff Price, Moc Morgan, Charles Jardine, Jean Howman, Donald Downs, Peter Cockwill, Ian Hay, George Westropp, Brian Peterson, Colonel Mark Conroy, Major Tim Glass, Colonel Alastair Drew, John Goddard, Michael Green, Ron Wilton, Trevor Housby, John Stewart, Brian Geraghty, Peter O'Reilly, David Porter, and Francis Lodge for their much-appreciated contributions.

Many overseas anglers have also greatly assisted in the project, especially Rafael de Madariaga Giraldo for his major help over Spain and the Argentine. My sincere thanks go to the others who have contributed: Bela Sarosi, Christian Fouvez, Paul Vekemans, Erik Berg, Philipe Mathieu, Bertrand Kron, Mogens Esperson, Joachim Bujok, Nigel Montgomery, Jagdip Inder Singh, Carlo Malvosio, Roby Colombero, Eddy Arnauts, Ladislav Elnetti, Jean Zender, Josef Jelenski, Jurek Kowalski, Markku Leinonen, Thorbjørn Tufte, Julius Ytteborg, Juliu Lungu, Robert Southey, Mike Oliver, Mike Scott, Rafe Mair and Janicek Pavel.

I send a fisherman's appreciation to the many who have shown me how to fish their waters. In addition to the above names I am especially grateful to John Sautelle Senior, Jean Delire, Marian Kwasnik, Tony Hayes, Henri Hosinger, Andrew Fink, Terry Piggott, Owen Nuttridge, Jason Garrett, Reinhard Resch and Gerard Tegelaar.

I am also glad to acknowledge the encouragement and advice from Air Vice-Marshal Pat Neville and the assistance from him and Richard Bollard in arranging for me to sample New Zealand's wonderful trout fishing.

Books and references which have been helpful to me include *The Truth about Trout* and *Trout Fishing in Tasmania* by Dr Robert Sloane, *Fishing for the Educated Trout* by John Sautelle, *Brown Trout Trilogy* by Cecil E. Heacox, *Fly Fishing* by Joe Brooks, *Taupo Fishing Guide* by Gary Kemsley, *The Trout* by W. F. Frost and M. E. Brown, *About Trout* by Robert J. Behnke, *Freshwater Fishing in South Africa* by Michael G. Salomon and various articles in *The Field*, *Country Life* and the *Journal of the Flyfishers' Club*.

Introduction

Trout have always had an almost mystical attraction for fishermen, who are captivated by their beautiful colouring and nice symmetry. God or Nature, whichever you will, made man a hunter-gatherer, and the catching of trout has exercised in him a timeless and world-wide fascination. The sport, and the skills that fly fishing for trout inspires, are some two thousand years old. Writing in AD 200, Aelian outlined the method of catching 'fish of speckled hue' in north-east Greece. These rose to flies on Macedonia's Astraeus river. Fishing for them with artificial flies was already well established, as he described: 'With an angler's skill the men circumvent the fish with this artful contrivance. They wrap scarlet wool round the hook, and to the wool they attach two feathers that grow beneath a cock's wattles and are the colour of wax. Their fishing rods are six feet long and so are their lines.' How far-flung and deeply ingrained is the tradition of fly fishing for trout!

Spain's *Manuscrito Deastorga*, published in 1624, gives expert advice on fly dressing and the catching of trout. Izaak Walton's *Compleat Angler*, first published in 1653, has run to over four hundred editions or reissues and been translated into many languages. Indeed, the chief collector of this book, the American, Rodolphe Coigney, recently described it as the world's most popular book after the Bible, though much of it is plagiarization of earlier works such as *The Treatyse of Fysshynge with an Angle*. Of all the great variety of fish Walton describes therein the trout remains his first love. His enchantment with it is clear even in the preface, where he writes that 'He that likes not the book, should at least like the excellent picture of the *Trout*'. Later he adds: 'The trout is a fish highly valued in this and foreign nations.'

That enchantment is enhanced for so many of us by the skill required to catch trout, by the magic of their sinuous movement, and by the instinctive thrill of watching them in the water. No wonder the trout has inspired artists and musicians, great writers, and poets, or that millions of dedicated fly fishermen are in tune with these lines of T. C. Yelland's:

The aeroplane that roars across the world
And back again before the day is out
May still evoke less wonder than the curled
Low ripples that are started by a trout.

That is the feeling of wonder which has made trout fishing such a favourite pastime in so many countries. The trout is beneficiary as well as victim of this passionate enthusiasm. Empire builders of several nations have stocked waters previously devoid of trout in areas where now they thrive. So man's love of trout fishing has made up for nature's oversight. In many countries where the trout is indigenous only the anglers have saved them from extinction by fighting careless pollution of waters, poaching with explosives or poisons, and the many menaces from industrialized societies that take little care of their countryside.

'Fishermen are born so,' said Walton, and certainly I was – and a trout fisherman at that. The feeling of wonder has been with me from childhood. My earliest memory is of peering over a bridge in the Scottish Highlands and being captivated by the whispering waters wandering beneath. The swirling eddies, now opening a clear window to the stones below, now clouding over like frosted glass, hinted at mysterious life below. Aged just five I was enthralled then and the fascination has grown stronger over the years. My hunter's instinct was stirred, too, as I slid down the bank, hid behind a bush, and lowered my worm. As if by magic the line went as taut as my nerves and a moment later a small trout sailed over my head into the heather. By six I was fly fishing for trout, and I have enjoyed the infinite variations of that technique as much as the infinite subtle changes in the colouring of the trout in different waters and different parts of the world. For me, part of the lasting attraction of trout fishing has been in sampling that variety of method and of flies. Wet fly or dry, nymph or daddy-long-legs, shortlining or long, dapping or bobbing the dropper, floating line or sinker – each has appeal for me. That appeal has taken me to many countries and the many expert contributors to this book have fired my ambition to visit others. Happily, my elder brother, Philip, shares that love of trout fishing and we have enjoyed it together over the years. He too has fished in many countries and has now made a major contribution to this book.

Trout fishing takes you to beautiful places and gives you a freedom of spirit and a heightened imagination with which to enjoy them to the full. Virginia Woolf in her essay 'Fishing' echoed J. W. Hills's evocative description of this aspect of the sport: 'I felt receptive to every sight, every colour, and every sound, as though I walked through a world from which a veil had been withdrawn.' When fishing we are indeed born free again and see with the clear and wondering eyes of childhood. In the countries covered in this book there are many trout waters where the scenery is as compelling as the fishing, and for most of us the surroundings enhance the sport itself. Robert Venables summed that up as early as 1663: 'Suppose the angler should catch nothing yet he enjoyeth a delightful walk by pleasant rivers in sweet pastures among odoriferous flowers which gratify his senses and delight his mind.'

All honest anglers, however, will admit that catching a few fish tends to heighten that pleasure. So the purpose of this book is not only to point to the range of trout fishing available and the many delightful places in the world in which it may be enjoyed. It is also to help the angler to plan a visit to any that excite, and to be aware of some of the best fishing and of the flies and methods most likely to bring success. Or you may simply share in imagination the variety of fishing experiences and characters portrayed in the tales from distant countries. The choice from over sixty, and the emphasis given to particular countries, reflects only a personal view, since space prevents covering all in detail. Many of them I have yet to visit myself, but writing this book has given me the excuse to try trout fishing in several new regions and the will to sample many more.

Fly fishing for trout has always been my passion, but that art has many subdivisions and if you add in all the other methods there are almost as many varieties of fishing as there are subspecies of trout. In the first such species classification in 1758 Linnaeus listed *Salmo trutta*, then added *fario* and *lacustris*. By now to *Salmo trutta*, the archetypal species of the trout, some fifty new racial variants have been added. Since Linnaeus's time trout have also spread more widely through the world as British, German, French and American anglers introduced them to distant lands. Antarctica is now the only continent without the trout which originated in the cold Arctic waters some 70 million years ago.

During the much more recent glacial epoch trout swam ahead of the ice sheet spreading southward. Then, when the ice finally retreated 10,000 years ago, they left behind resident populations in the furthest places they had reached, while others migrated north again, stocking the rivers and lakes as they went. Thus the natural distribution of brown trout ranged from northern Norway and north-western Russia to the Atlas Mountains of North Africa in the south, and from Iceland in the west to Afghanistan in the east, where their further progress was halted by the mountain barrier of the Hindu Kush. Similarly a separate species of trout, *Salmo gairdneri*, the rainbow trout, spread from the Aleutian islands along the west coast of America to the mountains of north Mexico, while to the east of the Rockies the rivers and lakes of Canada and the northern United States were populated by varieties of the closely related char, including brook trout (*Salvelinus fontinalis*), Arctic char (*Salvelinus alpinus*) and lake trout (*Salvelinus namaycush*), but no browns or rainbows. The third main subspecies of 'true' trout, the cut-throat (*Salmo clarki*), is indigenous only to the Rocky mountains of North America.

Subspecies of trout crop up in unusual places and new ones may be found at any time only to disappear again. Robert Behnke recently referred to three such from his own researches.

In 1974, during a fishery survey in Iran, Behnke was introduced to a previously unrecorded subspecies with a remarkable profusion of small red and black spots. This was local to one small stream, the Ligvan Chai south-east of Tabriz in the Rezaiyeh Lake desert basin. This was derived in turn from another subspecies, the Caspian basin brown trout, but isolation had brought substantial change.

In 1967 he received three specimens of a trout from Turkey which had no markings at all and which he named *Salmo platycephalus*. He is unaware of any others coming since from the Taurus Mountain streams. In 1924 the British Museum acquired four trout from Lake Algueman in Morocco, which he later examined. These had mottled markings on the head but none on the body, and he doubts now if there are any of this specialized variety left. In all its many manifestations it is the brown trout that has had attraction for skilful anglers, partly because it is the most difficult to deceive. So difficult, in fact, that some of the more romantic fishing 'philosophers' tend to ascribe a human brain to it and talk as if it is an equal battle of wits instead of man's intelligence against the fish's natural instinct. *Salmo trutta* is on all statistical evidence much harder to catch than the rainbow, which in turn is more difficult than brook or cut-throat trout. Naturally it was the brown trout that keen anglers first introduced to many new lands.

Typical of the drive for distant stocking was Lord Delamere's approach to the founding of a settlement in Africa. To a friend he wrote: 'What the white settlers will want to find there is wheat in their fields and trout in their rivers. You fix the trout, and I will look after the wheat.' It was the difficult job he left to his friend! Only after twenty years of failure had trout been stocked in Australia in 1864, and thence in New Zealand in 1867. Thereafter the pace quickened, but the problems remained in those days of long, slow voyages and no modern refrigeration. By the 1860s commercial trout farms had started in France, Germany and Britain, stocking brown trout into rivers. In America brook trout were stocked, with Seth Green pioneering many of the techniques of trout culture, hybridization and transfer. It was probably Seth Green who brought rainbows from the west coast to the east in the early 1870s. The first consignment of brown trout ova to the United States was sent from Germany in 1883 by Baron von Behr to Fred Mather, another eminent American angler and culturist. In the United States these were originally known as 'von Behr's trout' or 'German browns'. The following year ova of the Loch Leven strain of brown trout were sent from Britain to New York, and another consignment to Newfoundland, and about the same time rainbow ova from America were sent to Delaford Fish Farm in Buckinghamshire, in which Francis Francis and Frank Buckland, the men who stocked trout in Australia, had an interest. Others were sent to Howietoun in Stirlingshire. Also at this time rainbows were sent from America to New Zealand to start the legend of Taupo and the remarkable rainbow explosion there.

Trout thrive in well oxygenated waters with suitable spawning grounds and temperatures cold enough for their ova to survive to hatching (below 54°F for browns and 57°F for rainbows). Where the food supply is good enough they can grow to great size. In the new museum at Turangi in New Zealand there is a faded photograph of an angler with a day's catch from Taupo of 78 rainbows averaging over ten pounds. The current rod-and-reel-caught record brown trout recognized by the International Game Fish Association is a specimen of 35 lb 15 oz caught in Argentina, since the well documented brown trout of 39½ pounds from Loch Awe in 1866 is not accepted as authenticated. A commercial fisherman is said to have taken a trout of 68 lb from the Wolfgangsee in the early 1900s with many others over fifty pounds. The Caspian Sea area, now with only rare remnant populations of trout, was noted for even larger trout, with Berg citing a report of one of 72 pounds taken from the Kura River in 1897 and another of 112 pounds as unverified. The record rainbow of 48 pounds was taken from a Canadian Kamloops Lake after such mountain lakes had been first stocked in the early 1900s. When the feed was good enough such massive weights were possible, although conditions no longer seem to exist for such growth.

Following their success in introducing browns to Australia and thence to New Zealand, the British found that trout could thrive in many lands far beyond the limits of their natural distribution. Surmounting the daunting problems that had to be overcome in those days, they took them to the Cape area in South Africa, to the high streams of Africa's equatorial regions, across India to Kashmir, and to the far south in Argentina and Chile. It is a strange fact of nature that no indigenous fish of importance had earlier evolved to inhabit the cold high-altitude streams around the Equator, or those of the southern hemisphere where trout thrive so well. The rainbows of North America were soon to follow the browns to distant parts of the world – to Australasia, Africa and South America, as well as to Europe and the British Isles. The acclimatization of both browns and rainbows to these areas has left a wealth of choice for the trout fisherman in search of new experience, or an Eldorado of trout fishing. What follows is a sample from many countries, rather than an exhaustive survey.

Perhaps I have omitted your own Eldorado or done less than justice to a country rich in trout fishing. If so, please write and tell me. Who knows? This book might in time run to a revised edition. The chief delight of trout fishing is that there is always something new to learn.

May 1987
Manor House, Chilcomb
Nr Winchester
Hants SO21 1HR
England

Go Fish Australia!

From Tasmania to Papua New Guinea

'Go Fish Australia' is a slogan for the country's bicentenary year, 1988, which should have appeal for trout fishermen world-wide. For there rainbows and browns grow fast and run large, whether in Tasmania's myriad lakes or in the dark, peat-bottomed rivers and startlingly clear basalt streams of New South Wales, or in the swift waters of the Snowy Mountains. Apart from a cheap general licence all fishing is free, except for a few privately constructed and privately owned waters such as the beautiful London lakes in Tasmania. The growth rate is best illustrated by the giant trout of Lake Pedder in Tasmania and by two tales from John Sautelle, doyen of Australian fly fishing. In the Black Lake close to his home at Bibbenluke the largest trout taken recently was a wild brown of over nine pounds, which was only 2½ years old. Close by he pointed out to me a small pond, unfishable at the end of a dry autumn with the water barely visible amid the smothering weed.

'In bad droughts in New South Wales many rivers and small lakes may dry up and the trout be lost. They recover again quickly when restocked because the trout grow so fast. While restocking we put some trout in any water that may be fishable, even for a short period, to reduce fishing pressure on the rest. I even put some in that pond after a rainy year. Some thirty months later I stopped and had a few casts and was broken in the weeds by a big trout. Later a friend fished there with an exceptionally strong leader and caught one eleven pounds. Yet in some years that pond dries up entirely and in most the level hardly rises above the weed growth on the bottom.'

It is in its way a small miracle that there are any trout in Australia at all. Even after more than 120 years they are still not even accorded the status of 'honorary' native fish, and further imports are banned except under exceptional circumstances and with special licence. So only in a tiny window of time since the endless years from creation was it possible for trout to be introduced there. Of all those importations of trout into far-off countries in the past 150 years, that into Australia in 1864 is the most romantic and posed the greatest difficulty. For twenty years they had failed in attempts to ship in salmon as the fry died or the ova addled from the heat of the long voyages or were poisoned by acid from the holding tanks. Learning from successive failures, J. A. Youl finally worked out a way to ship the eggs the 16,000 miles to Tasmania.

Even then the venture seemed doomed when the promised salmon ova were not forthcoming only a fortnight before the sailing date. But a pleading letter in *The Times* brought a ready response, and not only from those donating salmon eggs. Frank Buckland sent 1,000 brown trout eggs – 'regular beauties, taken from the Itchen trout'. Admiral Keppel, who lived in Itchen House at Bishopstoke, had asked Buckland to send these eggs from trout taken from his garden pool. On his own the noted angling author of the day, Francis Francis, contributed another 2,000 eggs in equal lots from the King's Pond at Alton and the River Wick at High Wycombe. The ship's sailing had to be delayed a day to await their arrival and at first Youl was inclined to throw them over into the London Docks as he feared the trout would hatch first and devour the salmon fry.

Happily the eggs were put on board the clipper *Norfolk*, which sailed from London on 21 January, with all the eggs stored in a 56-ton ice-house. The boxes, stacked under 9 feet of ice, were built of one-inch pine and carefully packed to the formula Youl had devised. A couple of handfuls of charcoal were sprinkled on the bottom, then a thin layer of broken ice. A nest of moss was next made and drenched with water before the ova were poured in from a bottle kept full of water. Each box was finally packed with living moss and had pure water poured on until it streamed out of the perforations. A thin layer of ice topped it off before the lid was screwed down. 181 boxes were packed in this way, containing some 100,000 eggs of Atlantic salmon and 3,000 of prime brown trout.

The Itchen strain of trout is still renowned, but the King's Pond, near the source of the Wey, then produced a fine breed of Thames-type trout. With a cornmill in operation there the trout had grown so large that, as Francis wrote, 'The Wycombe and Alton trout reach ten pounds at times and when we went for spawn in the latter place we took out four at once that went much over thirty pounds in total.' The river at High Wycombe, the Wick as it was then called, also flowed into the Thames and also produced a superior strain of trout. Writing as 'Red Quill' in *The Field* in the last century, James Englefield recorded that the Wick *fario* were so much in demand that they had 'been introduced as ova, fry, or yearlings into a hundred rivers near and far, even to the Antipodes. The trout were remarkable for their perfect form, beautiful markings, and sheen of silver shading to gold.'

Only the best came from England to the antipodes, and though the trout fry did not attack the salmon they were the ones that really flourished in the new environment. The *Norfolk* arrived at Melbourne on 15 April, the boxes were rapidly transferred to the sloop *Victoria* en route to Hobart, where they were off-loaded on to a barge and towed up-river by the steamer *Emu*. 91 days after embarkation bands of volunteers fondly manhandled the boxes to the prepared breeding pools. These Salmon Ponds of Plenty are still maintained as a place of historic interest, with a waterside willow over a hundred years old taken from the grave of Napoleon Bonaparte. On 4 May the first trout hatched out and twenty-one months later there were still 171 surviving. Thirty-eight were released into the River Plenty, and the rest were kept for breeding. From this sole source all the waters of Australia were originally stocked. The legacy of that voyage of the *Norfolk* is some splendid trout fishing, not least in Tasmania itself. The opportunities in Australia were accurately described to me before a recent March visit by Robert Southey, grandson of the poet, who wrote:

'Rivers can be low at the end of summer, but in Tasmania at least you will be assured of good fishing, especially if your eyesight is sharp and you are not afraid of fishing in windy conditions.

'To deal with Tasmania first, there are three places you should fish: Lake Pedder, south-west of Hobart, where you fish from a boat and some monsters are caught (a friend of mine caught two of eleven and nineteen pounds one afternoon, and was too weary to recast his fly when he saw a third, even bigger, one); the Macquarie River, near Launceston, where there are famous red spinner hatches in the spring; and the Western Lakes around the Great Lake area, also near Launceston.

'Pedder is accessible by car at that time of year, and there would be boats for hire and no shortage of advice on where to fish and what flies to carry.

'So far as the Macquarie is concerned, I have never fished it in March, but it should be good and it is certainly in delightful countryside. You will probably be aware that water is not "owned" in Australia in the same way as it is in the UK. The water itself is regarded as Crown land (if you will forgive the absurdity) and may be fished by anyone so long as they hold a freshwater fishing licence for that state (it costs something like 20 Australian dollars). Of course the land surrounding the water may be privately owned, and in that case one must have the permission of the owner to gain access to the fishing. The Macquarie is within twenty minutes drive of Launceston.

'My personal preference is for the fishing in the Great Lake area, and there is good accommodation in a hotel called The Compleat Angler at Miena (telephone 002–596163), which is owned by an old friend and fishing companion of mine, Jim Allen. You will need (and can hire) a four-wheel-drive vehicle, and I am sure that if Jim is in Tasmania at the time he would be delighted to take you out fishing with him. Not only is he a marvel to watch but there are many (indeed hundreds) of lakes to choose from, and some local knowledge can be a help, particularly as to where to fish in certain weather conditions.

'There are three main types of fishing up there (and it is high country, so it can be perishingly cold even in summer): polaroiding the fish in shallow lakes, which requires blue skies; fishing to "tailing" fish – in other words, fish nosing around in shallow weedbeds feeding on tiny crustaceans; and fishing to dun hatches. All are demanding on eyesight, and speed and accuracy of casting. But the rewards are great, and Jim Allen and I have caught (and released) up to 30 fish in a day, averaging well over two pounds. For a good fisherman this is some of the finest fly fishing in the world, and if you can spare a week fishing these lakes (and the weather is kind, as it should be in March) it will be a memorable experience.

'If you consider going to these lakes with a local guide, there is one I could recommend – Noel Jetson, of Cressy (just outside Launceston, telephone 003–976272). Apart from being a knowledgeable angler and local identity, he is also a most expert fly dresser, and you would want to buy your flies from him in any event.

'To move on to the Snowy Mountains. The best fishing is in what is known as the Monaro, a flat area of high plain country around Cooma, south of Canberra. The most popular and well-known fishing spot in the area is Lake Eucumbene, but the fly fishing would be better in some of the lesser-known streams ("creeks" in the Aussie vernacular) and rivers.

'If you have to choose between Tasmania and the mainland (as opposed to covering both) my recommendation would be to opt for Tasmania, as I believe it is quite unlike any other sort of fly fishing in the world.'

Robert Southey had given the best possible advice as to people and places for autumn fishing down under. The easiest time to take trout may well be in the spring, when the fish are still uneducated, but the weather then can be very cold and windy. Even in late summer there was a temperature drop of some 30°F as I flew from the heat of Melbourne to the chill and wet of Launceston, which so contrasted with the warmth of the welcome.

From a small sample of more than two thousand Tasmanian lakes and some productive rivers, all with a good head of trout, it was soon clear that this part of Australia does indeed provide unusual trout fishing both in the methods used and in the size and condition of the fish. Polaroiding the shallow lakes proved an exciting experience if not a productive one for a beginner. Such 'spot fishing' depends on sighting the trout before they see you. Only when you have frightened off a number of large fish can you appreciate how good is their camouflage, how sensitive their reactions. Only after polaroiding with experts can you appreciate how the experienced polaroiders develop a sixth sense and second sight in spotting

—4—

distant fish which you fail to pick out, even when they are pointed out to you. With chest waders you can wander quietly over many Western lakes perhaps a hundred yards or more from the bank with the wide brim of an Australian slouch hat helping shade your glasses and making the trout easier to spot. Ideally you should move upwind with the sun behind you. During my week in Tasmania Jim Allen had one remarkable bag while polaroiding a Western lake. Spotting a wild brown, he floated a Geehi Bug past its nose without causing a quiver of interest. In mid-lake he then changed flies quietly and quickly. Finally the great mouth opened to swallow a floating nymph. That was the first of four browns weighing almost forty pounds in total, caught on permutations of those two flies.

The other unusual type of fishing is for 'tailing' fish in the shallow margins. In Tasmania this aspect of the sport is probably more practised and more widely developed than anywhere else. In September and October, when the trout are feeding on anything from worms to tiny frogs, tailing is a frequent sight in the stream backwaters and the edges of lakes. The huge tails will still be breaking the surface as the trout feed on tadpoles in November and December. Snails and the like produce similar 'rises' well into midsummer. Dawn and dusk are the best times, but tailing fish may be spotted throughout the day. Sadly, this was an experience I missed in the autumn, but it was described for me by Robert Sloane, an expert angler with many years of experience in researching trout behaviour for the Tasmanian Inland Fisheries Commission. His book *The Truth About Trout* has a wealth of practical information, especially on how to fish Tasmanian and other antipodean waters. On tailing, he comments: 'Tasmanian lakes and lowland rivers provide unique conditions which lead to the commonplace phenomenon of tailing trout and create a challenge to fly design, presentation and technique rarely encountered elsewhere and bearing little relation to traditional methods and fly patterns.' Robert Sloane's favourite areas for catching such trout are the marshes of Lake Sorrell, the tussocky margins of Brontë Lagoon and the flooded heathland of the Western Lakes. He rates Lake Sorrell as Tasmania's most productive brown-trout fishery and the tailing period in early season can provide especially good sport there after a wet winter.

On technique he lists the main rule for catching tailers as the need to work the shallow margins first before wading quietly towards the deeper gutters. The main fly Dr Sloane recommends is the Rabbit Fur Fly, tied simply from natural grey-brown wild rabbit fur, and a few turns of black ostrich herl added as a head. The fly can be cast with a splash, the sound often attracting distant fish. One tailing phenomenon can cause anglers as much exasperation as a caenis hatch, in which the trout are impervious to a fisherman's offering. The trout then are 'untouchables', preoccupied in picking up small amphipods from the bottom. Again Dr Sloane has worked out a method that is sometimes successful: he uses a 'Fiery Brown Beetle', size 10 or 12, tied with dubbed seal's fur and a slip of crow wing feather tied forward to form the back. The technique then is as different as the fly. The beetle has to be delicately cast close to the untouchable and allowed to lie on the bottom for the trout to pick up.

Apart from advice relating to special Tasmanian conditions, *The Truth About Trout* appeals for its general wisdom, and for demolishing a number of myths. This on flies, for instance: 'Many anglers believe fly pattern to be all-important, but I know too much about trout habits and diet to consider that this is the answer. I have checked too many bags of trout caught on different flies on the same day during the same rise to subscribe to this school of thought . . . what seems important is the general shape and size of fly and, in particular, the way it behaves on the water.'

For those wishing to fish down under this practical expert lists three essentials to success. First is the ability to 'see' trout and read water. Then, when a trout is spotted, correct presentation is the essence of effective fishing. Finally, correct presentation must be coupled with a fly pattern of suitable size and shape.

The Inland Fisheries Commission has produced a useful guide for visiting anglers entitled *Trout Fishing in Tasmania* which was also written by Dr Sloane in 1985 and is obtainable from their office at 127 Davey Street, Hobart. On the rest of the fishing it makes the point that because Tasmania is relatively small – only 88,000 square kilometres – the major lake and river systems are all within easy reach of Hobart in the south or Launceston in the north. For general advice on places and periods it is worth reading in full, but the following extract fills a few of the gaps so far left.

'The best rivers and streams for trout fishing are those flowing towards the north. Launceston is generally regarded as an ideal centre for river fishing. The Macquarie, North Esk, Meander and Lake rivers are all popular and fish up to 1½ kilograms are common. Many anglers consider Brumby's Creek to be one of the greatest trout waters in Tasmania. Year round it receives cold water from Great Lake via the power station at Peatina. The cool waters cause prolonged mayfly and caddis hatches, and produce fast trout growth. Practically all the small rivers of the island provide exciting fishing. The Mersey, Leven, Forth, Liffey, St Patrick's and Break o' Day rivers in the north and the Clyde, Ouse, Derwent and Huon in the south are popular waters. However, excellent fishing is to be found in out of the way places too numerous to mention.

'It is most important to choose the right time of year for the type of fishing that is preferred. In August and September, winter months at the start of the trout season, the weather is usually changeable and cold, but the early-season fishing can be rewarding. Bait, spinner and trolling are often productive in the lake country at the time. Often the rivers are high, creating ideal wet-fly fishing and worming. Spinning for sea trout in the estuaries of the larger rivers at this time can provide splendid fish. In late September trout feed ravenously on spawning frogs in the tussocky margins of many lakes, and wet-fly fishermen do well, particularly in Arthur's Lake, Brontë Lagoon, and Lake Sorrell.

'As the weather warms up in October and November, the famous red spinner mayfly hatches begin in the northern rivers with prolific rises in the Macquarie and Break o' Day rivers.

'At Penstock Lagoon, Lake Sorrell, Arthur's Lake, Brontë Lagoon and in many smaller dams and lakes fish can be found in the early morning fossicking for tadpoles along the shallow margins. The fish are said to be "tailing" and provide good sport on wet fly. Sea-run trout can also be taken at this time, and the opening of the rainbow-trout season sees good catches of fish on bait and lures. The warmer days of December and January produce mayfly and caddis hatches in the highland lakes and rivers. Little Pine Lagoon, Lagoon of Islands, and Brumby's Creek are well worth a visit from dry-fly enthusiasts. In January, the mudeye (dragonfly nymph) migration begins at Lake Pedder and the brown trout feed freely on them.

'Late in summer, during February and March, falls of terrestrial beetles provide good dry-fly fishing amongst the trees at Dee Lagoon, Lake Leake and Woods Lake. Lake Pedder also continues to fish well. In the small streams, fishing with light spinning tackle using a grasshopper for bait is a favourite pastime. Good evening rises to corby moths are to be found on lowland streams during the summer. Cold, frosty nights and warm, clear days are frequent in April and May, but the weather can change rapidly to snow in the highlands. The season is nearly over and the trout begin to develop spawn. Falls of jassid bugs and gum beetles result in spasmodic dry-fly fishing. Wet-fly fishing or spinning in the late evenings can be rewarding in the lake country, and autumn rains often provide some backwater fishing in the rivers.'

My own Tasmanian experience was gained in company with three knowledgeable anglers from Western Australia – Andrew Fink, Terry Piggott and Owen Nuttridge. All had been prepared to spend some six hours of flying time to attend the annual Australian Freshwater Fishing Assembly, which includes coarse as well as game anglers, and representatives of the Native Fish Society who hold little brief for trout, which are apt to snap up native galaxias and the like. In the two days of the assembly the papers presented by a team from the Liawenee Research Station on the Great Lake were of special interest. One in particular from Peter Davies confirmed that Tasmanian trout stocks are being kept prolific by improving spawning grounds and the ease of access to them, rather than by putting in large numbers of hatchery fingerlings which by comparison give a relatively low return in survival rate. A visit to the research centre gave a prime example of such work with the specially designed spawning stream around the station helping to keep the Great Lake full of trout. In our car-camper we made The Compleat Angler hotel a base for activities and a centre for information, as the necessary up-to-date advice on which of the many waters were fishing well was always available there. The drive up to the highlands had been made under leaden skies and sheeting rain. Dripping gum trees, muddy roads and dark water everywhere did not at first give any great lift to the spirits, and the warmth of the hotel bar was very welcome. Before a drink could cheer me further a local inquired: 'What do you think of our Western Highlands, then?' 'They have a certain rugged splendour' was the best I could manage. 'Rugged splendour nothing! They are f——ing beautiful' was the forceful response. And beautiful they were once the sun shone and the water sparkled.

The fishing was always interesting, but rarely easy. For me there was never a blank day and always at least the occasional large brown or rainbow to give a thrilling fight. Conditions were rarely ideal for fishing to seen trout, which is the highlight of Tasmanian experience, but the less interesting fishing blind proved productive. Particularly effective was a green-bodied Mrs Simpson, though red or yellow are usually to be preferred. For those not dedicated to fly fishing in the normal way, trolling in some of the lakes was still producing large catches. In the bar of the hotel a notice also pointed to a method more reminiscent of some of Izaak Walton's tactics than modern methods. 'A dozen wattle grubs $14,' it read. And these very large white caterpillar-like grubs are apparently very effective when pulled across the surface of the water, though this was hardly a method to appeal to most anglers.

For me three experiences indicated the range of Tasmania's fishing. The freedom to fish without pressure from other anglers was nicely illustrated on the first evening. Driving down to a favoured spot on Arthur's Lake, my companions nearly turned round again because there were two other fishermen visible within a couple of miles. Happily they stayed to fish on a windy evening where trout were rising in the quieter areas. These were shielded by a deep water screen of dead gum trees, the white eucalypts making a delicate tracery round the lake's edge. All four of us had frequent takes to a Green Nymph tied with a blob of white possum for a tail. Terry Piggott, however, was the most successful with his own dressing of a Red and Black Nymph.

'When the water is higher there are parts of Lake William which can be very productive. Once I was being maddened there by rising fish which wouldn't take anything I offered. Finally I tied up this experimental nymph and had a bagful,' he explained.

We didn't get a bagful in the couple of hours we fished, but his nymph took enough to prove its effectiveness, as it was later to do on the London Lakes. The most unusual fishing was on the Lagoon of Islands, so called from the clumps of Ti-trees breaking the surface to give the impression of a series of islands. Thick weed growths cover much of the lake and from the bank you need to stalk fish cruising down the narrow lanes between thick weedbeds. But it was the top of the Dee Lagoon which fascinated me. Where the river ran in there was a large sandbar which was wadable across the whole wide neck of the lagoon, with a tangle of tree stumps where it shelved off into deeper water. Large rainbows cruised the area and there were usually fish to be seen rising to the gum-tree beetles. But they were reluctant takers and not even the neatest imitation of the beetle appeared to attract them. However, the Mrs Simpson fished on a sinking line had occasional success, with some trout of around 4 lb landed and others breaking the cast as their first unstoppable rush took them to the shelter of the tree stumps.

That was fishing full of promise, though hopes and expectation were not always realized. The nearby London Lakes, however, provided complete fulfilment. The setting is unusual for Australia, with the two sizeable lakes privately owned. The enterprising Jason Garrett has constructed both and also owns the surrounding estate, in which wild life flourishes. Fishing one evening under his guidance it was somewhat unnerving to find my casting technique also under review by a dozen wallabies which had bounced down to watch. The abundance of animals was further confirmed as a rare black Tasmanian devil moved slowly from the path of the returning Land-Rover. But it was the morning that provided the unforgettable fishing. In the misty light of dawn big trout cruised the shallows moving so slowly that at first the tell-tale fin was hard to spot. Putting a black and red Robin fly close to the first fish triggered an explosive response, the water humping high behind the trout as it surged towards the fly. Surprise made for too hasty a strike and a lightly hooked fish which soon came off. Other such chances were wasted over the next hour and just before the glare of the sun dictated that it was time for breakfast a dry fly along the edge of the twisted branches of a fallen gum tree brought another good rise, another fish lost. Later that day, approaching the other lake to look for a rising fish, I found myself eyeball to eyeball with a five-pound brown in water that barely covered its back. The green nymph, shakily cast, was inspected and sucked in, but again the trout soon broke free. Two more of some four pounds then fell to the same nymph, tearing off line in long rushes before being netted. The delightful lodge, the expert instruction available, the abundant wild life, the beautiful and productive lakes, and the unusual 'spot fishing' to seen trout made this a unique experience even by Tasmanian standards.

The little stream running between the lakes is being expanded into a fishable river and the plan for further development included a helicopter pad to ensure rapid trips to other lakes and rivers in the area, though the London Lakes fishing is hard to match, let alone excel. The combination of fishing and luxury is similar to that provided by the best of New Zealand lodges – costly, but value for money for those able to afford a rare fishing experience. (For details write to Jason Garrett, London Lakes, c/o Post Office, Brontë, Tasmania.)

On the mainland of Australia my guides were John Sautelle senior and junior, a father-and-son combination recognized as two of the best fishermen in the country. John Sautelle's book *Fishing for the Educated Trout* is the other invaluable reference work for those wishing to fish in Australia. John senior is primarily a river fisherman for trout in the pellucid waters of New South Wales or the rivers of New Zealand. He has, however, already caught thirty-seven different species of fish on fly. His unbounded enthusiasm for fishing had recently found expression in New Zealand as a huge rainbow had him running hundreds of yards in pursuit with shouts of 'He's a fighter.' Shortly after that fight he was – perhaps unsurprisingly for a man in his seventies – in hospital with a mild heart attack, but in my own experience of fishing with him this had clearly done nothing to slow him down. First he took me to two of the peat rivers of the Monaro – the Quinburra and the Little Plains. The dark bottoms of these streams made it hard to see the trout, but there were some moving in several of the little pools throughout the day. A Geehi Beetle floated to the rises brought two trout on the Quinburra and another five on the wider Little Plains, all between 1 and 1½ pounds.

John Sautelle also caught and released seven, including one of around three pounds. He saw this make a characteristically violent rise at a grasshopper and there was the same surging take when he floated a Muddler over it. There was an even larger trout he hooked, but could not hold on fine tackle as it charged into a trailing branch. His yell of disappointment was audible several pools away, sounding to me like 'Oh bother', though perhaps the breeze distorted the sound. How different was the fishing in the basalt streams. The Bobundara runs for hundreds of yards like a little burn that you can jump across. Then it suddenly broadens into a long, deep pool with every stone on the bottom clearly visible.

One such pool is below a hillock with a sheer rocky side running down to the water. Driving up to the hill's edge, John recounted how he had been broken there recently by a huge brown. Perched more than 100 feet up we peered straight down into the water shadowed in places by the cliff face and rippled by a gentle breeze that gave relief from the burning heat. Before I could see anything John was shouting in excitement, 'There he is.' After much pointing it was clear to me too that there he was, and now he began to rise casually and consistently. Hurrying down the hill and over the little entry stream, I was soon crouched down in the tall brown grass amid the prickly thistles working out his cruising circle. Ably guided from above I cast a Geehi Beetle many yards ahead and let it lie in wait. There was a heart-stopping moment as the trout saw it, altered course ever so slightly, moved up under the fly then slid past. Twice more it did that, feeding busily the while as it circled round. The feeding pattern suggested a change to a nymph. As I was tying one on with shaking fingers the trout suddenly gave a massive chomp at a 'hopper' and sank from view, apparently sated. In an hour's fishing later on the McLoughlin River the big trout there eluded me too, though it was easy to appreciate John Sautelle's claim that this was the best stream of them all. For those who might wish to fish the area John junior and an equally expert fisherman, Kaj Busch, run fishing safaris supplying all the necessary guidance and instruction. Details of these can be obtained by writing to PO Box 103, Bombala, NSW 2632.

Time prevented a visit to the large lakes of Eucumbene and Jindabyne with their excellent rainbow trout fishing, or to the Snowy Mountain waters. There I had hoped to visit a stretch about which the landowner gives this advice to his guests:

Water The river is the supply and is potable. It complements the Famous Grouse.
Fishing What you came for. Fly only please – and you can fish both sides. Which brings me to fishermen and access. I cannot stop anyone walking down the middle of the river. I can stop them on my property which begins at the water's edge. Legally I cannot accost anyone in the river except to ask for their licence. This I do for people spinning or using handlines and worms – fortunately not too many.
The Environment Animal life abounds in the area and you should be aware that snakes, quite a lot of blacks and some browns, are active, particularly in summer and along the river. Dress accordingly and keep an eye out. There are wild pig which are pests, kangaroos are prolific. Wombats, echidna, rabbits, platypus, goannas, fox and a variety of bird life are also present.

Snowy Mountain Fishing Holidays, PO Box 122, Corryong 3707, Victoria, Australia, telephone (060) 76 8252, arrange holidays and describe the fishing as follows:

'The upper Murray area is in part made up of a 330-hectare lake pondage which is part of the Snowy Mountain Hydro Electric System. Most of the water on the south-western side of the Snowy Mountains flows into this lake and is then directed down the Swampy Plains River (about 10 km of fly-fishing-only water) to meet up with the Indi River which forms the headwaters of the Murray River. From here there are four bridges which cross the Murray River in a space of about 80 km from which most of our river float trips are run. Float trips are also offered down the fly-fishing-only water below the dam of the Swampy Plains River

'Nearly all of this area is made up of rich river flats with red river gum and willow being the main tree vegetation close to the river. Because of this, accessibility is relatively easy for the fisherman.

'The streams are rain-fed which means that there is the usual spring run off (Sept.–Oct.) from the snow in the mountains along with any rain that falls and the river is usually coloured and up. Worm, beetle and nymph patterns work well at this time. By early summer the streams have been established and are relatively gin-clear. With the annual rainfall at around the 34-inch mark you can naturally have fluctuations in the height of the waters and changes in their colour.

'The feeding habits of the trout seem to be about the same as most other places in the world with a tendency for the fishing below Khancoban Lake to be more wet-nymph fishing although certain hatches of various insects during the season (spinners, duns, grasshoppers, ants, midges, beetles, etc.) make dry-fly fishing most enjoyable.

'In recent times restocking programmes have begun on the Murray River and Khancoban Lake. These programmes have been privately funded and it is hoped that these moves will promote an even better fishing future.

'Guide services are available for daily river float trips plus a walk and wade guide service. Because we are located right on the river you also have the choice of exploring on your own with good fishing water in front of our location. We have modest fly-tying facilities should you wish to tie that special pattern. There are tennis courts and table tennis available for any periods of non-activity on the river. There is a wide range of other activities in the area, but a car is needed. Car rental service is located in Corryong, 9 km away.'

Before my visit I had queried whether chest waders were really necessary and had been told that even if I didn't wade they would ensure peace of mind against the snakes. The locals take no notice of these, which slither away when they hear anyone, but for those not accustomed to them such precautions are sensible. In any case, you need to put your foot down carefully so as not to tread on one that is sleeping and the advice to those who are polaroiding is not to wear the glasses until you are in the water as they cut out the tell-tale glint from a snake's back. Parts of Australia are still untamed and it is as well to remember that some of the wildlife is wild indeed.

Western Australia also has trout fishing of note, though one of its best lakes has suffered recently when an explosion of red-fin perch deprived the trout of their normal food supply. The opportunities on lake and river are well described in Neil Coy's book *Freshwater Fishing in South Western Australia*. In general, trout fishing is not so easily available, or so good, as in Tasmania and New South Wales. And perhaps the best of it is not much publicized, or easy to locate. One of my companions in Tasmania, Terry Piggott, is Australia's leading opal merchant and a former gold miner. He told me of one time when he and his partner came on a man celebrating a large and lucky strike. They promptly joined the celebrations hoping that an excess of drink might unlock the secret of the location of the strike. Before they rolled off to bed they felt they had achieved it at the expense of very thick heads. In the sober light of day all they could remember was that it was near a station, but whether railway, sheep or cattle they had no idea. So they never did find it. Not unnaturally Terry is equally close and difficult to deprive of his own secrets of some very excellent fishing on a Western Australian river.

Australian interest in trout fishing has been responsible for its availability in Papua New Guinea. This was one of the last of the equatorial regions with high-altitude streams to be explored and developed. It was not until the late 1930s that Europeans penetrated into the highlands. The country only achieved independence in 1978, and prior to that date it was administered from Australia.

During the 1960s and 1970s the Australian administration carried out extensive stocking, or 'seeding' as they call it, throughout the central highlands and almost all streams and rivers around Goroka, Mount Hafen and Mende were stocked with rainbow trout by helicopter, by Land-Rover and by enthusiastic patrol officers on foot.

The central highlands have many great mountain ranges with peaks rising to 12,000 feet or more. Throughout the year rain falls on their cloud-covered heights. It is a land of waterfalls and sizeable rivers pushing a never-ending succession of sand and gravel, rocks and boulders, down to the flat country below. There they converge on the floodplains of the huge Sepik, Wagi, Fly and other great watercourses.

The experience of catching trout in these unusual rivers intrigued Jonathan Niblett, who recently spent a year there. Based at Mount Hagen, Jonathan went exploring most weekends, usually fishing as well. This is his account:

'No fishing licences are required and very few people bothered to fish. Those that did, mainly Australians, invariably spun using all the usual bar spoons. I was treated to mild ribbing for sticking to the fly, but managed to catch almost as many trout as my companions and also caught the largest trout that I saw – just over three pounds.

'The reason for the general habit of spinning was that the streams were mostly very rapid and normal flies could not get down deep enough in the pools and pots before they were whisked away down the current. On the bigger pools also it was necessary to fish really deep – about six to ten feet – to have any success. Hence the use of the ironmongery. On the higher reaches the streams could be fly-fished in the normal way, casting upstream with a leaded nymph, but it was difficult to reach these places away up in the forest far from any road.

'If I were to return to Papua New Guinea I would bring a much heavier and quicker-sinking line than the size 6 that I used. A selection of size 9 sinkers, weight-forward or with shooting heads, ranging from fast to very fast and lead-cored, would really get down into the places where the rainbows lie. I would also bring some salmon flies tied on size 4, 6 and 8 doubles, plus some Waddingtons of 1–2½ inches and some heavy tubes. Leaders would have to be heavy for this type of fishing: anything from 7 to 15 pounds BS. Finally, the rod would be a salmon/seatrout type of 9½ or 10½ feet. The standard flies and leaded nymphs used in East Africa (see page 172) were just as killing in the smaller or quieter reaches. With such tackle I would dearly love to return to some of those fine rivers, and even with my inappropriate lightweight lines and flies I had much enjoyable sport.

'The heavy rainfall makes for high and luxuriant grass and bush along the open river banks, whilst in the forest gorges the going is steep, slow and very jungly. In fact progress can be a nightmare. Often more time is spent getting to the river, and then from pool to pool, than in fishing. An army assault course is a kid's playground compared with the approach to most streams, and I was thankful for the pig tunnels in the thick and prickly grass. We were once forced to climb a steep clay bank of about fifteen feet instead of progressing by the easier method of half-swimming and wading downstream. Our companion, David, who was much fitter and younger, climbed up on my shoulders and just managed to make the top. Next came my wife. Halfway up David's hand grabbed hers and she was making good progress when her foothold gave in the wet slippery clay. She swung pendulum-like on David's arm. It was really very funny and I stood back laughing. "Give us some help," groaned David, the bones in his arms creaking; "dammit all, she is your wife!"

'On that day David caught (and released) about fifteen fit little rainbows of about half a pound each, whilst I never had a touch. So the last laugh was with him. Generally, the higher you go the smaller the trout. The big fellows keep dropping downstream until they find deep enough water. The heaviest trout I heard of weighed 14½ lb and 5- and 6-pounders are quite common in many rivers.

'Your best bet as a fishing centre is Mende. There is a very nice little stream, the Mehele, beside the Mende–Mount Hagen road, whose lower reaches look very promising. I never had time to fish them, though I caught plenty of small trout upstream of the road bridge. My own favourite was the Kaugul River – with a fine piece of water for two miles upstream of the road bridge. Trout here averaged about a pound and I got my 3-pounder about two miles upstream, just before the forest begins.

'It is worth fishing any likely river that you come across, but local knowledge, local guides and local car watchmen are always useful, and sometimes necessary. There are hotels in Mende, Mount Hagen and Goroka, where there is a government hatchery and trout farm.

'At 6,000 feet days are warm but nights can be cold, and at 7,000 feet frosts are common. Good warm camping gear is essential, but most fishing is done from a home base, with hot baths a welcome luxury for the scratched and exhausted fisherman. The people themselves, known collectively as the Highlanders, are very picturesque, speaking a Melanesian pidgin, but are quite unpredictable. We were treated with great courtesy and kindness by gentlemen with bones through their noses and wearing nothing but "arse-grass", and on other occasions were mugged and robbed in midstream by youths in jeans. The rivers around Mount Hagen were the most unpleasant for fear of this sort of assault, but the people up in Mende district were far more peaceful and friendly. Tribal fights, however, are common and on more than one occasion we drove under an arch of arrows flying to and fro across the road, fired at each other by warring warriors hiding in the grass. It was wise to keep the windows wound up however hot the day.

'The coast was far more civilized and the fishing there easier. Indeed, the tackle I recommend could be used to good effect even in the saltwater creeks, lagoons and river mouths and out in the Pacific itself.'

The best of the trout fishing in Papua is clearly for the adventurous. Those with a desire to tackle the remote and the unexplored, and who relish a hint of danger, may well find this the most exciting of all.

2

Some Other Place in Time

New Zealand's Unique Trout Fishing

In Tasmania Terry Piggott told about a Western Australian angler with one eye on a large trout rising persistently, the other on a tiger snake swimming towards him. As the fisherman's casting grew more erratic the nearer the snake came, the trout finally had to leap up the bank to grab the fly. There are no snakes in New Zealand, but such is the reputation of its fishing that some seem to believe that the trout there will come crawling out of the water to take a fly however badly cast. It is indeed true that any novice can catch large rainbows by trolling in Taupo, with the charter skippers supplying all the necessary know-how. But most of New Zealand's remarkable waters will only reward the competent angler, while for the skilled there are riches indeed.

Nature made New Zealand one vast fishery, neglecting only to supply the trout. That deficiency was made up with the importation of the progeny of those 138 brown trout from the *Norfolk* shipment when the acclimatization societies of Otago and Christchurch each brought back 800 trout eggs from Tasmania in 1867. Brown trout of the Itchen and Thames type still abound in South Island, but in the North it is the rainbows that have proliferated following their later introduction from America's Russian River. But of all New Zealand's myriad lakes and streams few indeed are without trout of some kind to attract the fishermen. With countless miles of fishable trout water, and so many areas only sparsely inhabited, there is no great fishing pressure, no need to keep up stocks by improvised means. Conservation is aided by reasonable bag limits and a ban on the sale of trout. Visiting anglers are the more appreciated if they too help by 'catch and release'. Indeed, that is the obvious course to take unless you wish your hotel to cook you a trout, or you have a trophy fish to mount.

The New Zealand weather is unpredictable, changeable and extreme only in the sense that it ensures both heavy rainfall and more than average sunshine. So fishermen have to be prepared for both, and both within a short time. Fishing the Mataura I drove past one range of mountains bathed in sunshine, only to find the river and the suitably named Umbrella Mountains overlooking it blanketed by rain. Throughout the afternoon that situation kept reversing as downpour alternated with sunshine. There can be days of rain and wind that make fishing impossibly difficult in some places. So it is worth listening to the forecast since, because of the country's geography, there are always sheltered areas to be found. A feature of South Island is the central mountain chain, rising to over 10,000 feet in many places. The prevailing westerly winds are forced up over it and the Fohn factor, by which the temperature increases faster in the descent than it decreases in the ascent, helps ensure that the area is warm as well as wet. Be prepared for storm, but expect the sunshine that comes in abundance, and revel in the fishing when it does.

The visiting angler is made welcome in many ways. One cheap licence covers all except a few areas of the country though each acclimatisation area will have different rules as regards limits, seasons, fishing times, and the like. For the rest all fishing is free, and freely available. The 'Queen's Chain' gives anglers the right to access for 22 yards either side of nearly all fishing waters, and landowners are mainly helpful in allowing approach over their land, provided it is properly requested. In some areas, however, a fee must be paid for crossing land to get to the fishing. Subject to fluctuation of the New Zealand dollar, the cost of living is low for the visiting angler. The food and accommodation are excellent and cater for all pockets and tastes. Car-camper hire is increasingly popular, or you can hire a car inexpensively and stay in the excellent Tourist Hotel Corporation hotels, or in the Best Western chain, which covers much of the country, or in any type of lodging from bed and breakfast upwards. With local meat, fish and fruit in such plentiful supply hotel meals proved excellent value. For those who can afford to fish New Zealand in style there are also the luxury lodges, such as Mount Hutt on South Island's prolific salmon river, the Rakaia, or the award-winning Solitaire Lodge beside the Tarawera trophy fish lake in the North Island, which also boasts two delightful lodges near Taupo, in Huka and Tongariro.

Advice on all aspects of fishing and accommodation is readily available from tourist offices. There are also many helpful books on trout fishing. Some are general, like *Trout Fishing in New Zealand* by Rex Forrester, a former fishing officer with the Tourist Department, or *Fly Fishing in New Zealand* by the late George Ferris. Some are guides to each island, such as Ferris's guides to rivers and lakes, or his Angler's Guides. Some are local, such as Gary Kemsley's informative book on the Taupo area, or the *Rotorua Trout Fishing Guide* by the local anglers' association. For advice on flies in New Zealand, as in Australia, the book by the late Faj Griffiths is as comprehensive as any. For fly patterns world-wide, Taff Price's *Fly Patterns: An International Guide* is invaluable.

There are two main ways to approach a New Zealand fishing expedition. If you can afford it, you can make sure of successful fishing by the use of expert guides, or by arranging to be helicoptered to streams or rivers full of big trout and rarely fished. The Professional Guides Association of New Zealand has nearly a hundred members covering all parts of the country. They will provide transport, advice, flies, sometimes even photographs, and will take you to special places and show the best methods. Advice on guiding can be obtained from the Secretary of the Association.

Alternatively, you can offset the cost of flying there by enjoying the free fishing so widely available, informing yourself by following the advice of the guidebooks or the helpful local tackle shops. Best of all for the competent angler may be the compromise of enjoying one or two days' professional guiding, to get the basics right, and then exploring on one's own. My own opportunity to try out both methods was a fortnight in March 1986, though circumstances dictated that for the first week I fished South Island with George Ferris's *Angler's Guide* as my only mentor. Others may do better or worse according to competence, or fortune, or the mood of the fish. What follows is the experience of one happy-go-lucky angler – always happy, often lucky – with plenty of experience elsewhere, but none in New Zealand.

Queenstown was my starting point. The town is overlooked by the majestic Remarkable Mountains, their craggy faces veined by the years. From the selection offered by the Ferris guide there was just time in the day to fit in two contrasting waters. Lake Moke nestled in high hills, its tranquil surface so clear that from the road above I could see several trout cruising near the top. A Hare's Ear or a small green nymph had been the tackle shop's advice and, though many of the rising trout ignored them, each fly took one nice brown while another fell to a dry Twilight Beauty left in wait for a circling 2-pounder, the largest of the trio.

Then it was across Lake Wakatipu by water taxi, ignoring the blandishment of a proffered champagne and crayfish trip on the pleasure steamer. There the River Lochy's rapid stream yielded a good rainbow to a Mrs Simpson fished on a fast-sinking line. The local advice had been to go far up the river to get the best of the fishing, but time prevented exploring a delightful steam, unapproachable except by water.

Lake Wanaka was the next area visited, the good roads making for a swift journey never far from rushing rivers. The run-in was past the great Clutha River, which has the largest volume of water of any in the old British Empire though it is only the second longest in New Zealand. The upper reaches were listed as fishing well and again the downstream wet fly brought results with one good rainbow taken on a Mrs Simpson and another on a Black Pennell on the dropper. Both Wanaka Lake and nearby Hawea are full of trout and their settings are such that the signs 'million dollar view' don't seem excessive exaggeration.

But it was the rivers which beckoned me and Ferris's guide referred to the Makarora as 'very productive'. Only after a two-hour drive there did I read the next sentence: 'Unless you have a fly-repellent the sand flies will make fishing a misery.' Before leaving Australia I had been advised that taking vitamin B in quantity, topped up by a tablet a day, would be adequate protection against their bites, but I had not acted on it. Fortunately, the sandflies weren't feeding that day, and the trout were. I went down at random to one of the lower pools, which was shallow and yielded nothing. The next was as large as a small lake, with the water shelving down on the near bank and the main current running deep beside the far rockface. Again, a sinking line, and again the Simpson, now alternating with the Hamill Killer, proved highly effective. The first five rainbows were around a pound. Then there came the firm take of a big trout. The fight was a sluggish battle of strength, rather than the usual tearaway battle with the power of the river abetting the power of the fish, for this brown was the one poorly conditioned fish taken on my visit – some 28 inches long but weighing about six pounds.

With the Hawea River flowing down to join the Clutha close to Wanaka, and the Hunter River to explore at the far end of Hawea Lake, this is an area which would make a fine base for a fishing holiday, particularly as the Tourist Corporation hotel is ideal for anglers. But I kept on the move. Omarama was my next stop. There I stayed with friends, the Wardells, whose merino sheep flock the fields for miles around. Benmore Lake and the Ahuriri River provided more high-quality trout fishing. In the small pools of its upper reaches the Ahuriri is noted for big browns, but my concentration was on its outflow into the lake. You can wade out for hundreds of yards into shallow Benmore, and at first I went slowly down the centre of the rip, covering the whole of the broad current. That was not a good idea as the fish sensed intrusion. Once the switch was made to fishing from the side, several yards back from the edge of the current, rainbows and browns up to two pounds began to take. Several came in the deeper pockets and back eddies. Then in late afternoon larger fish moved close in. A big brown followed the fly without taking. Then, as it was dibbled into a deep hole close to the stream mouth, a four-pound rainbow seized hold, with a protracted struggle following in the shallow water.

The final two days in South Island were spent at Gore, fishing the Mataura River. This had been forecast as the highlight and how correct that forecast proved. In the tackle shop the advice was that the Mataura was fishing better than the Pomahaka and that size 16 Owakas were the local choice of dry fly. Further comment was that the stretch between Ardlussa and Cattle Flat was fishing best. There I went, expecting it to be crowded, but that day and the next, over some six miles of river, no other angler came into view. The first pool to catch my eye was a fast, shallow run. It was a wet and windy day with nothing showing in the way of fly life or rising fish. So a size 12 Royal Wulff was floated down the current. Soon it was sucked down so imperceptibly that the strike was slow. That was as well since the water then erupted as a four-pound brown surged away. This was a satisfying start and in each pool there seemed some inviting spot, usually in the faster, shallower water, where a trout could be attracted up.

With a small evening rise allowing a Twilight Beauty to snare a couple more, some eight good browns were caught in a few hours of fishing. The wild fish, and free water, had provided unrivalled sport, as good as any to be had on the stocked and expensive Test in England. The trout averaged over two pounds and were lively fighters. The following day the sport was as good, the number caught the same, but this time there was a desultory afternoon rise in which a small Owaka was very effective.

For South Island, Ferris's recommended dry flies had also included the Kakahi Queen, Dad's favourite, the Blue Dun (particularly earlier in the season), Greenwell's Glory, Black Gnat, and Peverel of the Peak. For wet fly, Hardy's Favourite, the Red-Tipped Governor and the Grey Ghost were added, with Craig's Night-time for late fishing. All these were still highly rated by local anglers. So was the fishing in the north-west corner of South Island, which I had no chance to sample. The current issue of New Zealand's main fly-fishing magazine, *Flyfisher*, contained an article by Frank Schlosser on the joys of fishing out from Nelson on the Motueka – reputed to hold the highest number of brown trout per mile of any New Zealand river. The flies he used were size 14 and 16 dry flies, with the Coch-y-bondhu an important addition. The other rewarding fishing for him was on the remoter regions of the Karamea, to which he was helicoptered in the popular New Zealand style.

For me the next experience was in the Rotorua area of North Island. At Solitaire, the ebullient host was Reg Turner, for whom only the best is acceptable in furnishing his lodge and in providing fishing facilities. Deep trolling is a normal daytime method on Tarawera and his boat had the latest gadgets to detect depth, and even fish. Much impressed by his powerful presence and a little bemused by his reiterated preference for harling, Scottish-style, with a team of flies, some American visitors later addressed their letters to him as 'Lord Harling'. That was now the name of his boat and harling is also the name of the game for the best fishing on Tarawera.

From the sheltered luxury of Solitaire Lodge a local guide, Mike Oliver, took me out for a couple of hours' night fishing on Tarawera, the lake where you expect any trout you hook to be over five pounds. Fishing in the stream mouth where the water shelved sharply away, one good fish was hooked and lost before the midnight deadline for fishing there. That brief experience was all I had in this area, but Mike Oliver gave me his summary of the Rotorua fishing, which is more fully described in the Rotorua Angling Association's booklet:

'The main Rotorua trout fishing season starts on 1 October, early spring. The dry-fly fishing on the rivers begins then with good hatches of mayfly (1½ inches in length), midge and caddis and fishing is very productive on Royal Wulff, Twilight Beauty and Turkey Sedge. Nymphing is effective all season using Pheasant Tail Nymphs, Hare and Copper, Flashback and Black Nymphs, all with varying weights to fish different depths. For really deep fishing two weighted Nymphs are used, one as the dropper.

'Terrestrials like the beetles begin hatching towards November and blunder into the water in large numbers as easy pickings for the rapidly mending trout. Smelt (minnows) start congregating in large numbers around the lake shores in November and this creates exciting sport with smashing takes on the floating line. Rainbow trout over five pounds are then quite easily caught on streamer flies such as the Parson's Glory or the Grey Ghost.

'As summer progresses the beetle and smelt fishing diminishes, but other terrestrials, like grasshoppers and cicadas, begin to carpet the water in some places and create remarkable dry-fly opportunities to fish for large browns and rainbows with "hoppers". During the height of summer the Rainbows head to cool water outlets from streams or springs in the shallow lakes, or into the deep cool layers in the deeper lakes. During these few months the trout can grow by as much as four or five pounds because of the abundant food supply and low stocking rates.

'Earlier in the spring large trout up to ten pounds seem easy to catch, but they become harder over the summer until the autumn spawning urge makes them congregate around, and in, the streams beginning about April. The weighted nymph and lures then become the main means of catching these very fat trout. Flies like the Red Setter and Glo Bug in daylight and Craigs Night-time and Scotch Poacher, Marabou and the new Glowflies (which glow in the dark like a neon tube) seem to be the most effective. This type of fishing continues right through the winter until the opening of the new season, although in limited areas. Large numbers of rainbows, many of them double-figure fish, congregate in small areas of perhaps 20 by 10 yards at stream mouths. It is an astonishing sight, with up to 200 fish boiling on the surface at once in a confined space.

'There are 14 fishing lakes and 4 major river systems in the Rotorua conservancy, plus all the feeder streams. This makes for some of the most unpressured rainbow and brown trout fishing in the world.

'Night fly-fishing is very popular, especially during the months of April, May and June for the spawning runs on Lake Tarawera, Rotorua and Rotoiti. The two major river systems are the Rangitaiki and Ruakituri, with excellent populations of rainbows and browns up to ten pounds and low angling pressure. Lake Aniwhenua is probably the best summer lake in this fisherman's paradise.'

Mike Oliver is typical of the helpful guides in the area who run what they reasonably term 'An enlightened Guide and Hosting Service'. They offer a variety of opportunity apart from 'internationally famous rainbow and brown trout fishing (no previous experience required)'. This includes taking visitors to see thermal, orchid, and private gardens as well as geysers and thermal activity off the beaten track. Since they can provide accommodation as well, this service can offer relatively cheap packages. As their pamphlet puts it: 'We offer: our homes for a night or two; self-contained cottages (with meals if required); day trips from your hotel or lodge; extended tours beyond Rotorua; our private cars; peaceful rural settings – but especially ourselves.' This last comment is apt enough for all the professional guides I met, and a pretty good offer it is. Details are available by writing to M. H. Oliver, Waikita Valley, R.D.1, Rotorua.

Rotorua Lake can be very productive with its massive head of rainbows. It is a relatively shallow lake, rarely more than fifteen feet deep. So in the heat of summer the trout congregate in the colder waters round steam mouths and even big fish are often easy to catch then. The Ohau Channel is as good a place as any, and Ty-llyn Lodge an excellent base from which to fish it. As the Welsh name implies, this is a 'lake house' on the northern shore of Rotorua beside the famous Ohau Channel connecting Rotorua and Rotoiti. The size of fish you may catch is graphically illustrated by the special offer in the Lodge's terms: 'A REFUND of one night's lodging is offered to all guests who land a takable BROWN TROUT from the Ohau Channel which weighs LESS than eight pounds.' That is not necessarily a very costly offer for owner Mike Scott. The browns are not nearly as numerous as the rainbows and those which get caught are usually double-figure fish.

Mike Scott found a most killing pattern for this area by aiming to tie a fly which would closely resemble the smelt on which the trout feed so avidly. The Silver Dorothy was the answer, and his success with it has made it a most popular fly here at certain times of the season.

New Zealand has been referred to as 'some other place in time'. There is indeed a timelessness about it, and for the fisherman a peace and a quality of fishing recalling bygone golden ages for anglers. To enjoy it to the full you should have a timeless approach yourself, but my schedule involved experiencing it on the run while wishing for more time in each enticing area.

Impressions of South Island had centred on the outstanding brown trout fishing, the placid beauty of the lakes set off by the gaunt, impressive mountain chains like the Remarkables, and the startling clarity of the water. The clarity was common in North Island, too, but in its more pastoral setting the rainbow is dominant. Lake Taupo is the famed centre and acts like a magnet, allowing the town of Turangi on its shores to boast the sign 'Trout Capital of the World'. In advance of my visit that delightful fishing writer Sidney Vines had given me this description of joining the famous 'picket fence':

'The Maoris call Lake Taupo "The Sea of Taupo". This is a fitting name, for the rainbows treat the lake as the salmon treats the ocean. They spend the summer feeding in the lake, and in autumn they run up the many rivers and streams that flow into it to spawn. In spring they fall back, spent, to begin the cycle again.

'Taupo is both a civilized and a wild place. Taupo town (population 20,000) is geared to the needs of tourists. It offers plenty of accommodation of all kinds. Good guides, boats, and a variety of aircraft are available. A tackle shop contains everything the visiting angler could want, including local advice and the hire of chest waders – which are essential.

'Despite the civilized comforts, there is a wild side to Taupo. Sudden storms spring up. Wading can be dangerous. Every year, there are a few accidents – caused invariably by those who venture out into wild places without a guide. Beyond the north shore there is a screen of steam about a mile wide from the thermal geysers of Wairakei. The whole vast lake of 240 square miles was formed by an earthquake 1,400 years ago – only yesterday in geological terms. Minor tremors are common. They are said to help tourists suffering from constipation.

'In company with that stalwart fly-fisher Tom Stuart-Menteath (who emigrated to New Zealand in the sixties) I set out one sunny March afternoon to explore the lake, and especially to see the famous "picket fence" at the mouth of the Waitahanui, 8 miles south of Taupo town. We parked our car, and walked through the bushes on to the shore, where the scene was revealed. About twenty anglers stood in water up to their chests, in a half-circle, casting out into the lake with heavy, powerful rods. Flies whizzed through the air. It looked a trifle dangerous and irresistibly comic.

'While we watched, a Maori angler hooked a fish, played and lost it. "You've come half way round the world for this," said Menteath "You had better have a go." I was not all that keen, but Menteath was right.

The picket fence was by no means the only reason for my visit to New Zealand, but it was certainly a major one.

'So, equipped with what Menteath said was an infallible local lure called a "Red Setter", I joined the half-circle and began to fish with my little graphite rod. One braced oneself against the water and cast out into the edges of the current. For some reason, this varied. The water of the Waitahanui flowed out hosepipe fashion, moving by ten or so degrees. The good anglers watched this, and always aimed for the edges, where the fish were running up.

'On my left was a venerable Maori with a battered black sombrero and a grey beard. His name was Barney Northcroft and he was deferred to by the other Maoris. He courteously made room for me, and they were all most friendly. But I sensed from their smiles that they did not have too high an opinion of the Poms.

'After about twenty minutes I felt my line check and instinctively tightened. Suddenly the rod was almost torn from my hands. The reel screamed and far out a huge silver shape leapt. The Maoris were greatly amused. What would the Pom do now? I heard Menteath on the beach giving instructions. "Lift your rod and walk behind the line. They will stop fishing while you do it. Then wade back up to the beach." This was accomplished while the fish leapt several times. I reached the beach and saw to my horror that almost all my 80 yards of line and backing had gone. I cursed my own foolishness. In the tackle shop at Taupo they had warned me that at the lake I would need at least 125 yards.

'With great care, I played the fish out and drew him in. A Maori shouted, "Bring out the landing net" – which was greeted with general merriment. The Maoris regard landing nets as effete. They let the fish flap up the beach, helped with a few kicks. "Let them laugh," said Menteath. "We're taking no chances." Skilfully he netted the fish. It lay on the beach, and I gazed at it in awe – a six-pound rainbow of perfect proportions, as silver as a fresh-run salmon. "A noble fish," said Menteath.

'Barney Northcroft called out, "You don't get them like that in the Serpentine", which caused another outburst of mirth. Then another called, "You're not giving up are you?" Indeed I was not, and they allowed me to resume my place in the line. Another twenty minutes, another check to the line, another fish – only three pounds this time, but another beauty – and all this time not one of the local experts had touched a fish. Barney shouted to his friends, "It takes a Pom to come out here and teach us how to fish."

'A typically generous remark, but I would have been foolish to believe it. The Maoris are fine anglers, with a natural rhythm to their casting. Over a fisherman's life the luck averages out, and that afternoon my luck was in. I was in the right place at the right time, with the right fly. Such occasions are rare.

'Not much skill is required at the picket fence. It is a sort of comic-opera fishing, made memorable by the charm of the Maoris and the quality of the fish. Experienced American anglers from Colorado, who have fished for the rainbow in its home – the Red River – say that the Taupo rainbows are in better condition. The environment is ideal for them. There are many places around Taupo where there is better fishing than at the picket fence, though not better fish. Its popularity is due to its accessibility and its safe wading – a level shingle.

'My abiding memories are of that magnificent six-pounder and of Barney Northcroft. He may feel now that not all Poms are whingeing, and sometimes they may even catch a fish or two. I like to think so.'

Obviously the picket fence had to figure in my own experience and I was able to sample it at its most crowded and conversational. There were indeed *two* picket fences that Easter weekend, with another row of anglers poised heron-like across the shallow neck of the pool above the road bridge, while others fished shoulder to shoulder down the lower reach of the river. The scene was reminiscent of an English reservoir on opening day. In so democratic a setting it seemed appropriate to give a go to a Nobbler. In England, of course, no one actually admits to *using* one although the Nobbler is by many thousands the fastest-selling fly because of its effectiveness in catching rainbows. In America and Europe they are often equally reticent, giving it pseudo-imitative names such as Jig Nymph.

In New Zealand there are no such inhibitions, no fastidious distinctions imposed by arbiters of fashion, no mumbo-jumbo philosophy. However much they may prefer the more delicate and skilful methods of fishing, the New Zealand approach is that if it is legal, and you want to fish that way, then that's fine. The term 'Nobbler' in fact covers a multitude of patterns from the unleaded to the shot-head type which the name immediately conjures up. Local Taupo rules permit leading of nymphs of any size, but only flies of size 10 or smaller – a rule with which my shot-head mini-nobbler complied. When cast, leaded flies are apt to pursue a somewhat erratic course, so the interested locals soon suggested the end of the line was the safest place for me. Several good rainbows were taken while I was there and my Nobbler proved its point by hooking a number of around four pounds – indeed it won itself a mention in the *Auckland Star* under the even stranger name of 'Dog Gobbler'.

In the car park by the Waitahanui bridge there is now a stone seat as a memorial to the man who did most to make Taupo famous, O. S. Hintz. He for certain would have preferred moving on to the upper reaches of the river or to the shallower, less crowded mouth of the nearby Hinemaiaia. There I followed the instructions culled from Gary Kemsley's *Taupo*

Fishing Guide, a book which gives clear and practical advice about all the fishing round Taupo. Floating line and a special green marabou fly was his recipe for success there. Marabou streamers are not basically different from the Nobbler – they just sound more elegant. In fact it was a green-bodied Mrs Simpson that had me another good rainbow from the Hinemaiaia. The spawning run had just begun up the Tongariro and that was a much more important priority than the picket fence. First I went for advice to the Tackle Creel, the Taurangi shop run by two very professional guides, Frank Harward and Frank Schlosser. Frank Schlosser's instructions were clear and practical: 'The rainbows will be running up to spawn. They are in superb condition and not looking for food. So you need to get the fly down to them. Downstream wet fly is doing well, but upstream fishing with weighted nymphs usually does better. In this torrential water you need a fast-sink no. 8 or 9 line to get the wet fly down in time.

When asked the best place to fish his reply would have done credit to the bet-hedging Delphic Oracle: 'Wherever the fish are! You must read the water to find them.' It wasn't difficult to read where people thought they were. Signs pointed anglers to all the best-known pools. Tracks on the bank showed all the favourite entry places. This weekend, too, the river was as crowded as the Waitahanui rip. It wasn't so much a case of reading the water as finding somewhere to squeeze in.

But in this home of fishing everyone seems keen to help the angler. A lady picking blackberries told me her husband had just left a place at the bottom of the Hydro Pool, where he had had a good rainbow and a large brown. There was indeed room to cover the tail of the pool and after I had fished hard for an hour the Mrs Simpson was violently seized by a rainbow which leaped high, tore off line, paused a moment on the lip of the rapid, then leaped and surged on downstream. The fly pulled out before he could be checked. With the leader strength increased to 3·5 kg there was then a quiet period. 'That used to be a good spot,' said a passing fisherman, 'when there was a big log in the water which acted as a pier, allowing you to cover the far edge of the rocks at the tail. But the great flood earlier this year swept it away and altered many of the other traditional lies as well.' That encouraged me to try a new tactic of wading out to the rocks and casting long upstream to let the fly sink. In a couple of hours that brought me two rainbows of about three pounds which were netted and released. The Hydro Pool was something of a magnet, with the high left bank lined with nymph fishermen and the right with those fishing downstream wet fly. That was not surprising for Gary Kemsley's guide book records: 'Right at the end of Kutai Street is the Hydro Pool. This would have to be the most popular of all pools on the river. Some great catches have been made from the pool. I have had more than a few limits from the Hydro myself. It is easily accessible and from the right bank can be fished from the shore. Wet-fly fishing is especially productive on this pool. Some large brown trout are caught here. The reason for their presence is that the Mangamawhitiwhiti Stream enters the Togariro here and the browns use this stream to spawn, waiting at the stream mouth to run up when the water is high and coloured.'

So far all my fishing had been a matter of reading or asking about where to go and what flies to use, and then following my instinct. But staying at the comfortable Tongariro Lodge, where Tony Hayes holds sway, I was fortunate enough to have him as guide for a day. No one is more knowledgeable about the area, or could have been a kinder companion. He drove me much higher up the river and was delighted to find no one fishing the pool to which he headed. Tony told me that there had been a dozen caught there the day before and advised two weighted nymphs.

A heavy Grey Nymph was put on the point, a smaller one as dropper. The second nymph is usually attached without any of the traditional link to the cast. Instead the lower part of the leader is tied direct to the curve of the hook; or the cast is doubled over and fed through the eye of the hook and looped back over the nymph, which then hangs direct from the cast. In the fast swirling waters of the Tongariro you need exceptional eyesight, or a small luminous indicator, if you are to detect in time the check of the line which indicates that the nymph has been taken. Despite being equipped with 'Uncle Jock's strike indicators', little luminous red or yellow patches pressed on the join of cast and line, the first check was so slight that only Tony's urgent 'Hit him!' had me tightening in time. The rod strained under the first rush of a five-pounder as his diagonal leaping run took him to the edge of the rapid at the bottom of the pool. There he was checked, and my instinct was to walk him. 'Walk back, not up, to avoid disturbing the rest of the water. Recover line when you can. Keep him playing in the quieter shallow water level with you.' Aided by such practical advice from Tony, after a stirring struggle I soon netted, photographed and released the rainbow. Tony Hayes had indicated the way to fish the pool, wading close in and fishing out the near water before searching the more promising main current near the far bank. He had also suggested casting long to give the nymphs time to sink deep, and the takes were indeed near the end of the pool as another three rainbows quickly followed, all much the same size. With a light rod and two leaded nymphs there were problems in long casting into the teeth of a gusting wind. Tony had advice for that too, showing how much easier it was to shoot the line out with only one false cast if first you let it trail in the water behind you to its full extent then flicked it forward when it was already taut.

Practising this new method had an amusing sequel. Trout are only meant to take nymphs swum down at the pace of the current without drag. But on one occasion, with the line at full length behind, as I waited for a gust to pass before casting, the rod was suddenly jerked down and a rainbow dashed away before coming off in its first run. Such nymph fishing is very different in any case from the classic nymphing with imitative patterns. The rainbows are not on the feed on the spawning run, and there is little fly life in the stony Tongariro at this time. But the leaded nymphs do get down to where the trout lie and provoke them into a grab as they drift by their noses. That stony bottom has its own surprises for the visitor. When you see a large one drifting by, for a moment you don't believe your eyes until you realize it is one of the pumice stones floating down the current. Floating down the current too were canoeists and white-water rafters in some profusion, though the fishing seemed none the worse for it. There was, however, a pause after the early excitement. Then, as Tony advised just a few more casts, a hard take which needed no indicator to detect was prelude to a wild fight with my largest rainbow of the day – about seven pounds.

At Tongariro Lodge I had read a recent letter from ex-President Jimmy Carter thanking them for his comfortable stay and the splendid fishing which had brought him the four largest trout of his life, including one of over eight pounds, with which he was photographed. Looking at my large rainbow before sliding it back in the water I could well appreciate how such trophy fish make even an enthusiastic 'catch and release' man like Jimmy Carter reluctant to return them. After catching this fifth trout I asked the name of the pool. 'It's the no-name pool, while it's fishing so well' was Tony's response. On free water the experts have to keep a secret or two! He had one other to show me in the pool below the hatchery and the fishing museum, built to celebrate the centenary of rainbow trout in New Zealand. The river there is wide and fast, the best lie under the far bank. There is no problem reaching it with ordinary casting, but the wet fly is usually swept too fast over the taking places. So Tony used a short fast-sink line as a shooting head. The light backing was paid out and caught by the current, leaving the fly and the heavy line to drift down hugging the run and at reasonable pace. Not an easy technique, and one I didn't come near mastering in the hour that was left.

The museum held two items of special interest. One was a faded photograph of 'the world record individual day's catch' – a bag of 78 rainbows weighing over ten pounds on average. The average now is less than half that, prolific though the rainbows still are in Taupo. The other special feature was the small feeder stream just outside. Tony pointed through the window to a score of rainbows in one shallow stretch. 'When you see them there you know the spawning run is really on. The fishing will be very good soon.' It had seemed good enough to me, though the wind was now too strong to try what can be the best of it, the river mouth.

The Tongariro Delta, as the river mouth is known, can provide some of the best fishing on Taupo, since so many rainbows channel through it. Wading varies from the impossible to the dangerous, so it is best fished from an anchored boat. In daylight the boat should be positioned on the lip of any drop-off into deep water. At night it is best to be some twenty yards back and to fish the lip itself. Fast-sinking high-density lines are important for consistent success as the flies need to go down quick and deep. For flies, Gary Kemsley recommends a Red Setter size 4 on the point, and a Parsons' Glory size 6 as dropper, but any similar lure types have a good chance.

The use of a shooting head also helps in getting good distance and rapid line sinkage. The retrieve should be slow, and with these tactics large catches are likely when the trout congregate in the several mouths of the Tongariro. In his book Gary Kemsley describes fishing there with Tony Hayes in Hayes's boat, Tyee. Tyee, the name for large pacific salmon, is an appropriate one for fishing the Delta area, which is noted for producing heavy rainbows. So tackle and knots were carefully checked as usual, with a light breeze promising good fishing. Casting some forty yards and using Red Setters and Dolls they caught consistently well. But the majority of the fish took close to the boat as the line was being lifted for a cast or the splice of the shooting head was through the top rod-ring. Perhaps the trout were lying close in. More likely they had followed the flies up from deep. When rainbows do this the English reservoir tactic of suddenly checking the fly near the end of the retrieve, and letting it hang or drop back, might help induce the takes.

While the crowds gather at Taupo there is as good fishing close by where you can wander undisturbed along miles of delightful water. Mike Oliver was my guide for a day on the Rangitaiki (not the Rangitikei, though that can be equally productive). Like all the professional guides I met in New Zealand not only was he able to take you to the best of the fishing, provide the most likely flies and nymphs, and demonstrate the more effective methods, but he was the type of encouraging and cheerful companion who can make the day enjoyable whether or not you catch. In fact he started me catching at once in a long run where the water bubbled and sparkled in the sunlight.

Again, two nymphs were advised: 'A pair is twice as effective, as I proved on this run a few days ago. The lady I was guiding fished it down with a single nymph and missed three takes she didn't see. Then a heavier dropper nymph was added and going over the same water without resting it she had eight takes and hooked three of them.' On technique, Mike's advice was to keep the forefinger up the rod when casting for better

control, then to retrieve smoothly over that forefinger to keep in touch
with the nymphs coming down the fast stream; to keep the line straight
without dragging; to lift the rod as the nymphs came close, then lower it to
go on working the nymphs behind, still without drag. He commented that
the trout averaged about a pound and a half with a three-pounder a rarity
in this stretch. It was with a start of surprise that I saw the indicator check
second cast and my hesitation meant a missed take.

'Strike as soon as you see a check and strike hard, as there is a lot of slack
to take up' had been Mike's instruction, and as my reactions quickened
two average rainbows were caught out of five takes. One hard strike also
hooked a rock and my Hare and Copper Nymph was lost, presumed
drowned. As we neared the broken white water at the head of the run Mike
held out hopes of a bigger fish: 'The more aggressive ones get the best lies
and you are coming to the best of them.' With concentration heightened, it
needed only a quiver of the yellow strike indicator for a fierce strike to get
an explosive response as a large fish tore downstream. The trout, when
landed, was about four pounds, as large as any from that area that season
according to Mike. But it was larger fish that we went seeking next in a
quiet part where large browns could usually be found. They weren't
feeding this time and a big rainbow sighted was soon spooked by a careless
cast. Only one trout rose steadily, and as steadily ignored the dry flies and
nymphs cast up to him.

'Let's try and surprise him,' said Mike, 'On the Hinemaiaia I was
nymphing upstream and saw a large rainbow in midstream. When I
shaped to cast he was away before the rod was back. The same happened
when I crept back later. Then I reasoned that he must be used to anglers
trying that approach. So I had a third try by coming down from above and
floating a nymph to him. He sucked it down without hesitation.' So too did
this smaller fish when I tried the same tactic. Most of my takes had been to
an unusual nymph – the Flashback. This has a small patch of silver on the
body which seems to attract the rainbows.

Variety is the spice of New Zealand fishing and the Rangitaiki provided
every variant. We ended the day at the top of a canal-like stretch where the
rush of the stream slowly dissolved into a wide deep pool – virtually a small
lake. In the swirling eddy at the top Mike and I each had two rainbows,
taken from the opposite banks. By then the swifts were skimming the
water as a hatch of fly made it sense to switch to a dry Twilight Beauty.
Wading up a shallow sidestream, we quickly caught another five. A chill
wind put paid to the evening rise which Mike had hoped might come on
the canal stretch, but it had been quite a day.

One-third of the batch of 3,000 trout eggs which provided all the
original stock of brown trout for Australian and New Zealand waters came
from the stream at High Wycombe in Buckinghamshire then called the

Wick. The best stretch was in the Abbey grounds and was characterized as 'a place where a man might fish and dream'. On the Rangitaiki and a hundred other New Zealand waters you can do just that and take pleasure in some of the best trout fishing in the world. No wonder Zane Grey publicized it as the Eldorado of angling.

3

Midnight Sun and Northern Chill

From Iceland to Sweden

Iceland can provide wild brown trout fishing of exceptional quality. Having learnt his skills in troutless Holland, Erik Berg has travelled far to practise fly fishing for them. Of all the countries he has visited, Iceland has had the greatest appeal – as he describes below:

'If somebody asked me where I would choose to live if I was able to spend all my time fly fishing I think the answer would be Iceland. I find it hard to explain exactly why. It has to do with all the emotions a fisherman experiences while he is fishing and travelling. For me wild brown trout, strange new surroundings, and complete loneliness are the most important ingredients for a perfect fishing day, and you can find them all in Iceland.

'My choice may seem strange considering that fishing with natural imitations gives me the greatest satisfaction, and especially when fishing upstream. Alas, this is not the way of fishing in Iceland. Usually water and wind are just too rough to use small nymphs or dry flies. A rod capable of throwing a heavy line is essential. Why? In Iceland's bare landscape with no trees to screen you strong winds and rough water make it hard work most days. In this situation a rod rated lighter than six is uselsss. It *is* possible to use a floating line combined with heavy weighted streamers, but these will land like small bombs. I have learned that it is much more comfortable and effective to use a fast-sinking line. As to flies the good old Mickey Finn proved its effectiveness all over the world and so it does in Iceland – but don't rely on it exclusively. Flies like the Muddler Minnow are also killers, and you need to experiment. If you are travelling through a big city like Reykjavik or Akureyri try to find the local fishing shop and ask for typical Icelandic streamers such as Thingeyingurr and Homefridor. These flies belong to Iceland as the Greenwell's does to England. The size should be 6 or 4 – rather large for the European fisherman, but the trout are also large, up to 5 pounds or more. Remember, big fish, big fly.

'Streamer fishing is one of the simpler kinds of fly fishing, and can even get boring. But here in Iceland the fish make it worthwhile. I have seen big trout swim up to my fly like submarines, and strong nerves are needed not to strike until you feel the fish. However, one morning I was lucky enough to find trout feeding just below the surface in knee-deep water. The dry fly called! I tied on a kind of Hawthorn imitation, only bigger (size 8). The natural, the *kaltra fluge*, is one of the more common members of the limited Icelandic fly population, which otherwise consists mainly of millions of tiny mosquitoes, the major food of the trout, and two or three types of small sedge. I started fishing the dry fly and it worked! After my third cast a large trout took my fly with a lazy roll and . . . I got him, I got him! I had to play the trout hard to keep him out of the weed which grows on every inch of the river bottom. After a splashing surface fight I landed a fish of 3 pounds – not at all bad. This trout was followed by four more on the dry fly to make it one of my best fishing days. All these trout came from the upper part of the Laxa, just where it flows out of Myvatn Lake. This large lake is surrounded by volcanoes and contains millions of tiny mosquitoes. Because of this the trout can feed almost the whole year through. An Icelandic friend told me that this is the best river in Iceland for big trout, and after five days fishing I had to agree with him. Apart from the Laxa there are thousands more lakes and rivers which can be fantastic fishing waters for trout and arctic char. It is very important to inform yourself in advance about the water you want to fish. Water "A" can be a fantastic water while water "B", ten miles away, can be worthless. So get some information about the conditions from the nearest farmer, petrol station, or hotel before you start. The cost of fishing can be rather high. A day on the Upper Laxa costs about £20 but that river is the best in Iceland. Other rivers and lakes are cheaper, sometimes even free, as long as they contain no salmon. And Iceland has a lot of salmon, some of the best rivers in the world, though you need a deep pocket if you wish to fish them. On a good river like the lower part of the Laxa, for example the daily price can be up to £100. Such prices bear a close relationship to the quality of the fishing. If you pay £50 a day you can expect salmon worth that amount. But if you are unlucky . . .

'For up-to-date information one contact is Arni Baldursson, Melbear 11, 110 Reykjavik. Fishing cards for the upper Laxa can be obtained from Mrs Homefrido, Arnarvatn 3 (in the corner where the Laxa flows out of the Myvatn). Or just go and explore and enjoy the experience where the fishing is more than worth the expense.'

The Laxa river is best for trout in its upper reaches and my own experience confirms Erik's that there it rates as one of the finest trout rivers in Europe. It was a pleasure for me to fish there despite the bare, wild landscape and the wind that swept in a snowstorm even in August. For the river there ran clean, clear and fast, so different from its lower reaches where catching salmon and sea trout had been made more difficult by the moving kaleidoscope of weed tendrils drifting down in endless profusion from the cluttered lakes in its middle stretch. In the uplands near Myvatn the banks were grassy, the fishing easy, the river an intriguing succession of swirling pools as the river ran bright and sparkling over its rocky bed. For a change there would be the occasional broad, quiet pool like a small lake.

It was in one such pool that for me too the trout fishing proved as good as any I have experienced. Over its broad expanse the bottom was firm and of uniform depth, allowing me to wade its whole length and width, easing along with the water close to the top of my chest waders. The fast run-in was full of trout; so was the edge of the current sweeping over to the far bank; so was the quiet tail of the pool. Occasional anglers appeared on the opposite side and fished the current down with spinners, but without success. No fish showed on the surface either. But fishing that pool all day with fly there were few dull periods. The trout took eagerly, striking hard at the size 8 Black Pennell on the tail, or the Blue Pennell on the dropper bobbed across the current. The slashing dropper rises of trout of between two and four pounds were heart-stopping in their sudden eruption. Once the tail fly was taken quietly but so firmly that it might have been anchored in a rock. When the rock moved at last there was an explosive fight before a marvellously coloured brown trout of six pounds was finally beached.

In just five days I had 67 trout from that pool alone, from ¾ pound upwards but averaging 2½ pounds. Eighteen were over three pounds and three over five pounds, the big trout taking most freely when the snowstorm blotted out the sky. Those spinning on the far bank saw the success of my flies and, before I left the farmhouse where I stayed, some came to ask for samples of the catching pattern. The most successful had been the Blue Pennell on the dropper, well hackled, but old and faded so that the colour was nearer grey. I left the Icelanders all I had and never again have I been able to match those faded 'Blue' Pennells, or the fabulous fishing they inspired, when the large wild Icelandic browns found them so attractive.

Ian Hay, of the Rod Box in Winchester, has researched trout fishing in Iceland and he endorses my view of the Laxa:

'Iceland has some excellent salmon fishing, and some splendid sea trout fishing in the south in rivers like the Brerau, but there is only one river to visit for exceptional trout fishing. That is the Laxa. The big trout, the *urridi*, come into the river from Myvatn lake and the fishing is fabulous. There is also a fine lodge run by Askell Jonasson, which caters splendidly for fishermen, their peculiar hours and their need for instant meals whenever they come in. Like everything in Iceland it is very expensive by

English standards, but there you do get your money's worth in outstanding fishing, easy travel from the nearby airstrip at Husavik, and ideal accommodation for fishermen. There are gillies available, but at a very high price – £100 or more per day, including transport. There are many other trout streams and lakes in Iceland, but none of this quality or ease of access. You can fly in, or hike in to little-fished waters, but in terms of size or numbers it is unlikely that it will be worth the effort or expense, except as part of a general exploration of a remarkable country.'

My own holiday had been fixed up through contact with Iceland Air in London. That is a good starting point for inquiry since aircraft are the main transport to outlying areas of the country, and Iceland Air officials are often knowledgeable about local fishing and the best waters for trout.
    Ian Hay has tested out the fishing in Greenland:

'There is one salmon river of no great distinction, and no worthwhile trout fishing. But for those who look on Arctic char as the equivalent of trout there can be an unusual fishing experience. Again transport will be a problem, as Greenland's few miles of road don't extend outside the town of Gothab, where the tourist office will issue the necessary fishing licences. In the small rivers running down into the fjords, and particularly in their brackish mouths, you can catch your fill of char up to double figures. They are formidable fighters, so you need a strong leader to deal with them. But you should have plenty of opportunity to work it out. They are as easy to catch as most wild trout which have never seen an artificial. We took them on traditional dry flies, traditional trout and sea-trout wet flies, and on nymphs. Upstream or down, they were equally eager. The problem was getting to them. The only way to do it is by boat, exploring fjords, most of which have a river at the head. It is an exciting and unusual experience, but needs planning in advance. But if you do start from the Tourist office in Gothab you will find you get every help and excellent advice.'

A look at the map is enough to suggest Finland's potential as one vast fishery. The country appears to be as much water as land. Visiting it, my impression was of an endless vista of lakes and forests. There are in fact over 62,000 lakes in Finland – some very large, three of them vast. The largest of these is Inari in Lapland and, appropriately, it is there that the Finnish record brown trout was caught. At 15.1 kg, over 33 pounds, this is close to the existing world record from Argentina.
    The only limitations on Finland's potential as a trout fishery are the quality of the water and the spread of industrialization. The lakes are shallow and rich in humus, the water soft. Ice covers the waters for many months, preventing oxygenation. The 20,000 kilometres of river in

Finland have been harmed for fishing by the building of over 150 hydroelectric dams, by dredging and canalization for water traffic and by the floating of logs for pulp mills or timber projects. That figures largely in my own first experience of fishing there. Visiting the United Paper Mills of Finland with a sports team I did not neglect to take a rod. Once the managing director saw it he turned to an aide and announced that Mr Pawson *was* to catch fish. Juuso Walden had a humpty-dumpty figure, but a very powerful personality and I thought the aide turned a bit pale. The only chance of nearby trout, it transpired, was by fishing at 3 in the morning on a river full of floating logs. The logs were all I caught, so my unfortunate guide was instructed to take me further afield. Instead of joining in the great Midsummer Eve celebrations he had to row me back and forth across the rapids below the Vierumaki Sports College, near Heinola. There I caught several trout while the oarsman looked wistfully at the bonfires beginning to blaze in the gloaming. To prove that his job was done he asked me to keep a couple of trout to present to Juuso. I was proud of my 1½-pound fish, but they were dismissed as 'very small'. How was I to know then that the limit for brown trout was 35 cm and most years fish of up to twenty pounds are caught.

One who does know all about it is Markku Leinonen, who runs one of the country's main tackle businesses:

'The guidebooks may say that as in Norway the further north you go the better the trout fishing, but that is not the case. The trout may be more plentiful in the north, but they are generally much smaller. We call them brook trout, not because they are *Salvelinus fontinalis*, but because they are so little. Obviously there are big trout in Lapland in lakes like Inari, or in some rivers like the three-river Kuusinki system, flowing on past Kuusinkijoki over the border into Russia. But in general the Lapland rivers are clear, rocky, and without much fly life. They have many good-sized grayling, but only small trout by Finnish standards.

'The best region for trout fishermen is the centre of the country where there are many fine lake and river systems, often with a chain of lakes linked by short stretches of runs and rapids. These *viitaasaaren reitti* are best fished at the outflow or the entry to the next lake or in the fast river reaches. Fish of a kilogram are standard trout, five-pounders nothing to get too excited about. The trout tend to lie deep and mainly it is a case of wet-fly fishing with sunk line. My favoured method is long casting upstream with an appropriate nymph or fly with a shot nipped on the leader an inch above the fly. As soon as there is a check you tighten and can expect a good trout. In half an hour this season I had three up to six pounds, while my heaviest this summer topped eight pounds. There is always a good chance of wild browns in double figures and in the system I fish most, the Rautalammen reitti, two of over twenty pounds were caught.

'State licences cost only about £3 and local permits about £15 for a 24-hour day's fishing, starting whatever time you please. You can get cheaper twelve-hour permits and most villages have shops with signs in all languages indicating that fishing licences can be bought. In good fishing areas there are usually farmers who provide good bed-and-breakfast accommodation, or cottage-type rooms to let in rebuilt barns, or small hotels. The Finnish Sportfishermen's Association, Suomen Urheilukalastajain Liito, is a useful source of information and publishes a fly-fishing magazine, *Perho-Kalastus*.

'In my view the best river systems in central Finland fall into four main areas. There is a fine river and lake system between Karna and Kymankoskio. Then the town of Vittosaari has a wealth of good fishing within a radius of hundred miles. Huopanankoski, some 400 kilometres north of Helsinki, is another good system with several rapids, as the name *koski* implies. But for me the outstanding system for inland trout, the *taimen*, is the Rautalammen reitti north from Mankasalmi. Biologists studying these waters estimate there are 1500 trout per hectare, compared with the normal 250 to 400. They also report that the minnows on which the trout feed average over 7 cm. in length. That is why much of the fishing is with spinners or wobblers or very large streamer flies on size 2 hooks.

'There are many special Finnish fly patterns, such as the Kalkkistenvaalea – the light-coloured fly from Kalkinnen. In general, dark or brown flies are effective. So are big caddis imitations and some fully dressed traditional salmon flies like the Silver Grey. Dry flies are sometimes effective in quieter waters. One popular pattern tied with a variety of body colours is the Nalle Puh.'

This Winnie the Pooh fly has its wings tied with bear's hair, hence the nickname. Of the streamers the Matuka-type or Yellow Grouse Sculpin streamers are often effective and several Finnish flies are often tied with flashabou. As a general rule the flies are big because the fish feed on big items in their natural diet. In general it is also best to fish deep, often using a shot near the fly.

There is also good fishing for sea trout – meri taimen – particularly in the Gulf of Bothnia rivers. Typical of several delightful rivers where you can catch sea trout, brown trout or grayling is the Isojoki.

Lapland is famed for its salmon rivers, especially the Teno and the Naatamo. The Teno is also called the Tedna in the Saami language spoken by the Lapps. More than 10,000 fishermen go every year to try for the Teno and Naatamo salmon, and special rules apply to fishing there. In Lapland there is also good fishing for char and grayling. The helpful guidebook, *Leisure Fishing in Finland*, published by the Central Association of Finnish Sportfishermen and the Finnish Tourist Board, comments that 'The peaceful environment of the rivers of Lapland, with the reindeer and the midges, helps the angler to forget the bustle of town life'. The midges aren't quite as big as the reindeer, but are a lot more hostile and a good repellent is desirable if you are to enjoy the peaceful surroundings. When contemplating a trout-fishing trip to Finland it is desirable to get from the Finnish Tourist Office both *Leisure Fishing in Finland* and *Finland Fishing*, which give all the necessary information about seasons, laws, licences, and fishing areas. If you enjoy fishing in remote isolation and pursuing large trout, Finland is well worth a visit. Contact with the Suomen Urheilukalastajain Liito at Toimituksen osoite, Pihlajatie 12–14, 00270 Helsinki (Tel.[90] 414 851) is a good starting point. For tackle Markku Leinonen's Perhoporssi Oy, Hietalahdenkatu 18, 00180 Helsinki (Tel.[90] 6949 088) should supply your needs, but there are some 350 tackle shops around Finland, a country which has had a great boom in sport fishing with about a million now estimated to take part and many excellent fly fishermen among them, though worming and spinning are the most popular practices.

Finland's northernmost vacation centre is the Morgamin Lemakeskus on the Teno River. As their brochure comments, 'You have wonderful fishing possibilities on the famous Teno River. Row-boats are available with rower if requested. The Alakengas Rapids casting area is only 6 km away. The fishing season lasts from June to August. Nightless night with the midnight sun is a truly enjoyable experience.' Tourist offices have the leaflets for this and other centres in a country to delight the trout or salmon angler.

Another such country is Norway.

Sea trout are a diversion in a book devoted primarily to brown and rainbow trout, but how can you write about Norway without at least a mention of its extraordinary sea-trout fishing. Some of my happiest memories centre on catching large sea trout at night, whether in the Cothi River in Wales or, even more excitingly, in Norway's Laerdal River. In late August you could indeed fish the Laerdal round the clock, with the night warm and glowing, light enough still to be able to chase after huge sea trout as they stripped off line at alarming speed. By day small black dry flies would bring the occasional fish looming up suddenly and silently, soon visible in the clear water as it sailed up from the stony bottom. By night the streamer flies would be seized, and great fish would surge away down the fast current, perhaps playing deep, perhaps leaping to send the spray flying white and luminous. In the enclosed valley of the lower beats, the sheer mountains would shut out the sun from ever touching river, road or village through long winter months. But in the summer the only fishing problem was when to stop and sleep. It was here that my host's son, Einar Wahlstrom, took a record sea trout of over 25 pounds on a size 10 Butcher. It was here that I battled for four hours with a huge salmon seen in awe as it porpoised up the far side of the current, only for my sea-trout cast with its team of droppers to be finally broken as I tired faster than the fish. The brown-trout fishing, too, can be fabulous (rainbows are seldom encountered in Norway).

For details of Norway's immensely varied fishing the Norwegian Tourist Board, in conjunction with Nortrabooks, has produced *Angling in Norway, a Comprehensive Guide to Fishing Facilities*. Comprehensive it is indeed, and the English edition is especially well presented, having benefited from the advice of Peter Tombleson, Director of the National Anglers Council. The editor, Erling Welle-Strand, admits the impossibility of knowing everything about more than 200,000 lakes and a multitude of rivers and streams. At one point the guide contains this delightfully honest comment: 'The Skaitielv river is a tributary of the Junkerelv, which joins the Lonselv to form the mighty Saltdal river. All this happens in North Norway, near the Arctic Circle. The Junkerelv is noted for its wild beauty. We can give no description of the Skaitielv, but it looks worth trying.'

Angling in Norway underlines the limitless opportunity for fly fishermen, and for those favouring other methods. It notes that the best fishing is in the north, above the timber line, and in remoter areas. As general advice, the massive Langfellene, the long mountain chain running from the Seresdal uplands above Kristiansand to the Sylene range north-east of Roros, provides the best of the southern trout fishing. The huge Hardangervidda plateau, up to 4,000 feet above sea level and covering the counties of Buskerad, Telemark and Hardaland, is another favoured area. But the best is probably the Finnmark plateau near the Finnish border: 'The word Finnmark sounds specially sweet in a fisherman's ear. Here can be found lakes and rivers seldom, if ever, visited and offering splendid sport.'

Thorbjørn Tufte is well versed in Norwegian trout fishing and adds this advice:

'One main rule must never be forgotten when it comes to fishing in Norway: the further north you go in this long and remote country, the better will be the chances of making a fine catch. This applies to all kinds of fish, even sea fish, and of course has something to do with the great concentration of people in the south of the country. The pressure on the lakes has for years been much greater there than in the north. In addition to this, the south of Norway has for a long time suffered constant air pollution. Regrettably, most of this pollution comes from the British Isles, with the south-westerly winds bringing so much tainted rain to our part of the world. Large-scale testing of the water has shown that nearly all lakes in the south of Norway suffer from this pollution, which makes the water far too acid. It is a fact that trout have disappeared from great areas during recent years, though in some districts heavy applications of lime have brought water back to a standard that makes life possible for trout again.

'Notwithstanding this negative aspect, Norway remains without doubt a leader in Europe when it comes to fishing for trout and also Arctic char, a fish which in many ways may be compared to the ordinary brown trout and which you will find more and more numerous the further north you travel in Norway. In many lakes – for instance in the extreme north of the country, on the great Finnmark mountain plateau – trout and Arctic char live and thrive in the same lakes. The char take a fly well and provide additional interest for the keen angler.

'In Finnmark alone there are thousands of lakes with a relatively good stock of fish. In Finnmark foreigners may fish only within 5 kilometres of the roads; the remote areas are kept for the use of the local people, who include the Lapps. Fishing is very cheap in these mountains, which are owned by the government. This is also true of the north of Norway. There are many more government-owned areas from the middle of the country northwards than in the south, where the lakes and the rivers often are private property, with little or no opportunity for fishing. I must emphasize, however, that areas with free fishing for all can also be found in the south of the country, where perhaps 50 per cent of the fishing is in private hands, whereas from Trøndelag northwards the mountain areas are 100 per cent government-owned, and fishing is open to all.

'Mountains are the key to fishing in Norway. The best and most interesting trout and char fishing is to be found in these areas, where the lakes and the rivers are numerous. As a general rule, the further you are willing to walk into these mountain areas, the better the fishing will be. The Norwegians make veritable expeditions when they go into the mountain areas to find the really big trout. They pack all they need in a rucksack, carry their tent and sleeping bag, and walk, often for a day or two into the most remote areas. They know that the big trout are never found close to the road. The further you adventure into the wilderness, the better are your chances of finding the virgin lakes where perhaps only a few people have been before and where the stocks of fish are entirely wild and natural.

'It is possible to find fishing near the roads in Norway, but the chances of catching a big trout are low. The sad fact is that seven out of ten Norwegian lakes contain too many fish for the available food supply and, since there is no interest in fishing for small fish, the stocks remain unculled and the cycle of ever larger populations of ever more stunted fish continues.

'Because the most interesting fishing for trout and char is concentrated in the mountain areas of Norway, the season is rather short. In the north the lakes are covered by ice until the end of June or the beginning of July, and fishing is good only from the middle of July until the end of August, before winter returns to the mountains in September. In the mountains of the south the season starts a little earlier, but only a fortnight or so. In the lowlands, however, the season starts in May and ends in September. But the really good fishing is not found in the lower areas, again as a result of too many people and very limited management of the lakes and rivers. The shortness of the season is compensated for by the fact that in summer it is possible to fish right round the clock. In the north the sun shines for twenty-four hours and even in the southern parts of Norway it never gets dark during the fishing season in June and July.

'As to tackle and techniques, remember that the Norwegians learned to fish from the British, and if you walk into a tackle shop in Norway you will find all the flies you have in your own fishing bag with the same English names. Because water temperatures can be very low, especially at the beginning and the end of the season, sinking lines with flies or nymphs retrieved deep down can prove most effective. A very useful item of equipment is a small inflatable boat. This may be the real key to successful fishing, since it is often impossible to reach the fish – particularly the char and the bigger trout – from the bank because of the extensive shallows, the ever present daylight, and the fact that the fish prefer the cooler depths.

'Do not be put off by the thought of remote mountainous districts and iced-up lakes. The fact is that the summer in Norway can be fantastic. The sun, shining day and night, makes the summer season a short and very intensive one. You can almost watch the plants growing and flies and insects abound in quantities which will amaze the visitor. A good supply of insect-repellant is essential and mosquito nets are to be recommended for the north. Good footwear and weatherproof clothing will also be required.

'Norway gives the angler the special thrill of fishing in a land where nature has not been spoiled by man and where the fish you catch have not been planted by man. And it is certainly nothing unusual to discover that the water you have walked for hours to reach has been fished by you and perhaps no more than a dozen other anglers.'

Julius Ytteborg, a member of London's Flyfishers' Club and a very experienced Norwegian fisherman, has this to add:

'From the early 1960s Norwegian trout fishing has deteriorated rather rapidly, and is today only a shadow of what it was immediately after the war. The chances of catching a trout of, say, four pounds on a fly are very slim unless you are prepared to walk five or six hours from the nearest road. In the extreme south of the country it is virtually impossible to find fishing even for trout of a pound or so, but if you are able to find your way to the upper part of the Klara River, also called the Trysil River, which flows out of Lake Femund not far from the Swedish border south-east of Trondheim, you will have a chance of good fly fishing (if you are lucky with the weather). There will be more grayling than trout in these waters, where dry-fly fishing is the best method during reasonably warm periods of the comparatively short season. Try grey, brown, yellow and black artificials in sizes 10–14. This is the only good fishing in southern Norway that can be reached by car, and where it is possible to find lodging in a farm or boarding house, but even here you will stand a much better chance of catching the big ones if you bring your own tent and walk into the wilderness.

'Other places worth exploring in southern Norway are the mountain areas on the peninsulas between the deep fjords in the Western parts of the country, especially in the counties of Sogn, Möre and Romsdal. Here, however, anglers are even more exposed to the weather, since lakes are situated more than 1,000 metres above the sea, but big fish are certainly to be found.'

The National Tourist Office in Oslo can provide many useful names and addresses, especially if you have already decided on a particular area. A brochure, *Sportsfiske i Norge (Angling in Norway)*, lists the general rules for freshwater fishing. Two will especially appeal to trout fishermen: the use of live fish as bait is prohibited; then there is the regulation that ensures the continuing dominance of trout and char in many areas – 'Trout and/or char are the only species in large areas of Norway. To prevent the spread of unwanted new species of fish section 34 of the Act relating to freshwater fishing prohibits the introduction into watercourses of species of fish not existing there before.'

There is also a reminder that you have to pay a fishing insurance fee to the Government Fishing Fund. All fishing in government territory in Finnmark is administered by the Directorate for Wildlife and Freshwater Fish through the Finnmark Land Commission in Vadsø. More detailed information can be obtained from the Directorate for Wildlife and Freshwater Fish, 7000, Trondheim; the county governors' environmental protection departments; and the local lensman (a police officer with administrative duties).

Sweden

The following summary of Swedish fishing is also provided by Julius Ytteborg:

'Conditions for trout fishing in Sweden are not unlike those in Norway, but in Sweden there is generally more forest and less mountain fishing. Even there the fishing becomes better the further north one goes, and it is generally also better in the western districts of northern Sweden, towards the Norwegian border. In southern Sweden brook trout of less than one pound are rather numerous, and there are also found two outstanding sea-trout rivers, the Em, with some of the largest sea trout in the world, and the Mörrum. In southern Sweden there are also rainbow trout in numerous lakes, even in lakes quite close to the capital, Stockholm. All the rainbow trout have been introduced by man since the Second World War. They are usually stocked at half a pound or a pound, and under favourable conditions they grow quickly. The size of rainbow trout in the Swedish lakes also depends on how long fishing in a particular lake is closed to anglers after stocking to make catching more difficult. Today, fishing for rainbows with a fly is a very valuable addition to Swedish trout fishing and absolutely vital to the fly fishing in the southern part of the country.

'As in Norway, a type of very large lake trout, up to more than twenty pounds in size, but not of interest to the fly fishermen, is found in the largest lakes. In Norway, Lake Miosa and Lake Tyrifjorden, both an hour's drive from Oslo, are famous for their large trout, and in Sweden you find the fish in very large lakes such as the Vanern, the Vattern and the Lake Hjalmaren, all in the southern part of the country. Normal brown trout from half a pound up to four or five pounds are found in increasing numbers from the county of Jamtland, roughly as far north as Trondheim in Norway, and it is to the north and north-west of Jamtland that Sweden can offer good fly fishing to the visiting angler. Grayling are plentiful and the northernmost lakes also hold some char. Seasons and tackle are similar to Norway. Information about Swedish angling can be obtained from the Swedish angling association Sveriges Sportsfiske – och Fiskevardsforbund, Box 11, 501, 10061, Stockholm, Sweden.'

With over 96,000 lakes, numerous rivers, an area twice that of Britain and a population less than Greater London's, Sweden has little angling pressure. Again the general advice is to make for the north and the high ground for big baskets of sizeable trout. But for sea trout there is at least one outstanding southern river. The Mörrum is justly famed for large specimens and even larger salmon. When reporting the World Football Championship in 1958 it was to the Mörrum that I hurried as a change from watching Kopa and Fontaine, Pele and Garrincha pile up the goals. Unfortunately I could not bring as many to the net as they managed. That was no blame to the river but to dredging and bridge-building above my stretch, which turned the Mörrum into a wide cocoa-coloured stream.

No doubt the fish could see well enough in that opaque world, but it was still a surprise to me to catch even one sea trout and a salmon. Muddy as the water was, the potential quality of the fishing was clear enough. Huge fish kept porpoising up the current. They looked vast to me and probably were as salmon of up to 50 pounds are caught in the Mörrum. The National Board of Crown Lands and Forests, the Domänverket, issues permits for a 3-mile stretch with thirteen pools. The Board also provides an opportunity to fish throughout Sweden, issuing permits for thousands of lakes and many miles of varied river fishing. In Sweden the sport is very much a family affair and the Domänverket is one of the few organisations to recognize that aspect for visiting tourists as well. It issues a special Turfiskekort for families on holiday, covering parents and all children under the age of sixteen.

Apart from the Mörrum it is mainly in the north, in Norrland, that the sea trout and salmon surge in quantity up the rivers. From mid-July to the end of September, when the season ends, is the best period for the northernmost rivers. In south Norrland April and September are particularly good for sea trout. In the broad Swedish rivers the sea trout, which keep close to the banks, are easier to catch than the salmon, which swim up the main currents. For sea trout in the far north the Torne and its tributaries, the Pite and a few smaller streams on the coasts of Norrbotten and Västerbotten offer the best opportunity. These rivers are at present free of hydroelectric dams. Elsewhere these barriers tend to limit the fishing to the lower reaches, as with the Buden rapids in the Lule, the Angermanälven at Solleftea, the Indalsälven downstream of the Bergefersen rapids, the Ljungan around Njurunda and the Dalälven at Älvkarleby. For west-coast rivers the pick of the fishing areas are the Atran at Falkenberg and the Orekilsläven near Munkedal.

Brown trout, along with Arctic char (*röding – salvelinus alpinus*) are numerous in the high mountain areas, the fells, and in the north Swedish forests from the province of Dalarna in the south to Norrbotton in the north. *Salmo trutta* run large and wild in the mountain regions. In fell areas these brown trout usually run to a maximum size of 6½ pounds, but in major forest lakes they have been caught up to 24 pounds. In smaller streams and brooks the trout are pan-sized, weighed in ounces rather than pounds. The char is the most characteristic cold-water fish and it thrives in the high country. Occasionally char up to seven pounds are taken, but in general a fish of two pounds is a good one.

The Swedish Tourist Board provides a most helpful pamphlet, *Angling in Sweden* (the printed broadsheet as opposed to the uninformative pictorial *Sweden Angling*). It includes the following advice:

'Grayling (*Thymallus thymallus*) are found in many rivers, but also in lakes in the north. Where you find grayling they are usually numerous. The following are good examples of where the fisherman looking for trout,

1 Author and son play fish together on Austria's Gmunderer Traun; John with a big grayling hooked on a leaded nymph, father with a rainbow on a dry fly.

2 John using the difficult Traun technique of swimming a leaded nymph down some thirty yards without dragging and keeping the fly close to the bottom.

3   Moc Morgan stalks the hard-fighting half-pounders of the Upper Teifi.

4   A typical, quiet-flowing Danish river.

5   Peter Cockwill takes time from catching trophy trout and steelheads to land a chinook on Oregon's Wind river.

6   The author plays a four pound rainbow in New Zealand's Rangitaiki river.

7   Henri Hosinger fishing on Belgium's Amel river.

8   Marian Kwasnik of Poland, in the foreground, prepares to show the Spanish World Cup
team the subtleties of nymph fishing for grayling on the San river.

char, or grayling can establish his base. From north to south start with Kimuna. Flights leave here for the sources of the rivers Laimio and Kaitum. Next is Arjeplog. The tributaries of the rivers Laisälven and Skellefteälven lie in this district. For summer fishing planes depart from Sädvaluspen about forty miles north-west of Arjeplog. From Armannas you can reach a number of good waters in the Vindelälven river system. Tärna is a good centre for a number of fishing waters in the upper tributaries of the river Umeälven, while to the west of Vilhelmina are some fine fishing waters in lakes and rivers, including the upper reaches of the Wojman and Kultsjöan.

'From Östersund you can fly to many excellent trout waters in the high mountain region of Oviksfjällen and the lake Rogen district. The southernmost waters with a good head of salmonidae are those in Fulufjällen and Idrefjällen in north-west Dalarna. The best time for trout in upper Norrland is from mid-July to September. In south Norrland some waters begin in late June and there is even fishing in the ice, particularly for char, which are best caught in late winter and spring.

'In many areas of Sweden coarse fish are being eradicated by treating waters with rotenone and the like, then restocking with salmonidae. This has led to a number of artificial waters stocked with rainbows, browns, brooks and char, thus making available a range of trout fishing in southern and central Sweden. There are a number of fishing lakes in the Skåne, the fishing district of the city of Gothenburg, in the neighbourhood of Tideholm, in the Stockholm area and in the Malingsbo-kloten fishing district north of Orebro, and a couple of areas on the coast of the Gulf of Bothnia.'

4
Trout Fishing in Europe

From Denmark to the Pyrenees

Denmark can provide some very interesting trout fishing, and some outstanding sea trout catches. Indeed, it was for many years the source of the world record sea trout. One of the best of Danish fishermen, Mogens Esperson, gives this personal view of Danish trout fishing:

'It was one of those days known to every angler – perfect, had the trout only known. Plenty of casting, but no fish interested. It was early April, one of the first real days of spring: a mild southerly breeze, clouds with flashes of blue sky, the stream in the southern part of Jutland clearing and falling after the torrents of the thaw.

'Having tried upstream spiders and wets, downstream pupae, shrimps, local flies and several others now forgotten, this angler decided to do something stupid, as trout apparently didn't read fishing books and so were ignorant of what was their proper behaviour. I decided on an impossible team of flies, a Black Ghost hairwing at the tail and a leader Goddard Shrimp on the dropper. I knew, of course, that as far as centuries of angling wisdom goes no elver preys on freshwater shrimp in mating clothing.

'But they do. Or, rather, brown trout occasionally believe so. A brownie, which didn't look particularly stupid, hooked itself and went deep. It was landed eventually with the shrimp securely in the scissors. Great, I thought. Two shrimps then. Nothing happened. Then back to the impossible, which worked again.

'After a few brace of nice brown trout the stream went back to sleep, and the elver-shrimp combination has not worked ever since. To this day, many trout later, I do not know what went wrong – and right – on that early April morning.

'The story without moral is not recorded to indicate that trout in Danish streams are maniacs. They are not. They do take flies according to books, but compared with British steady risers trout in Danish waters may from time to time behave without respect for tradition and angling style – for two reasons probably. First, most Danish streams are rainwater-fed.

Second, insect life is very different from the chalk streams where dry-fly fishing was more or less born. Blank days in a row do happen, and then suddenly, without any visible warning, the trout seem to go crazy, bless them.

'Trout fishing in Denmark with the fly is about 150 years old, spread by visiting British anglers hunting salmon, sea trout, brown trout and grayling. At Hagebro Inn at Karup Å there was a room prepared especially for the British. A closet built into the chimney contained two chambers – one for drying wet clothes, another for drying tobacco.

'The first recorded Danish flies are from about 1875. Round the turn of the century a leaded nymph of local tying, not unlike Frank Sawyer's Killer Bug, was widely used for grayling and brown trout, fished upstream, of course.

'Most of the fly fishing in early days was after salmon and sea trout, but in the early 1930s Olav Krogsgaard decided to find flies for brownies. He collected insects at the streams of Jutland, preserved them, and sent them to Hardy's for imitation. The result was a series of twelve wet flies, still known under his name and widely used. The Krogsgaard flies, which are mostly sedges, are recorded in A. Courtney Williams's *Dictionary of Trout Flies*, as are several other local Danish patterns.

'As fly tying is spreading the number of local Danish flies, many of them excellent, is growing fast – but a visiting angler would be well off with some leaded nymphs, sedges, palmers, spiders, and some tiny hairwings, all on the darkish-brown or olive side. Flashy patterns seldom catch steadily because most Danish streams are of slightly brownish colour. Sizes for brown trout and rainbows are 8–14. Browns and rainbows, the latter escapees from the many fisheries, are often fished for with a team of two flies, although large brown trout are best taken on a small streamer or hairwing. Dry-fly fishing is not effective in all Danish streams, some being too fast and others too stained. Duns are not as widespread as in British waters, and patterns should be sedges and the like, sizes 10–14.

'Most Danish streams are association water, but day tickets are normally easily available. They can be obtained through tourist boards, travel agencies, and local tackle shops. The Danish anglers' association, Danmarks Sportsfiskerforbund, Woersaaesgade 1, DK-7100 Vejle (telephone 5–820699), will be happy to provide the necessary information.

'There are hundreds of excellent streams, mostly in Jutland, with a few on Fuhnen, Zealand, and Bornholm. In Jutland are many streams with Lindenborg Å, Uggerby Å, Stor Å, Karup Å, Simested Å, Gels Å, Skjern Å, Sneum Å, and Vejle Å examples of good fishing open to visiting anglers.'

The streams contain certain stocks of wild brown trout, a few grayling, and rainbows. Sea trout should also be mentioned, as fly fishing for sea trout in streams and from the beach is developing into a Danish speciality. Karup Å, for example, breeds some of the biggest sea trout in Scandinavia.

The biggest Danish trout recognized as records are a brown trout of thirteen pounds from Sneum Å (south Jutland, 1981), a rainbow of fourteen pounds from Guden Å (central Jutland, 1973); and a sea trout of nearly thirty pounds from Karup Å (central Jutland, 1939). For many years this was the biggest sea trout recorded on rod and line world-wide, and Danish sea trout and trout fishing still has considerable attractions for the visiting angler.

The Fishing regulations in Denmark are simple, relating mainly to minimum sizes – 40 cm for salmon and sea trout, 25 cm for brown trout, unspecified for rainbows (these may be highest on association waters) – and to seasons. The close season for salmon, sea trout and brown trout is from 16 November to 15 January, with none specified for rainbows. On many association waters a close season from 1 November to 27 February is applied, so check before paying a winter visit. Salt-water regulations forbid the killing of coloured trout between 16 November and 15 January.

Belgium

The 1915 edition of Hardy's *Angler's Guide* did indeed give a favourable mention to salmon from the Meuse and Ourthe, but the king of fish no longer swims up these rivers, nor does Belgium today enjoy any great reputation as a trout-fishing centre. So is the country worth a visit today from the keen trout angler? The Belgian Fly Fishing Committee of Rue de Wijnants Straat 33, 1000 Brussels (Telephone Brussels (02) 511 6848), would no doubt put you straight on that. One of its leading members, Christian Fouvez, whose expertise in dry-fly fishing I have long admired, gave me a lyrical general description of the pleasures to be experienced and full details of the best of the trout fishing, all based on his own wide experience:

'Our loveliest rivers wander majestically across the south of Belgium, unrivalled as our country's most beautiful region. Deep valleys, vast pine forests of vivid hues, the wild scenery still as nature intended – all this makes me delight in fishing the rivers in our part of the Ardennes. On each visit they reveal to me new marvels and new secrets. It is also a region rich in history, with the many relics of past centuries lovingly preserved.

'The salmon may have gone, locals jealously guarding their favourite places from foreign invaders may talk of scarcity of fish, but in many areas the rivers are very rewarding, with trout and grayling especially plentiful.

They are well worth the fishing permit, which currently costs 250 Belgian francs, or 1000 if you want to wade. To avoid annoyance get the more expensive wading permit, because you will always find good reason to want to enter the water and won't want to risk having your equipment confiscated. Permits can be obtained at post offices, which are normally open Monday to Friday from 9 a.m. to 4 p.m. Armed with one you are entitled to fish anywhere from the bank or wading the water.

'Where better to start than the Ourthe? This magnificent river runs for more than 200 kilometres through the wild beauty of the Belgian Ardennes. The Ourthe is a fine grayling river and has a store of trout as well. In the higher reaches it seems to run in an unreal setting. So steep are the Ourthe's banks that as you wade down you feel they will engulf you and swallow you up. But once you return to reality you enjoy a perfect communion with nature, and can spend many relaxing hours there. Access to the river is difficult, but this helps to keep it a tranquil place where you can take pleasure in the solitude.

'Apart from grayling there are some wild brown trout, but stocking with rainbows has been necessary to ensure good baskets. However, Jean Servais, the President of the Union des Pêcheurs de l'Ourthe et de l'Amblève, has been trying to increase the numbers of wild brown trout by the use of "Vibert" hatching boxes in the Ourthe near Hamoir. The early results have been satisfactory and Jean, an excellent fly fisherman, is also delighted by the reappearance of several flies which had become rare in recent years. So the yellow ephemera, Aulnes flies and other sedges will again make a meal for the fish – good news for Ourthe anglers.

'To summarize the opportunities on the various sections let us start with the unexciting stretch between the bridge at Nisramont and the one at Comblain-Fairon. Wading is permitted between the Nisramont dam and that of Maboge from 1 June to 30 September and this is the best time for fly fishermen who enjoy this wide but irregular water. Access to the river can be difficult here, but those courageous enough to get down to it will find few other anglers to disturb them. My own favourite spots are at Hérou and Ondes, and my favourite patterns are Blue Dun, Universelle, Aulnes fly, Coachman, Red Tag and Yellow Ephemera. Avoid the sides of the Nisramont dam and the village of Maboge. From Maboge to Jupille the river is narrower, and is mostly bordered by meadows. Fly fishermen have many opportunities here in the quiet flats and the streams full of trout. There is no wading and the same flies should be successful. The harder the river gets fished, the smaller the flies you need – probably down to size 22 by late summer.

'Avoid the approach to Jupille, and miss out the water between Jupille and Hotton. From Hotton to Deulin there are some fine trout in the runs. Thereafter the river divides, and it is best to follow the larger stream, which has many trout and grayling. Keep trying both the streams between Deulin and Fronville, one of which makes a wide circle, while the other runs straight.

'Let us return to the area round Hamoir. From Hamoir bridge to Fairon there are many hot spots, but the best are beside the little wood, and also from the bank opposite the camping site before the village of Fairon. There are popular but crowded places near the camping ground before the bridge at Hamoir, where large grayling are to be found. For these areas I find that Black Gnats and other dark flies, Hare's Ear, Grannom and Autumn Dun are also effective.

'The area between the Nisramont dam and Fairon is worth prospecting again. There is some fine fishing over 80 kilometres of water, but it is very popular at the start of the season and in July and August, so don't go there if you don't like being crowded. Another very interesting part of the Ourthe is the stretch owned by the Trout Society of Houffalize. This is exciting water, with 18 kilometres of alternating flats, runs, cascades and deep pools.

'Quite simply, it provides fantastic fishing, but only for experienced anglers. For there are obstructions in many places as nature interferes with the normal course of the stream.'

The best places are between the Bilstain Mill and Engreux. There is no wading, but happy innovation of 'fly only' on one part. Permits to fish here can be obtained from M. Jacquemain, 3 Rue du Pont, Houffalize; M. Wathelet, Rue de Schaerbeek; and the Hotel de la Vallée des Fées in Achouffe. There are many pleasant hotels in the area, such as the Hostellerie de la Commanderie, 44 Rue Haute, and the Hotel de l'Ourthe, both in Hotton; or the Relax Hotel in Houffalize. There are also camping sites at Florenville, Hotton, Houffalize and La Roche. So no problems about accommodation or food, with many good restaurants in an area which stirs memories for an older generation. Old American tanks in many squares recall the Battle of the Bulge and the heroic defence of nearby Bastogne. Sad some of those memories may be, but the fishing ones can only be pleasant.

For a visitor's view of the Ourthe, here is Geoff Clarkson's account of his experience when first fishing there with Fouvez in late September. The fish had been hammered all season and it needed skilful fishing to tempt them:

'I was introduced to the Ourthe in magnificent autumn weather, crisp air and warm sun. The river was very low and crystal-clear after weeks without rain. The local experts advised fishing fine, with small dry flies, for the wily grayling. When I reached the river I was encouraged by seeing some rising fish, and started full of confidence. Using a 3-pound point and size 16, then 18, dry flies, after three-quarters of an hour of covering fish I hadn't even risen one.

'I walked to the bank for further instruction from a friend of Fouvez's. He told me I was fishing too large flies and too thick a point. He then superglued on a couple of feet of 1½-pound nylon and selected a size 20 Red Tag from my box. Immediately I started rising grayling. Now the problem was to hook them, since they grabbed and spat out the fly in a split second. One helpful tactic was to fish with the sun behind, which helped to see the grayling on the way up to the fly aiding an earlier strike. Another useful tactic was to find a shoal of grayling – easily done since they rose consistently – and then stay with the shoal. Surprisingly, in view of their disregard of flies attached to 3-pound nylon, it proved difficult to put them down despite repeated casting.

'I was unable to fish in the evening, but was back on the river very early the next morning. This proved to be the most productive time, both with grayling and trout, probably because they were undisturbed. It was the only time I was alone on this popular and heavily fished river.'

It is not only the Ourthe which can provide memorable fishing in Belgium. As Fouvez reasonably comments, 'There are many rivers with abundant trout fishing and an ambience which makes it a pleasure to be there. You should soak yourself in the atmosphere of these streams, where there is a magical quality, particularly at the time of the evening rise. The catch then is occasionally disappointing, but you will usually see some large fish and enough of them showing to stir the emotions. Exciting fishing there will be for you, but the rule to remember is to relax and enjoy yourself.'

Of the other rivers which appeal to him the Lesse has a special place. It was there he caught his first trout at one of it most productive spots – Donation Royale à Villers-sur-Lesse. It was there that he spent days trying in vain to snare a monster chub, which ignored every fly, and scorned every trick. The Lesse rises at Ochamps then flows for a hundred kilometres to Anseremme, where it joins the Meuse. It is a fast and winding river with many large grayling that make fishing a joy. There are wild brown trout too, but more difficult to deceive.

For Christian's brother Daniel, the princess of rivers is the Semois. Such is its reputation that Noel-Hubert Balzat, well-known Belgian author and editor of *Le Pêcheur Belge*, wrote of it: 'To describe the Semois is a dangerous task for its praises have been sung by poets before me and much better qualified than I. This sovereign and majestic river makes me feel like a straw swept away by the flood.'

As Fouvez puts it:

'The Semois is a seductive stream, enchanting you with its tranquil beauty, only to deceive you with many a trap of slippery rocks or deep holes. Again, as water is released from weirs you may need to avoid the mass of floating weed and vegetation. Despite such drawbacks this is an endearing river teeming with fish, including many trout. One of these typified for me its charm and its perils. To reach a big rainbow rising steadily, I edged out until the water was close to the top of my waders. My joy at hooking the fish changed to a cold sweat as I realized that I was stranded with deep potholes on either side, and in danger of slipping under. In the end I needed help from a passer-by to reach the shore, happy at the relief of nervous tension and that my catch was safe too. My brother Daniel is my favourite fishing companion. He is an expert on the Semois and can talk for days about his rewarding experiences on a magnificent river with so many fishy areas. He may exaggerate just a little, but certainly the Semois, some 200 kilometres long and between 25 and 50 metres broad, has catching places without number.

'The Lhomme is one of the smaller streams with a big attraction for fly fishermen. It is best in the Namur region and is very popular with local anglers, despite the fee which has to be paid. This was where I caught my first grayling – just a small one. Many larger have followed, though grayling can be difficult to catch in this river, which is never more than ten metres wide. Namur and Liège are the best areas for fly fishermen, and you get some good trout there. Some surprises too, as when I thought I was anchored into a monster trout near Mirwart, only to find it was an average-size fish which had dived under a submerged log.

'The Sûre is a river precious to both Belgium and Luxemburg, as it runs across the border. It is some six to ten metres broad and good for fly fishing. It is full of fish at the start of the season, but is so popular that the easy ones are soon caught. The Sûre becomes more interesting then, as it needs skill and planning thereafter to catch the trout – which are well worth the effort. The river runs through Martelange, the home of Mark Reckinger, a fly-fishing world champion. He owns a watchmaker's shop in which he also sells tackle. If he likes you he might even show you some special places on the river he knows so well. Of the many big fish I have lost the most surprising was one on the Sûre. It went off with all my cast, my line and my Universelle fly. If anyone ever caught it they would indeed have a tale to tell.

'The Amblève has been badly polluted and will take years to recover. The Sambre is another suffering in this way. There are, however, many smaller streams – such as the Viroin, the Chiers and the Rulles – which are popular with the locals, and others like the Boch which are kept mainly private – a source of much argument.

'Our rivers are full of fish and adding stocked adult trout to them is a short-term policy. There are still plenty of wild browns, chub and grayling, which are more intriguing to catch than these 'circus trout', as I call them. To pretend that Belgian rivers have not suffered from industrial development or the spread of camping sites is not to face facts. To promise full nets to everyone fishing in Belgium would be equally unrealistic. What I can promise the visiting angler is that he will enjoy his fishing, the relaxation, and the beautiful scenery. And if France is justly appreciated for gourmet cooking, so some of our own chefs are equally qualified. You can be fisherman and gourmet at the same time in Belgium.'

Luxemburg

Luxemburg has many excellent fly-fishermen, though no waters that are reserved solely for fly fishing. My first experience there was in the best of their stocked stillwaters, at Weiswampach, which boasts two small lakes, one with trout only. Well managed by Jean Ballman and Henri Hosinger, who is also an expert fly dresser, this had a good head of rainbow trout. On that early October day they were very choosy, but responsive to size 10 Tadpoles and Vivas fished slow about a foot below the surface. Naturally their moods and feeding patterns change with changing seasons and conditions, but standard stillwater flies and bank techniques should prove rewarding.

The general average was around the pound, but there were a number of larger trout too with some up to six pounds. A daily permit costs about £4, a fortnight's fishing there about £25. There is good variety in deeps and shallows and pleasant lakeside facilities. Close to the Belgian border, this Ardennes fishery has a high enough reputation for the Belgian Fly Fishing Committee to stage their annual European open competition there. There is a limit of five trout per permit on both lakes, and a limit to two permits per day. Small trout caught on fly may be carefully returned after being handled with wet hands. Those caught on worm or spinner must be killed and count towards the total.

A member of a fishing party from Luxemburg who came to join our Izaak Walton tercentenary commemorations was Jean Zender. This is his description of the rest of the fishing in his country:

'Clervaux is close to Weiswampach and also has two similar, but smaller, lakes. Again one holds trout only while the other has a variety of fish to match the variety of permitted methods. A few years ago Lake Echternach was a great trout fishery, very good for bank fishing with the fly. There I caught my largest trout in Luxemburg, a ten-pound rainbow and a five-pound brown. It was there too that the first World Fly Fishing

Championship was staged in 1981. But sadly the lake has been allowed to decline and no longer rates as a trout fishery worth a visit. The reservoir of Esch-sur-Sûre is interesting, but difficult for fly fishing. It is divided into two zones and only in the second is fishing allowed. Bank fishing is hard because of the rocks and the forest coming down to the water's edge in many places. The boat fishing is interesting and can be productive – the snag is that there are no boats for hire so you have to bring your own. All you need to fish there is a state department licence, but there is a limit of six salmonids.

'Our river fishing for trout and grayling can be attractive to fly fishermen, but much of the best is in private hands and barred to visitors. In general you need a state licence and a daily permit from the owner of the water, whether a proprietor, private club, or Syndicat de Tourisme. The Clerf river in Kautenbach is a delightful stream, but only short stretches are available to the public. The permit costs about £5 and there is a limit of six trout per day. Another pleasant river somewhat similar to the Ourthe is the Our. This flows down to the German border, but again only short stretches are open to the ordinary visitor, with some especially good fishing around Vianden. The cost and the fishing available are much the same, and the limit includes grayling. There are many good hotels around Vianden and the Syndicat de Tourisme can advise, as in other areas where there is trout fishing.

'By far the best of our rivers is the Sûre, or Sauer. This flows from the Esch-sur-Sûre dam to the German border, then along the border to join the Moselle. Most of the inland reaches of the Sûre are privately owned, but there are many beats where tourists can fish. Below the dam there is a stretch which winds in and out around the town. This is not easy for fly fishing as the casting is difficult. As all along the Sûre the fishing is cheap and here the limit is six trout or grayling.

'The cream of Luxemburg's river fishing open to the ordinary tourist is in the next three open stretches of the Sûre. Flowing through the most attractive part of the Luxemburg Ardennes, the river is very rewarding to the good angler, but also tests his skill. My own club, Pêcheur Ardennais Wiltz, owns the fishing from the Dirbach bridge to the bridge at Goebelsmuhle and daily permits can be had. All types of accommodation are easily available along the Sûre and the next available beats also have camping sites close by. This stretch is owned by Georges and Marie-Jeanne Kremer and the fishing fees for 1986 were: daily permit 250 Belgian francs (£4); monthly 1,200; annual 8,000. These can be obtained from the Um Gritt and Du Moulin camping offices at Bourscheid and cover the water from Barrage Camping du Moulin to the railway bridge at Brahmuhle.

'The hotel beats between Bourscheid-Moulin and Erpeldange are particularly good. Three hotels – the Dahm, 9145 Erpeldange/Ettelbruch, Du Moulin, 9164 Bourscheid-Moulin, and Week-End, 9164 Bourscheid-Plage – have rights to the water. For brown, rainbow, and brook trout there is the usual limit of 25 centimetres, and a bag limit of five trout or four trout and one grayling. The hotel brochure also points out the best seasons and the potential problems. In its words, April, May and June and then September, October and November (the trout season closes at the end of September, but grayling may be caught until the end of December) are the best months. In July and August the Sûre is often very low, while all the world also wanders along the beautiful meadows beside the river. To add to an angler's distractions at this time there are also kayak events with canoes frequently disturbing the water. So avoid the high summer months if you want good and peaceful fishing. Bourscheid has a striking landmark. High above you as you fish stand the ruins of Bourscheid Castle. Once a dominating stronghold, this ranks in importance with the magnificent Castle of Vianden and has unusual features in its double surrounding wall and ring fence for jousts.

'It is no wonder that the fisherman is disturbed in the holiday months by walkers, for the scenery here is superb – as it is in most of the Ardennes area of northern Luxemburg. For the rest of the river from Ettelbruch to the German border at Wallendorf and then along it until the Sûre flows into the Moselle (about the only small stretch of that river where you are likely to have a chance of catching trout) only the state licence used to be required. From 1987, however, an additional permit is required. By agreement between Luxemburg and Germany, the money raised by these permits, whether you fish on the Luxemburg side or across the border on the German side, will be used to keep the river well stocked and well managed. This should ensure excellent fishing.

'There is German co-operation too in the German-Luxemburg Nature Park area of the Ardennes Luxembourgeoises du Nord. This is a popular area to visit or fish because of the varied scenery, with steep hillsides covered with pine and oak, then narrow valleys with clear fast streams alternating with wide expanses of lush pastureland. This is a good centre for fishing the stocked lakes, or the Clerf and Our rivers. Information is freely available from the Syndicats d'Initiative at Clervaux, Weiswampach, Troisvierges, Binsfeld, Hosinger and Lieler.

'Standard English tackle and flies do well in Luxemburg. For dry flies Sedge and Coachman are the most generally effective; of the wet flies the Butchers, March Browns and Mallard and Clarets are favourites of mine; for nymphs use Pheasant Tails, or Ritz-D, or Hare's Ear; on stocked lakes any type of streamer may be effective, as well as small flies. The trout in the rivers run up to 35 centimetres, with any above that very rare, though I have had a 4½-pound rainbow. Grayling go up to 45 centimetres – again with a very few larger. Certainly there was one bigger one for which I fished one year for twenty hours without ever interesting him in nymph or fly. When I came back the following year there he was again; and again I spent twenty fruitless, but enjoyable, hours trying to tempt him. He was a wily one all right! In the clear water I could watch my nymph sail down at the right pace and angle. Just as it was about to bump his nose he would shift disdainfully sideways, then move back with a contemptuous flick of the tail as soon as the nymph had glided past. There is much to enjoy in Luxemburg's rivers and many helpful anglers to advise and wish you "Bonne Pêche!" '

Jean is himself very used to catching large fish: he has been to Yugoslavia's Gacka river for over twenty years, regularly catching trout up to ten pounds, and on the first day I took him to Avington near Winchester in England he had a double-figure rainbow there. But in Luxemburg it is not size that matters as much as the challenge of catching trout and grayling in clear streams in idyllic surroundings. Walton and Cotton would have approved.

France

In France it is easy to indulge one's gastronomic interests and at the same time to enjoy some varied trout fishing, much of it good and inexpensive. You don't have to be the man who broke the bank to enjoy fishing a trout lake in the romantic setting of the Bois de Boulogne in Paris. My own first experience of French fishing was in the well run Lac du Château at Dreux in Normandy and in the equally attractive and more varied La Chaise Dieu du Theil à l'Aigle, with its small streams, clear lakes and delightful setting. These two lakes are typical of many stocked stillwaters developing rapidly there. The explosion of this type of fishing, which has so added to English resources in the last thirty years, is now being followed by similar growth in France.

Dr Bertrand Kron was one of the talented French trout fly fishermen who came over for the week of commemorative Izaak Walton celebrations in 1983, and proved more successful than some of England's leading anglers in fishing at Patshull and Avington. His Escargot, or Snail Fly, was soon copied for use sunk or floating when trout are feeding on that type of food. Fished dry, this deerhair fly, looking like an enlarged Muddler head, should be left stationary, then twitched a few feet along the surface, then left still again.

Bertrand gives this account of the recent French boom in fly fishing for trout and an outline of the available fishing:

'Until 1970 the image of fly fishing in France was as a preserve for a small élite. Only the few could indulge in it because of the high cost. Good rods were priced at the equivalent of a working man's monthly pay. There was the considerable expense of private waters, or the discomfort of the public waters, overcrowded and with constant badgering from the trippers. You also needed to be leisured to enjoy trout fishing to the full as the best seasons were outside the holiday month of August, and the famous evening rises made the night too short for those who had to go to work at 5 a.m. That situation has changed rapidly as cheaper tackle has become available, particularly from Japan with the Daiwa and Kunnan ranges, allowing a fly fisherman to be completely equipped for the equivalent of a week's wage.

'The situation was further improved by the increasing importance and strength of national associations emphasizing the importance as a national resource of the salmonids. The TOS – Truite, Ombre, Saumon (trout, grayling, salmon) – associations and the Atlantic salmon societies (AAPPS and AIDSA) fought pollution and spread the idea of 'catch and release' to protect stocks. These associations also soon widened the interest in fly fishing through free instruction in fishing techniques and in fly dressing. That is how I learnt myself, from Andre Vesco of the Boulogne TOS, and for a dozen years I too have helped to instruct beginners in this delightful art.

'In the eighties France made a great leap forward in trout fishing with the development of stocked stillwaters of high quality. This started with Pierre Affre initiating at the Lac du Château in Dreux an excellent fishery run on English lines. This 15-hectare reservoir had an impact similar to that of Blagdon for English stillwater fishing. Suddenly there was good trout fishing available at reasonable price and from 1 January until 31 December there was an opportunity to fish with some hope of a monster trout. Indeed it was at Dreux in 1981 that I caught myself a French record rainbow of 16½ pounds on an Escargot fly tied to a 0·16 mm leader point. Since then fly-fishing clubs and reservoirs have multiplied rapidly, even if few have as yet attained the fine quality of the water at Dreux.

'These clubs have themselves contributed to the establishment of fly-fishing instruction classes and to attracting many new followers to this fascinating sport. For example, in 1970 there were only ten or fifteen fly fishermen in the whole Drouais region but now the Fly Country Club alone has well over a hundred members and there are probably twice as many in the area. We have a long way to go before we reach British standards, but the improvement is rapid. Another good sign is that in our friendly competition events we can see that French fishermen are improving technically all the time. Tony Pawson and his son John, with others such as Brian Peterson, Peter Cockwill, Gary Brooker and Steve Windsor, have done well over here and helped us learn from them. Equally, it was a pleasure to me to come to the Izaak Walton event and enjoy greater success than many of the best-known names in English stillwater fishing and to see the steady improvement in the ability of our fishermen at Dreux judged against some of the best in Europe. Events like the European Open at Dreux are a splendid way of forming international friendships and imparting technical knowledge which helps countries to develop skills in fishing and in fishery management.

'Brown trout are spread all over France, but very unequally. The minimum keepable size is 18 centimetres in the mountains and 23 centimetres in lowland areas. All true fly fishermen, however, regard this as too low and have pressed for it to be raised by 2 centimetres in acid rivers and 4 centimetres in chalk streams. Several societies set reasonable bag limits but this is far from being systematic or general. Unfortunately there are also numerous streams where the wild trout population are small of size and of poor quality because of the ravages of "meat fishermen". As for rainbows, at some fisheries they are of excellent quality, as at Dreux or nearby Chaise Dieu du Theil. Too often, however, rainbows stocked in rivers and lakes are not of adequate quality.

'In recent years the stock of sea trout has appreciated considerably, particularly in the Touques, the Bresles, the Canche and the Orne in Normandy. The electronic counter on the Orne registered more than 300 in a recent year, without counting the small finnock. The weight of the true sea trout is remarkable, often running to twenty or twenty-five pounds. I well recall an evening when I had a fierce take and was then broken by a sea trout of about twenty pounds after it had jumped within a few feet of me. Despite my 0·3 mm leader it broke me in a headlong dash for freedom. It could not have been a salmon as none come up this river. Unfortunately, there are no sensible laws relating to sea trout. The legal minimum size is 23 centimetres (leading to a massacre of the immature); the season closes on 15 September despite the main runs being from July to November; and no night fishing is allowed, denying anglers the best chance of catching them.'

An overall view of how best to plan a fishing holiday in France comes from Philipe Mathieu, managing director of *Plaisirs de la Pêche* magazine:

'Trout are today among the most popular fish in France. This is only right in view of their fine sporting and culinary qualities, though, if you look at a map of French fishing waters, it is difficult to explain the trout's popularity in terms of any abundance of this type of fishing. Indeed, a large number of classified trout waters are in fact streams in decline, or those with only stocked trout, or "catch and release" waters. This is not to say that trout fishing in France is a myth, but it does mean that you take care in your choice of where to fish, especially if you are only going for a short holiday. The following suggestions are intended to help in that choice, and if they also show that there are still opportunities for delightful trout fishing in France then my purpose will have been achieved.

'French trout waters no longer have the reputation they enjoyed thirty years ago. In many cases standards are lower, especially when compared with Austrian, German or British waters, which set a European standard in the quality of game fishing. There are many causes of this decline, including pollution, dams and greater fishing pressure. To look on the bright side, however, it is still possible to find highly enjoyable trout fishing – especially if you plan well in advance.

'The best waters naturally tend to be situated in, or close to, mountainous regions. Another important rule is that the best trout areas are well away from big towns and industrialized or heavily farmed areas. This reduces the options considerably. Nevertheless there are many hot spots in France, many varieties of trout rivers, and opportunities for every type of fishing.

'THE ALPS   For most of us the Alps evoke thoughts of skiing rather than fishing, but all those rivers you see at the bottom of the valleys are usually splendid trout streams and their little tributaries will also have a good head of fish. Again the industrialized or urbanized valleys should be ignored. Concentrate on those known for their fishing qualities. There is the Chéran, a superb location with excellent fishing in its gorges; the Isère in the Albertville area, full of fine trout and with many grayling; the Guiers, very similar; the Bourne where it descends to the valley of the Rhône; the Durance, the Ubaye, the upper Verdon, and all their tributaries, which often yield the best results.

'All these rivers are swollen by melting snow for several months and are at their height from mid-April to the end of July. Fishing then is very difficult, sometimes impossible. The start of the season is often good, but the best times are undoubtedly August and, above all, September. Don't forget either the Alpine lakes which have many fine trout.

'As always, the most accessible lakes are often the least interesting. Except perhaps at opening times, which are often different from those of rivers, it is best to walk to the distant ones, and probably to bivouac if you want the best fishing. Do that and you will really experience the thrill of catching our famous mountain trout.

'BURGUNDY   The Burgundy region does not immediately bring trout to mind. Good food and wine, yes, but not trout. However, administratively speaking this is not only the region of vineyards but also of the Morvan to the west and the hills of the Côte d'Or to the east, where you can find excellent trout waters.

'In the Morvan there are mainly small trout, but very numerous and with occasional beauties. The Cure and all its tributaries offer the best fishing. On the plateaux of the Côte d'Or it is the Seine with its large trout and grayling that commands attention. In these clear waters, with thick beds of weeds waving below the surface, fishing is indeed a sight to delight the eyes. Though not really located in Burgandy, the Ource, a tributary of the Seine, and the upper Aube are equally pleasant to fish, as are many other small and little known streams in that area (the well-known ones tend to be too heavily fished). In these regions pay attention to the special rules which often severely limit the fishing rights and are often different from district to district.

'BRITTANY For several years past the rivers of Brittany have been some of the best as a result of the efforts in fishery management and the great work of restoration accomplished by the Brittany AAPPS. As a result most of the rivers of Brittany have been restored to high standards, and for salmon even more than for trout. Each year the fishing there is more rewarding, and the trout tend all to be of a very acceptable size compared with those in some other regions. The best rivers are without doubt the Elle, the Elorn, the Scorff, the Aulne, the Léguer, the Blavet and their direct tributaries, but the streams of the Côtes du Nord department, though less well known, offer equally good fishing. A rewarding stillwater is the Quénecan reservoir, a well stocked and reasonably priced fishery of 10 hectares.

'THE JURA Without doubt the Jura region possesses the greatest density of excellent trout rivers renowned for the quality of their stock. There are several big rivers with clear water and a good head of sizeable trout. Sadly, intensive agriculture and hydroelectric dams have seriously damaged certain remarkable watercourses typical of this hilly, chalk, region where the trout have exceptional growth, attaining 40 centimetres in their third year on the Loue river.

'There is, however, still much fishing to enjoy in this region, particularly away from the beaten paths. The gorges of the Doubs around Goumois, the tributaries of the upper Ain, the Bienne, the Valserine (flowing down from the Crêt de la Neige), the Séran and the Furans before summer offer great attractions for a fishing holiday on waters still little known within the country itself.

'All along the Jura mountain massif you must be aware of the numerous anglers of the Ain, Doubs and Jura departments. They fish assiduously all season, so don't expect these rivers to be devoid of fishermen. Except in the department of the Jura – where one federal licence gives complete coverage, as instituted by the excellent President Granvaux – fishing is controlled by different AAPPS. As in the rivers of Burgundy, there are different rules in different areas and often severely restrictive ones.

'THE MASSIF CENTRAL This area provides some exceptional trout fishing, since there is little urbanization or industrialization, though some pollution from the extensive agriculture. The only shadows on this rosy picture are the hydroelectric dams. But a real plus for this region is the quality of its trout. It is one of the few places in France where you can find a large supply of natural trout, truly wild fish which reproduce naturally. Remember only that the weather can make this a hard place, and a deal of caution should be exercised. It has often been said that the trout here are small, but you will also – and more often than people would have you believe – come across some very fine fish. These fight like the devil and have very succulent flesh – trout to satisfy the most exacting anglers.

'It would need a book on its own to detail all the trout fishing in the Massif Central. Every water down to the tiniest stream winding through the meadows of the high plateaux can be happily and productively fished. Another advantage is that every method of fishing is permitted here. It is impossible to list all the good fishing areas but some of the best are: the Lot, the Tarn, the Bès, the Allier, the Chapeauroux, the Santoire, the Alagnon, the Dordogne, the Corrèze, the Vézère, the Vienne, the Creuse, the Gartempe, and the Lignon.

'A final important word of advice. Most departments of the Massif Central belong to Club Halieutique which has one general federal licence, which greatly simplifies the paper-work before fishing.

'NORMANDY Normandy long figured as one of the best trout regions especially for fly fishing. Sadly, that has changed of late. The rivers have suffered from pollution and most of them are only of secondary interest now. Some rivers, however, can still be very attractive to anglers, especially those fishing for sea trout. But many of the best waters are private and it can be difficult to get permits to fish. The few waters of the AAPPS tend to be overfished and of poor quality. The best opportunities are on private fisheries such as the Dame Blanche at Bernay on the Charentonne, but in general there is nothing to justify coming here for a fishing holiday alone.

'THE PYRENEES This region of sun and high mountains is less well known for its trout fishing than it should be. Rivulets, torrents, beautiful rivers are very numerous throughout the range and, even more important, they are richly stocked. The best bets are in waters of repute like the Nives rivers (though the Nive de Balgorry has suffered damage from road works). Others are the Gave d'Oloron, the Gave de Pau, the Nests, the

Garonne, and the Arros. Once again the most interesting fishing is away from the beaten tracks on small rivers far from tourist centres. Despite the high altitude, the trout often run to a good size. Except at the start of the season these trout are often difficult to tempt in these crystal-clear waters and you should use the finest tackle and a careful approach to the water, if you wish to have any success.

'As with the Alps, you should avoid at all costs the period of the snow melt from mid-April to mid-July. Here also the mountain lakes are very numerous and particularly interesting to fish. Often the reward of many hours of walking in exceptional surroundings is to come to the best of waters. A large-scale map is a great help in finding these. All the departments of the Pyrenees and the pre-Pyrenees belong to the Club Halieutique so that formalities before fishing are greatly simplified.

'THE VOSGES   The Vosges is the oldest of France's mountain areas, and today is rarely mentioned as a fishing region, but that is certainly a mistake because the rivers holding trout and other salmonids are very numerous there and, indeed very beautiful and pleasant to fish. Certain valleys like that of the Moselle still have waters of acceptable quality, despite industrialization and omnipresent urbanization. By contrast in Haute Saône, for example, you will find superb small streams running through tranquil and verdant surroundings where you can have fine fishing from spring onwards.

'The best opportunities are provided by the Meurthe, the Moselle and its tributaries (particularly the Moselotte and the Vologne), the Breuchin, the Lanterne and its tributaries, the Ognon, the Combeauté and several streams from the Alsatian part of the Vosges.

'If you except the Haute-Saône, where one federal licence covers most of the AAPPS, the fishing rights are often parcelled out between a multitude of fishing societies. On the Moselle, on the initiative of the dynamic President Salvèque, a successful effort is being made for reciprocal coverage of all first-category rivers as far as Épinal.

'CORSICA   This island of beauty, as the publicity slogans rightly christen it, offers varied fishing opportunities, which are largely ignored. Rivers such as the Golo, the best known, would largely justify a week's stay. There is also a special form of itinerant fishing which can make Corsica particularly interesting. Leave with a back pack, rods, and a tent and in the Corsican mountains you will find marvellous views and memorable fishing. The best times of the day for fishing are early morning and late evening. Another advantage of Corsica, in addition to the sun and the warmth, is that the lovely beaches are always close at hand. The countryside is superb and the Corsicans much more hospitable than they are reputed to be. The fishing is usually very good from the start of the season, except during the period of snow melt.'

5

The Spanish Tradition

Spain, Portugal and the Azores

Spain's tradition of fly fishing for trout is at least as old as England's. Almost thirty years before *The Compleat Angler* was published in 1653, the *Manuscrito Deastorga* gave advanced lessons in fly tying. This went far beyond Walton's reliance on twelve standard patterns, and is in some ways more impressive than Charles Cotton's intelligent contributions on the subject in Part II of the fifth edition of the *Angler*. Appropriately, this Spanish work originated from León, and it was León that gifted the original manuscript to that ardent angler General Franco – appropriately since León is in many ways the trout-fishing capital of Spain. There are five splendid trout rivers – the Orbigo, the Porma, the Esla, the Torio and the Curueno – within a few miles of the city, apart from the one that flows through it. León is also the centre for Spain's annual international week of trout fishing and it is from the famous cocks of León that the best Spanish flies are dressed.

Trout fishing in Spain varies as the country varies. In the north is the green belt with reasonable rainfall and rivers of the Scottish type, such as the Sella and Narcea, with their run of salmon and sea trout, and the brown trout fishing best in the tributaries. You can also fish in beautiful surroundings in the Pyrenees. The streams there are fast and sparkling and it is a delight to fish them in the clear air amid the grandeur of the mountains. The wild brown trout are there in plenty, mainly small to medium in size, and best caught on wet fly. In the hot southern regions, however, where you seem to go straight from winter to high summer, the trout have difficulty surviving below 2,000 feet. And in some rivers it is not low water that gives problems in summer. The middle Carrion, in Castile, may be unfishable from June because so much water is released from the reservoir at its head in order to irrigate the increasingly parched land around its lower reaches.

While there is superb trout fishing in Spain, particularly for dry-fly experts, little effort is made to attract foreign anglers. Indeed, there is a sensible belief that these fine, but limited, facilities are best preserved for the locals. This is evident in some of the pricing policies, which set a

Spanish rate with the locals only paying half and the foreigners double. On controlled waters getting a permit to fish is not easy. You need to apply many months before, sending your passport details and the necessary money and going into a draw, which may not give you what you want. Since each region also guards its own independence, and has control of its fishing rules, you need to check current regulations and current seasons carefully. Fishing seasons can vary from the first Sunday in March to the last and may be over by August or October, according to region and river and changing provincial decisions. In general, and in the León area in particular, the last week in June and the first in July provide the best fishing.

Fishing is relatively cheap if you can get your permit. For one of the best beats on the Orbigo the cost was only about £10. The beat was some 7 miles long, but about eight other anglers also had permits that day. In Spain some million permits are issued to anglers annually, but only about a thousand of these will cast flies. The vast majority will only fish flies on spinning rods and bubble floats, or will rely on spinners or worm. As you fish upstream dry fly you must get used to a loud splash close by not indicating a large trout but heralding the approach of a bubble-floater. Similarly, you may be taken by surprise by what appears to be a small fish leaping wildly across the river. This will not be a little trout pursued by a pike, but a bubble-floater retrieving fast. It is easy to dismiss bubble-float fishing as a simple method for the unskilled. In fact, as with most fishing methods, there is a vast gulf between those who hurl their bubbles in hope and the experts who skilfully adjust the amount of water in the bubble, the position of the bubble, and the speed and depth at which the flies are fished. Normally the bubble is fished at the end of the cast with four or five flies higher up. Sometimes, however, there is a tail fly below and the rest above. In the midday sun the dry fly will heavily outscore the bubble, and it will, of course, do well in the evening rise. But it is in the evening that the bubble, with its team of flies, may catch more and heavier fish.

On controlled permit waters there is no significant problem of interference from the bubble-users, since they don't put off rising trout and the different methods don't clash. But the easiest way of getting a permit to fish trout in Spain is to acquire a general one to fish free water. Some of this free water can be excellent, but there is great pressure there from bubble floats and spinners, particularly at weekends. There is, however, one unexplored area which might provide fine free fishing with no competition. No one seems to fish the fly in the many reservoirs, which hold large numbers of trout. In Salamanca I was told that the reservoir at the head of the Tormes was only occasionally fished by boys with worms who caught trout up to ten pounds. Much the same was said about those at the head of the Pisuerga and Carrion rivers. There are no boats on these reservoirs and I have had no opportunity to try the bank fishing, much though that promises. If boats are launched those expert in the lead-core methods of taking large browns might have a field day.

Because of the problems of organizing a fishing holiday in Spain it is desirable to take early advice about procedure from their tourist offices, or get in touch through them with the provincial fishing authorities of the region to be visited. The central fishing body, the Federación Española de Pesca, has an office in Madrid, but is not equipped to answer queries or arrange fishing. In my own case there was the ideal solution of having kind Spanish friends who made the arrangements for me. Rafael de Madariaga Giraldo is an expert fly fisherman whom I first met in the World Championship in 1982. He is also a regular visitor to England, fishing on rivers such as the Itchen. Rafael was my guide and companion on a 1985 visit to fish four dry-fly rivers brimming with sizeable trout.

On the long drive down to Castille from Madrid airport Rafael gave an ecstatic description of the Dulce river. This is within a hundred miles of Madrid and is Spain's closest equivalent of an English chalk stream. The river is relatively narrow, but the previous day Rafael had taken over fifty trout on his dry fly. 'They were only about ¾ pound, but as round as balloons and in fine condition. This is a "no-kill" river and in a few years it will be truly remarkable, with many really big fish, so good is the feed.'

All fishing water in Spain is state-controlled, with two exceptions. The owner of the ground where a river rises has rights over it until it leaves his property, and some clubs with a hundred or more members can control stretches of river to the point of issuing half the permits, as in the case of the Dulce. I began to regret that our itinerary did not include this sweet-sounding stream, but the others were to prove as delightful as any trout fisherman could wish. We stopped at the fishery office in Pallencia, a town dominated by a vast 200-foot-high effigy of Christ on the small hill outside, symbolic of a region with a profusion of old churches of striking design. Apart from collecting permits we talked about the desirability of introducing rainbows or grayling among the wild trout of the Pisuerga river, to which we were heading. There was information too that construction work had temporarily affected some of the best of the controlled stretches, the silt deposits having driven the fish away into the free water to the delight of local anglers. Fortunately, our stretch for the morrow was on the clear upper reaches close to Cervera de Pisuerga. But for that evening we sampled first the free water of this attractive river with its fast runs, its weir-type waterfalls, and its long, quiet flats. Rafael's advice was to match any hatch, but otherwise use Sedges to bring up the trout – small or medium by day, large at dusk. Since no evening rise developed I decided to give wet fly a try on the fast runs at the head of a long pool. Equipped only for dry fly I had to rely on the inevitable few flies hooked into the lapel of my fishing jacket. A weighted nymph on the tail, and a Black Zulu on the bob was an unlikely combination, but instantly successful, taking five trout of ½–¾ pound. By now I had bubble-float fishermen on either side, but as it grew so dark that I had to work the bob by instinct there was a slashing rise and a wild fight with a trout of over a pound. This I kept to sample for taste, and very excellent it was with its pink flesh.

It was a reasonable assumption that if the bubble float worked well, the bobbed wet fly would also do well, and the evening seemed to have proved that. Indeed, the makeshift wet fly had outscored the bubbles seven to one by the end – the same score by which England beat Spain in their first-ever football international with the famed Zamora in the Spanish goal, as I refrained from mentioning to the bubble-floaters. By then it was eleven o'clock and many hours since we had eaten so I was relieved to find the local restaurant still in full swing *and* ready to cook that sample trout for us. Come midnight, I inquired anxiously of Rafael if we ought not to book into our hotel and asked which it was. 'I don't know yet,' said Rafael, 'I haven't booked anywhere. But there should be no difficulty.' There wasn't. No surprise was expressed at the hilltop Parador Hotel and no problems in getting two fine rooms for £20 a night – or what was left of the night.

We were not too bright and early to try the Quintaluengos beat of the Pisuerga, but Rafael assured me that no rise was likely before midday. There were, however, a few moving trout as we surveyed the top of the beat with a series of waterfall pools below the weir at the bottom of a long, still pool. The first I saw was in the small mill-leat running off one side and it rose confidently to the first cast of a medium-sized Brown Sedge. That was a nice fish of about a pound which Rafael released for me when it burrowed into weed. The others were not so accommodating so we went to the shallow runs below the weir. These provided the most exciting fishing as I waded up the fast, shallow water. Rafael had advised casting in the shallowest water under the overhanging trees and bushes or the quiet edges of weed beds. How right he was! Nothing came in the main streams, but in those places there was a profusion of eager risers. The first was around a pound, and seven slightly smaller ones were soon caught and released.

Rafael then gave an expert demonstration of how to fish the really fast water with a dry fly. He held his rod very high and, having left slack in the cast as it landed, kept the fly from dragging, despite the swift and contradictory currents. No doubt a bobbed wet fly would also have scored, but he had six good trout, ending with one under the weir of well over a pound. We had been watched by a fisherman relying on a spinner, who expressed considerable surprise at the number caught and at their being returned, rather than kept towards the limit of six which the permit allowed.

As we went down in the car, leapfrogging on to Rafael's 'special' stretches, the day left increasingly vivid impressions on my mind. In the hot sun there were always some fish rising, and the places to catch them were mainly the fast shallow runs near the heads of the pools. Picking out your litle size 14 dry fly floating down amid the ripple of water and glint of sunlight was never easy, but in the turbulent runs at least you could take fish on this size of Sedge, or perhaps even the larger 12. In the deeper, quieter water nothing above size 18 aroused any interest.

The most fascinating fishing was in the cascades below another long weir, where a broad, quiet stretch some half-mile long was at last broken into a series of rushing waterfall pools. Chest waders were never more essential than here, as some of these pools had to be approached by wading along the lip of the weir. At a casual glance the little pools seemed hardly worth the scramble down the sloping stone face of the weir, with the white water lapping the ankles. Only a few casts appeared possible, with the dry fly difficult to fish in the swirling waters before each separate cascade disappeared into a tunnel of trees to link again into the main stream. Nothing stirred in the first, but as the eyes became accustomed to the shimmer and shake of the darker water beside the central white flurry the shadowy shapes of trout became visible there. A look through polaroids then revealed a hundred or more packed close together. Too close, perhaps, for none showed at the fly. In the next run there was a quieter tail of some five or six yards, but it curved past a tangle of tree roots. The first time the Sedge sailed down properly cocked a pounder took viciously and darted into the roots before I could haul it past. Happily the cast ran through and Rafael waded out to gather in the trout for photographing before release. Three more of similar size came from the same yard of water and others from higher up. After a short rest the tiny pool yielded several more to Rafael and later he hooked others on a heavily leaded nymph in the fast rush immediately below the dam.

A couple of dark shapes, like minisubmarines, then cruised into view. That French expert, Pierre Affre, had once taken a nine-pound trout on a streamer fly a mile below this weir and these might have been similar monsters. Rafael, however, pronounced them more likely to be barbel. But certainly there were some heavy trout swirling at flies in the reach below, though not, unfortunately, at ours.

In the quiet of the dusk it was the long pool we fished. 'If there is a proper hatch tonight it will be alive with trout,' said Rafael. No such hatch developed and most of the fish that rose appeared only once and moved on. One of the few persistent risers ignored my larger Sedge for a time, but finally swallowed it. That was my heaviest trout of the day – over 1½ pounds. As it grew dark there was at least one small patch of regular risers at the limit of my casting length. Most of them I moved, and two were played and released. Twenty-six such trout in the day, and another fifteen or so for Rafael, who had spent more time guiding than fishing, seemed a marvellous tribute to the river. But as we drove back for our midnight feast at Rafael's favourite Cervera restaurant he was full of apologies: 'What a pity it has not fished well today for you. We had nothing over two pounds and I cannot understand why there was no true evening rise on such a warm day.' Having never experienced the Pisuerga at its best, the worst was fine for me.

Moving to León, we had the added luxury of staying at the San Marcos Hotel, so imposing a building and so splendidly appointed inside that it well deserves its five stars. It is one of the city's showplaces, with the chapel alongside filled with effigies wonderfully wrought. Our cluster of fishing rods and bags looked a little out of place in such surroundings. But in León nothing to do with trout fishing is ever out of place and everyone from the porters to the reception clerk wanted to talk about it with Rafael. 'The hotel electrician will be coming with us to the best places on the Porma, when we fish it later,' Rafael told me. 'He is a very keen dry-fly fisherman whom I helped to teach.'

The Orbigo, rather than the Porma, was our first target. The lush comfort of the hotel delayed us rather too long and it was nearly midday before we were taking a late breakfast, or early lunch, at Patricio's, the fishermen's pub in San Martina. The bridge close by is the dividing line between our Sardonedo beat and the most prestigious of them all, which Rafael told me now had problems with an invasion of large pike. The walls of Patricio's were covered with trout pictures ranging from a photograph of a Frenchman with a double-figure wild trout from the Orbigo, taken on spinner, to posters for León's Trout International week dating back to the late 1950s. That put us in the right mood, but it was not to be one of the Orbigo's best days. We appeared to be a little late for the best of the morning rise, as there was instant action when I started in a couple of gravelly runs, which reminded me of a beat on the Usk. At once I hooked a good trout, and had four more, one over a pound, at the shallow head of the furthest run. There were no rising fish to be seen, but these were attracted by a sizeable Grey Sedge, and four more followed in the delightful pools above. Then for a long spell nothing moved, even when we went up to an island pool where Rafael expected to find trout feeding in a small side stream. A freak winter storm had uprooted hundreds of trees round this area and the débris had changed the course of the river for the worse.

The controlled beats of the Orbigo cover some fifty miles and the two other main trout rivers near León, the Porma and the Esla, are of much the same length and quality. This beat of the Orbigo covered about seven miles, so we were not short of choice. When a rise started in the tail of the island pool, I had three in quick succession and then opted to return to our original stretch. There trout were rising freely in a long flat above the runs where we had started. A small Black Gnat brought me three quickly and then I twice struck too hard to lose flies in good fish. But in the final hour the trout defeated us. Rafael, with his great knowledge of the fly life, soon identified the emerging nymphs they were taking. But all our artificials were ignored. Such periods are both absorbing and frustrating. As I kept trying for new fish I went deeper and deeper in my chest waders. Only when I splashed out at the end did I realize that my backpack had been hanging down below the waterline with my camera in it. It was a wonder the films could be developed later! While we caught nothing during the final rise at least it showed us the profusion of trout there for the taking.

The controlled beats near León are all well keepered, with an excellent intelligence network. To whatever remote part of a beat you drove, by whatever unlikely tracks, the car of the uniformed keepers would soon bounce into view. On our de Condado beat of the Porma there was an entertaining variant as the cheerful and friendly river watcher came pounding up on horseback to check permits and dispense information. To our park under the trees came also two delightful Basque anglers who immediately endeared themselves to me by inviting us to share a lunch of nectarines, cherries and rosé wine, which ideally suited the mood of a happy day.

They also hurried me down to the bottom of a long pool where trout were rising freely above a low weir. They had themselves already hooked a number in a shallow run above and the signs were promising. Kindly, they offered me the rising fish, but when I asked where they would go they said they were staying to watch. Under that pressure I missed the first two which rose to a Brown Sedge before catching one of about a pound. Rafael suggested a small hackled Gnat, size 18, when others ignored my offering. Edging up under the bank with its overhanging trees I caught two more trout and many more branches on the back cast. But honour was satisfied and I picked up a couple more in more relaxed fishing, while Rafael had three in the nice long run below. Just before the lunch session a large trout was pointed out to me lying in midwater, but not rising. Without much hope I put a Greenwell over it – not an ordinary Greenwell, but a special dressing by Colin Steele-Perkins of Romsey, tied with two long tails, which seem to make it outscore the ordinary by two to one. Certainly it rose this trout, but I struck too soon for the slow rise of one of over two pounds.

The afternoon was very hot, the trout as sleepy as ourselves. So there was a chance to look at the profusion of wild flowers beside the river. Particularly striking were the orchids, with the common early purples and occasional specimens of the rare lizard orchid. Rafael and I also practised a pleasant way of fishing, working side by side up the shallow run where my

Basque friends had had good sport in the morning. Each could cover one side, with the quieter streams close to the bank the most hopeful areas, and the friendly chat compensated for the trout's scorn of our flies. In a deeper pool above I took three fish from the middle, for once, while Rafael found a pocket near his bank from which he extracted several, one close to two pounds. On the way back we passed an unlucky bubbler. He had lost fish, his waders had sprung a leak, and now his car mat, which his wife had been washing, had dropped into a deep and weeded eddy where none of us could find it for him. It was the sort of day we all suffer from, but with the evening rise now in prospect he still bubbled cheerfully on.

For me it was back to that long glide on the far side of the weir. The rise there was of unbelievable intensity, as the rings of rising fish almost overlapped for the twenty yards above the dam. The third I covered took the Grey Sedge, and five others up to 1½ pounds soon followed. By now I was so eager that I failed to watch my back and a slight altercation with an overhanging tree necessitated a new leader. Tying it in the near dark was not easy and my old eyes could only see to thread a larger Sedge than the medium size that had been so successful. This the trout scorned, but clearly I should have had three or four more had I kept my head and my original fly.

The lottery system had yielded no controlled beat for the next day so we drove some sixty miles to good free water at the head reaches of the Esla with a prime fishing area of different streams not far beyond, and one of the best Esla beats not far below. The Esla is another clear, fast stream such as those in which Cotton and Walton delighted to catch trout. Again we waded up together through a promising run, only thigh-deep throughout the long pool. Nothing was moving, however, though we had a couple each in the shallow runs above. A bubble-float fisherman, who had parked his car close to ours, talked enthusiastically of the day his friend had 84 trout up to 3 pounds bubble-floating the Esla, but no one was having that sort of bag today. It was hard going in the afternoon and, while I had a look at a new cluster of wild flowers, Rafael pursued his different collector's interest by sampling the insects. One he put in his clear container was a large stonefly with two-inch tail. He had told me the trout were usually wary of taking anything so large. But earlier in rough water I had seen a large trout gobble one up. It seemed certain he must also take my large Sedge, but he merely swirled at it.

There was just one hour near dusk when the trout moved well in that first pool and I had five of them, including a large one from the deepest part of the run. There was no great evening rise, but I caught a couple and this time kept them for the occupants of a caravan with a GB disc on it. They were surprised to meet another Englishman in this remote place, and charmingly grateful. Rafael was less enthusiastic about them. 'I saw one using binoculars to study the hilltops. Why should he do that? Maybe he was one of those who come here to sight and steal young falcons. Their export is banned, but the price for them is so good that many smuggle them out.' So if you take binoculars to look at the scenery, don't give anyone the impression you are looking for young falcons! According to Rafael, the overcast thundery weather had made it a bad fishing day, but thirteen trout on free water hardly seemed a disaster to me. I never did see any falcons myself, but could hardly miss the profusion of kites, with their trout-like forked tails, or the storks nesting on roofs and pylons.

My last day on the Porma was an abbreviated one as I had to get back to Madrid before an early morning flight. The weather was now brilliantly fine, and once more the prospects good. We were now on a much higher beat of the Porma in Cerezales, which once belonged to the same Condado. Clearly the property had extended far. The fishing river the Condado had owned certainly looked noble enough with its sparkling water, interesting weedbeds and varied pools. But there was nothing special about the fishing at the start. We explored the shallows, the inviting runs, the edges of the weeds, but nothing stirred. Then in a backwater at the head of a long pool a trout of over a pound sailed up unexpectedly to mouth my Sedge. Another rose a few casts later, but I missed this one.

We were joined now by two partners in Rafael's tackle business – F. L. Fama-León, which makes millions of hackle flies annually for Spain's bubble-floaters and a wealth of dry flies, mainly for Europe's anglers. They were a splendidly balanced pair. Jon spends most of his time fishing or shooting. Rafa was perhaps an even more expert angler, but a workhorse as well, severely rationing his visits to the river. Not even they were able to conjure fish out of the unyielding water until we reached the top of the beat with a long inviting pool said to contain many big trout. 'Wait for the rise,' said Rafael, but by three o'clock still nothing was stirring and Jon waded in to catch a two-pounder.

Going back below I had just caught another trout when two visitors arrived who had helped to make my fishing possible, Aureliano Creano, inspector of rivers and mountains, and his delightful wife, Begona, who had been over in England for the Izaak Walton tercentenary celebrations. 'Rafael is still worrying that I have had no two-pounders, but it has been fine fishing,' I told them as we went in search of the others. No sign of them on the top pool. Where could they be? Then Rafa appeared at the double. 'Jon and Rafael have caught nine or ten big trout. Come and join us.' 'Where?' I asked. 'Surely this is the top beat.' 'Yes, but the trout are rising in the free water above.'

There was an irony in that, and the keeper was not too pleased that the free water should outscore his. But a hatch of olives had many large trout rising freely in a narrow stretch of fast water. As I had a Sedge on my cast

Rafael simply handed over his rod and I waded up level with Jon. We had to avoid tangling so close were we as each took the rising fish on his own side. Three good trout I hooked on the size 16 Olive, or an emerging nymph pattern, and missed twice as many. The two-pounders had waited until the end to excite us, and when that hatch died out Rafael and I each had one more in the controlled water. Then it was time for the long journey to Madrid, accomplished in less than three hours as Rafael played the rally driver. On the way I wondered what it would have been like had we had time to stay for the evening rise of those splendid trout. Even without that it had been a marvellous week of trout fishing.

Spain is memorable for me not only for such a week of pure pleasure but as the place where I won the World Flyfishing Championship in May 1984. That hardly deserved its prestigious title, being in essence a European competition, but it was still a great occasion for me, and the Tormes near Salamanca will always be a favourite river of mine. This was how Rafael described the Tormes when he was kind enough to give us advance notice of what might face us in the championship:

'THE RIVER   The part of the Tormes you will fish in the competition starts at Santa Teresa's dam and ends in Alba de Tormes, about eighteen miles downriver. The water is regulated by the dam so the level on competition days should be normal. It is quite a big river, from fifty to a hundred metres broad. In the area you fish the average width should be fifty metres. It is essential to use chest waders if you are to fish it properly, and even so some parts will be deep to wade. The river flows along a plain with only a slight gradient, so it runs in a series of long flats with variable current, and only occasional strong streams. There are many shallows and some deep pools. The banks in the upper part are mostly clear, but in the lower there is more vegetation and some large poplar woods. Casting is not often difficult, even from the bank. The area is quite windy, with the wind usually in your face as you fish upstream dry fly – isn't it always, everywhere?

'THE FISH   There were very few trout in this part of the river before the construction of the dam, with summer drought and high temperatures in the water making it unsuitable for them. When the dam was built they introduced wild brown trout from the high upper waters in the sierra and also stocked with wild trout from the Orbigo.

'That was twenty years ago and after the first five years the stock of trout was enormous and they also ran large. In the past six years, however, the stock declined and in the last two the sport has been poor. There is no pollution and the river hasn't been overfished, so I believe that this is due to the artificial nature of the river, controlled as it is by the dam.

'The river has a lot of natural food and the trout are very selective. They will take only the fly of the day, or of the last few days. Small dry flies down to size 24 are most likely to tempt them. They do rise well on the surface, normally under the brightest sun at noon. A few stock trout are likely to be put in, but it will be a negligible quantity for this length of river.'

There was also much useful advice about the fly life and the likely hatches. But in fishing you must always expect the unexpected. It was late May, but when we arrived at Salamanca the Tormes was a muddy river in spate. It had been Spain's worst spring for nearly fifty years and the area had been carpeted in snow a few days before. So the classic dry-fly river we expected was now quite unsuited to that technique, and only just fishable in the higher reaches where the competition stretches were marked out.

There is much more to fishing than catching fish, and that applies even more to world championships than to fun fishing. The hospitality and the friendly exchanges between the forty anglers from different countries would have made it a worthwhile visit even had the fishing been cancelled because of the conditions. It was quite an experience to take part in the opening ceremony in Salamanca's old main square before a crowd of several thousand. The Plaza Mayor, built between 1729 and 1755, is rightly rated the most beautiful in Spain. Three storeys high and including the decorated façade of the town hall it looks a masterpiece of simplicity, but on closer inspection the architecture is intricate, the shape irregular and trapezoidal, the whole effect startling, as with so many buildings in Salamanca. But it could not divert us long from the fishing.

Even in the upper reaches the Tormes ran high, slightly coloured, and very cold. It averaged about sixty yards wide and was normally shallow, but the trouser waders we had been advised to bring were now an essential. So too was wet-fly fishing as there was little hatch of fly and few rises.

In practice, too, we found stock fish among the wild trout, and they were eager both for black flies, like the Bibio or Pennell, the bright ones like the Dunkeld or Cinnamon and Gold. After the last practice day we lost Mike Childs, who got the worst of it when he joined some of the Luxemburg team and the locals facing the young bulls in a corrida. Fractures to his leg and arm put a damper on our enjoyment and meant that David Swatland, our non-playing captain, had now to put his rod where his advice had been – and most successfully he did it, to finish nineteenth.

Viewing your first beat is always an anxious moment in a major competition. Can I cover it properly? Does it look a good holding place for fish? Where are they likely to be lying? Are there signs of any feeding? These are the queries that race through the mind. In this stretch the Tormes flows fast, wide and shallow and though wading would normally be easy the river was now so high that in many places it was hard to get out, even in chest waders. But the sight of the water I was to fish gave an instant lift to my spirits. This was the type of pool which had entranced me in boyhood and was just as attractive more than fifty years on. An island above divided the river so that the main current flowed fast under the far bank while a series of small, quiet streams ran across to join it leaving a long still backwater down my bank for the remaining 200 yards.

First cast I rose a small trout, and third cast I caught one, only to find it was just below the limit. But, with the trout taking eagerly a Bibio fly bobbed across the streams, I had eleven by the end of the period. One gave me problems. There was a heavy penalty for keeping one undersized fish, disqualification for keeping two. So it was important to measure any borderline trout. One such I netted when wading down the middle of the river. As I hurried to the bank too hastily I tripped on a stone and fell flat in the water. When I recovered the net the dropper fly was caught in it, the trout swimming clear still held by the tail fly. Fortunately, when re-netted it proved large enough to justify the effort, and the incident certainly kept the spectators amused.

That proved the best catch on any of the top three sectors in the first session, but there had been more fish taken below on D and E sectors of the competition stretch, with one Italian catching twenty. However, I was more than happy to have a good start and not worried to have a bad draw for the next 5.30 to 9.30 period. This was a beat I had fished on practice day without moving anything when I was catching a lot elsewhere. It had been fished that morning by a Spaniard who had caught nothing, though he was a previous World Champion and on his home water. So I decided that the best hope was to fish as differently as possible from the normal method. By using a high-density line, which took the fly down fast, I had five trout from a deep eddy at the end of the beat and lost one really large fish as well.

Weigh-in and dinner at a local hotel meant that it was past midnight before we were back in Salamanca. Positions were redrawn after each period and David Swatland returned after the next morning's draw to say that we were lying second as a team and that I was third in the individual placings, which were based on scoring 1 point per gram of weight and 100 points for each trout caught. But David added that we had drawn number 8 beats, on which others had not done well; and I had drawn B8, on which nothing at all had been caught. However, an Italian had had a good catch on the beat below, so I was confident they *could* be caught there. How well you fish is often a matter of how confident you are, and once I had a sizeable trout early on I fished with keen expectation throughout the four hours, alternating between a slow-sinking line and a high-density one. Six more trout came to the net, some taking the dropper bobbed on the surface, some following it up from deep.

The final weigh-in was at a hostelry where the congratulations began as soon as I arrived, but I refused to believe that I had won the World Championship until it was formally announced. The Italians took the team prize and very expert anglers they were. To win once may owe a lot to chance; to win twice in succession is more than coincidence; to win three years running, as they had done, is proof of excellence.

I have found that occasional competition provides a new stimulus to your fishing and brings you in contact with many better anglers, introducing you to new friends and new techniques. But it is not to be taken too seriously and the more relaxed you are the more you can enjoy it. León's international week of the trout has the right balance. You can fish in the competitions on the rivers of the area, or you can just fish for fun and enjoy the company of trout fishermen of many different nations. It could be a good way to start to sample the splendid trout fishing round León. Sixty-four places are reserved for foreign visitors and early application might well get you one.

Another less established festival is the Jornadas Internacionales at Sanguesa-Yesa in Navarre, organized by the Baetis Rhodani Ulixta Nivelle Club. This only started in 1984 and involves much variety of fishing and fly dressing.

Fishing in the World Championships has given me many helpful Spanish friends with whom to explore other areas of Spanish fishing. The most successful of the Spaniards on the Tormes was Bela Sarosi. The Pyrenees provide his favourite fishing, and this is his description of it:

'The mountainous chain of the Pyrenees forms the natural border between France and Spain, extending from the Bay of Biscay in the west to the Mediterranean in the east. The highest mountains lie in the central part, with peaks of over 3,000 metres.

'The provinces of the Spanish Pyrenees are, from west to east, Guipuzcoa, Navarra, Huesca, Lérida and Gerona. The tiny Principality of Andorra lies also embedded between France and Spain.

'The snow-fed rivers are very clear and fast-running, and most of them have low water levels in July and August. Their rocky beds are full of big boulders and rounded stones which make trout angling a physically demanding sport. Trout can be easily spotted in these transparent waters and can as easily spot the angler.

'The construction of a network of reservoirs for irrigation and electricity production has provided another opportunity for trout anglers. Lake or reservoir fishing is not much practised by local fishermen and then it is mainly bait-fishing from the bank. British anglers could find good opportunities with their sinking-line techniques, although it must be said that the bottoms of these reservoirs are full of obstructions in the form of tree stumps, old hedges, and the like. Boats are not available for hire and permission for the use of private boats must be applied for at the fish and game office of the relevant provincial capital.

'For those wishing to combine trout fishing and high mountain hiking there are the "Ibones", which are small Alpine-type lakes well above the tree limit. These natural lakes are ice-covered during almost five months in winter and are seldom fished because of their remoteness.

'The Pyrenees are one of the European regions where the naturally spawning wild brown trout is still common and predominant. Stocking with rainbow trout was discontinued years ago as they do not reproduce naturally, and are often captured in a matter of weeks, or even days, after their introduction. The present policy is to rear brown trout and stock the rivers with fingerlings, closing the seeded stretch for one or two seasons until they reach legal size.

'No success was achieved with the introduction of the brook trout. Barbel up to 6 kilograms appear in the lower reaches of the rivers, but move upstream in summer as waters warm up, mixing with trout, much to the annoyance of the trout anglers. They sometimes take the fly readily and their fighting power puts heavy strain on the tackle as they are normally well above the kilogram mark. Some reservoirs contain carp and the imported American black bass. This first-class sporting fish developed very well in Spain and can be caught on the fly rod with streamers, poppers and big bushy flies, as well as by spinning.

'The great majority of the Spaniards use spinners, bait, or the plastic bubble with a team of flies. Early in the season, spinning with a fresh dead minnow accounts occasionally for some very big trout up to 8 kilograms. For the fly rod conditions are rather more difficult as the waters are clear and fast, which means that a careful approach into casting position is most important.

'The traditional English fly patterns do well here too. March, April and May are good for wet flies like the olives, Hare's Ear and March Brown wet, fished quartering downstream. Dry-fly adepts can also do well at any time, but June, July and August are the best months for the morning and evening rises. A rod of from 8 to 9 feet with a 5 or 6 floating line is all you need here. Chest-high waders are seldom required and hip boots suffice.

'Due to changes in the powers of the provinces, fishing regulations can vary. Basically, a foreign angler visiting Spain needs a national fishing licence, which enables him to fish all the many free waters in Spain. The licence is valid for 15 days and costs about 450 pesetas. Licences can be obtained from the local fishing guards and the fish and game offices which are located in the provincial capitals. The following regulations of the province of Huesca are fairly typical of the Pyrenees region, although there may be variations:

'Brown and rainbow trout under 19 centimetres must be returned and the catch limit on free waters is 20 fish per day. The season starts on the third Sunday in March and ends on 31 August. Waters 1,000 metres above sea level are considered high mountain waters and the season there starts on the second Sunday in May and runs until the end of September.

'Besides the so-called free waters, which of course are more heavily fished, particularly at weekends, there are the *cotos*, or controlled stretches. They are clearly marked and can be fished on a day-ticket basis. They differ from the free waters as they have access limited to between 8 and 20 anglers, and the bag limit can vary from 6 to 12 fish a day. All *cotos* have two-day tickets reserved for foreigners at a price of about 2000 pesetas. These can be obtained from the local fishing guard. Unlike trout, there is no close season for the carp, barbel, pike and black bass.

'Of the five Spanish Pyrenees provinces, Navarra, Huesca and Lérida are the most interesting for the trout angler, and Huesca is the province with the least angling pressure of them all, as it covers just the central and highest part of the range.

'Prices are reasonable compared with France and many other European countries. One hotel room and full board including three meals would cost from £15 to £40, depending on the category of the establishment. For example, in a mid-class hotel full board would be around £20 (1985). Bed and Continental breakfast for one person would range from £8 to £25. The best time to come is early in the season up to May or June, as July and August are Spanish holiday months, with more people and anglers around and sometimes low water levels. Those who also like skiing can choose the months of March and April.

'Although here too trout and trout fishing were more plentiful in the past, the Spanish Pyrenees, and especially the central part, the province of Huesca, still offer the angler better conditions to catch trout than in much of the rest of industrialized Europe. Free-running clear rivers, wild brown trout, natural insect life and large areas of uninhabited land are what every trout angler longs for. They are still common here, and I trust they will remain so, for the benefit of locals and visiting anglers alike.'

Portugal and the Azores

Portugal has a similar potential for excellent trout fishing in clear streams amid impressive surroundings, but the stocks have not been well preserved, nor the best waters so well managed nor the poaching kept within bounds.

Big game sea fishing rather than the freshwater variety is the name of the game in Portugal, though the trout angler can still find places to enjoy himself. The spectacular scenery may also compensate for any shortage of fish. The season is an early one, running from 1 March to 31 July. Of the rivers the Alge stream in the north is as good as any. For lakes, the Lagoa Camprida and some others in the Serra da Estrela are worth a visit. In the Azores there is entertaining fishing on the islands of San Miguel and Flores, amid the profusion of flowers the name implies. The lack of readily available information on Portuguese trout fishing reflects the poor quality of it and the failure to develop this resource in a country which proudly claims to provide every sport under the sun and gives itself the nickname of Sportugal. Perhaps too much diversity has distracted the authorities from preserving and improving freshwater fishing in the way so many other European countries are doing. Some details can be had from travel agents or tourist offices or from clubs like Clube Fluvial Vilacondense, Avenida Jose Regio 13, 4460 Vilea do Conde, in the Costa Verde, which have some interest in trout fishing as well as ocean angling. But if you want to go to Iberia for trout fishing Spain has to be the main attraction.

While lack of control has greatly diminished the possibilities for catching trout, the River Minho and its tributaries in the north do offer some reasonable salmon and trout fishing. The Minho and Limia rivers, both of which rise in Spain, also offer at times some excellent sport with sea trout. This can be good in the Minho estuary near Moledo, and on the Limia in the Viana area. To get information or permits, which are needed in Portugal, may require patience. On a recent visit to Guarda to fish the Mondego river, Merlin Unwin found it resembled a treasure hunt. Each helpful person gave a clue as to the next place to probe, whereupon an equally helpful person would put him on the road to somewhere else.

Trevor Housby has enjoyed good trout fishing in several rivers in the north of Portugal, but most of these are privately owned and not accessible to visitors. Trevor is a fishing consultant to British Airways and is also Consultant to the Regional Government of the Azores. As a talented all-round fisherman he is well known there for his record catches off the coast. He had a record 856 pound Blue Marlin fishing near the island of Faial and also holds records for Wahoo and White Marlin. But Trevor is perhaps even better known as a trout angler. As inventor of the Dog Nobbler he is responsible for the most successful and controversial fly of the past fifty years. Whatever fly he is using, the Azores is for him a very special place for trout fishing.

'There has been a hatchery in the Azores for nearly a hundred years and San Miguel and Flores Islands have idyllic trout fishing in their large lakes and rapid rivers. The lakes are formed from volcanic craters and are mostly over a thousand acres in size with marvellous bank fishing. You can take good baskets of trout on anything from Nobblers to March Browns.

Whether fishing the stillwaters or the streams the tactics are the same as for flyfishing in England, or any other country with good fly hatches.

'The special feature of the Azores is the pleasure of finding excellent and varied trout fishing with no clutter of other anglers, and no expensive formalities involved beyond getting a permit from the local police. All that and remarkable scenery too! The Logoa de Fogo, the lake of fire, is my favourite in San Miguel, but the river fishing is very good too. There is nothing more enjoyable for me than trout fishing in the Azores where weather and scenery so enhance the experience.

'There is a long-established hatchery in Madeira too and you can take large brown trout of up to a couple of kilos in its rivers. But you need to be a bit of a Tiger Tenzing – good with crampons – to enjoy the best of the fishing there. It is a case of climbing into remote and difficult mountain areas to catch well. Take your trout rod if you are going to the Azores for a holiday. Better still arrange a holiday trout fishing there and it should be one of the most rewarding of your life. Certainly, I have found it so.'

Trevor spends several months in the Azores every year, usually between April and October. The attraction is as much the beauty of the islands as it is the sea and trout fishing.

6

Rivers of Delight

Austria and Yugoslavia

Austria

'Never look back' is usually good advice for fishing as for life in general. You may not be turned into a pillar of salt, but you are likely to be disappointed if you try to recapture long-past pleasures. So it was with some anxiety that I returned to fish in Austria after a break of thirty-five years, for Austrian trout fishing had a special place in my memory.

It was at the war's end that I first crossed the border into that enchanting country with its fairytale castles and romantic scenery, so pleasant a contrast to what had gone before. We marked our route from North Africa to Italy with our armoured division's emblem – a clenched mailed fist. But here it was depicted with the thumb up. Thumbs up indeed! We had all struck it lucky, but especially the fishermen.

To ensure a happy ending to war my brother's artillery unit motored in just behind our tanks and he was made town major of an area that controlled Carinthia's Gurk river, then the most prolific trout water I had ever fished. It is also a stream of breathtaking beauty, which sparkled in the May sunlight as it tumbled down from high mountains with its racing waters clouded by melting snow. Even with rods crudely fashioned from the wireless aerials of armoured cars we had remarkable catches of trout and were later to find grayling in quantity in the lower reaches. It was not hard to keep both our cookhouses well supplied with trout and when the signal came that General Alexander was to visit us the Pawson brothers were ordered to catch a hundred trout for the banquet, which proved to be one of the easier assignments the army gave us.

We produced the hundred trout by using a strange assortment of flies rather than the more explosive methods sometimes employed by the Lovat Scouts encamped along the river's upper reaches, with the stock of trout apparently inexhaustible. Mostly they were a pound or less with the occasional two-pound fish. But on the nearby Glan, slower and more prolific of fly life, my brother stalked and caught a four-pound brown.

Such was the rarity of the feat that he celebrated by drinking a stein of beer while standing on his head to the delight of the mess.

For several years after demobilization I returned annually to these entrancing waters before other commitments absorbed my time. Then an Austrian friend pressed me to return in 1985. Reinhard Resch gave me details of the present fishing and the river he recommended above all others was his own favourite.

The Gmundner Traun is indeed so good that there was certainly no need to look further. But for those wanting more general advice about Austrian fishing their tourist offices are a helpful starting point. Or there is the book from Verlag Jochen Schuck of Nuremberg, *Gastliche Fliegen Strecken '81*, which gives specific details of most good Austrian waters, as well as those of Germany and Switzerland. The format is to give precise information about the waters and the local accommodation under the same headings for each. Those covered range from the Gmundner Traun and the Gurk to 'brooks' like the Tuxbach, small rivers like the Ischl, and large ones like the Drau or Salza. The pictures and text underline their great variety, from the turbulent streams of the high mountains to placid lakes.

For those interested in the development of Austrian fishing there is the centenary commemorative book *Osterreichische Fischereigesellschaft 1880 to 1980*, produced by the Fishery Department. The Osterreichische Fischereigesellschaft is at 1010 Vienna, Elisabethstrasse 22, and can give useful information. The colour illustrations in the centenary book are enticing enough, but the reality is even more attractive, particularly if you fish the Traun.

As bait, Reinhard sent me pictures of the Gmundner Traun with its clear wide waters, wooded banks, and large fish. 'Come in September,' he wrote. 'That is the most rewarding time, when the fishing is the most interesting, if you are good enough, and the river is least crowded, because many find it hard then.' My son John and I were met at Vienna airport by Reinhard and Peter, an Englishman for whom Austria has proved so irresistible that he is permanently resident there. It was a surprise to me to see a cricket match in progress on the outskirts of Vienna, no surprise in that dreary summer that the rain was beating down when three hours later we peered at the Traun over Steyermuhl bridge.

The drive down had only hinted at the remembered beauty of Carinthia with its wild mountains, lush meadows, and sparkling streams. But the landscape on the way from Vienna was still pretty enough and rural enough, with the houses neatly blended, the churches with their onion spires and the endless fields of maize. Typical of the contrast with England were the motorway lay-bys, all of them set in pleasant wooded surrounds with picnic tables and the restful atmosphere that encourages a break. So it was a momentary disappointment to get a first glimpse of the Traun in city surroundings with a papermill by the riverside, at the outflow from which huge barbel were said to gather. The sight of its swirling waters, however, soon gave a lift of anticipation. Only where it flows from the Traunsee in Gmunden and at this lower part of the fishable water, before pollution takes its toll, is the Traun urbanized or industrialized. For the rest it flows through a valley with steep wooded banks, so shut in that it is often windless on windy days, so natural that access is never easy and there are no well beaten paths along its banks.

We lodged at the Wirt Am Bach Gasthof, four miles from Gmunden. It is a typical Austrian inn, with excellent food, clean and comfortable bedrooms, and a landlord whose spacehopper figure is a tribute to his establishment's cooking. Bed and Continental breakfast cost us less than £12 a day and the fishing too at less than £10 a day was very cheap considering its quality. There was an early start the first morning to get licences, since the forestry office in Gmunden puts some of our officials to shame by opening for business at 7 a.m. Indeed, if you are lucky you can get one of the *limited* number of licences from the fishmaster, Mr Gebetsroither, from the second-floor office on a Sunday (with the information and regulations made available in a leaflet printed in English).

The rules of the Gmundner Traun embrace a season from 1 May to 30 September and fishing from sunrise to half an hour after sunset. Only artificial flies are allowed, and only those dressed on barbless hooks or hooks with 'pressed down barbs'. Though the rules don't specify this, a single fly or nymph is the standard practice. Spinning rods are banned, as is the use of split-shot sinkers for nymphs, not surprisingly in view of the profusion of swans. Any fish caught must be 'returned immediately with care', with one possible exception. All grayling *must* be put back, but up to seven trout or pike may be taken each week *if* you pay £1 per pound for trout and less for pike. We were not to see any pike, but the most expert of the Traun fishermen, Roman Moser, takes forty or more a year on his special pike streamer flies. The information leaflet also includes the helpful comment: 'If desired the fishmaster will advise the fisherman.' It is certainly sensible to take advice. As Reinhard commented to me, 'Those who don't know how to fish the Traun may come here and catch only three small fish in a week. But if you fish it right it is the best grayling river in Europe, with the largest grayling you will ever catch, and the wild rainbows are the fiercest fighters you can hook.'

By the riverside Reinhard was soon demonstrating the technique which brings daytime success. It is a peculiar mixture of traditional nymph fishing and coarse-fishing skills. 'Most of the fish lie in the darker, deeper water. You must go as close as your trouser waders will take you, then use these full-function, fast-join casts to work your leaded nymph right down on the bottom. If you let it drag, or rise a few inches too high, you won't catch a thing.' The full-function casts are of the braided type, to which Rafael had also introduced me in Spain. The particular version for this method of fishing had thin slivers of copper wire inserted within the braid to ensure fast sinking. The fast join aided rapid change of leader, which needed to be down to 0·16 mm, or even finer. A tiny red wooden indicator was slid up the line to be positioned at the estimated depth of the water. Reinhard then demonstrated the casting method – one false roll cast, then the operative one, checked like a parachute cast so that it fell loosely coiled close to the indicator. This allowed the nymph to sink deep before the fast current dragged it. At once the line had to be mended and paid out, and then you had to keep mending and paying out so that the red indicator went bobbing down without drag, the nymph bumping the stony bottom. It looked easy enough as Reinhard demonstrated with fluent casting and sure control. But two hours were enough to convince us that plenty of practice was needed for reasonable competence.

Nor was there any success to encourage, with not even Reinhard or Peter provoking any reaction. So we moved to a new area near the Steyermuhl weir where a channel of water streamed back to the main river. 'This is often good for grayling' said Reinhard. Like myself, John had not appreciated just how large those grayling would be. When his indicator checked in the swift current his instant strike seemed to have caught the bottom. Looking across, I saw him yanking the rod to free it. But suddenly the bottom moved, and he was playing a grayling, whose sail-like dorsal fin gave it great power in the racing water. It played like an autumn salmon, now holding deep, now running purposefully, now jumping. When it gave up we measured it at 51 centimetres before returning it, a remarkable fish close to the UK record of 3½ pounds. At least, we thought it remarkable. How were we to know it was just average? At once Reinhard hooked a couple of similar fish and I had one much smaller before the sidestream was fished out. Higher up in the main river John had a brown trout of about a pound to confirm his growing confidence in a method, which I still found difficult.

A late and protracted lunch back at the inn ended with Reinhard saying: 'The morning has not been good. The evening will be better.' From my point of view it was. On the leaded nymph I had a small rainbow before changing to a Sedge for the evening rise. It was almost dark when the river around me began to boil with rising rainbows. One of around a pound and a half gave me a fierce fight. I then hooked one which played so hard that after ten minutes I was only just on terms when Reinhard came to inquire what was wrong. 'It must be six pounds or more,' I told him, 'but it's under control now.' It wasn't, and it got off before I had a proper view of it. Reinhard was too polite to challenge my opinion of its weight, but I thought he smiled knowingly. He had caught a lot of the Traun's wild three-pound rainbows, and I hadn't as yet any experience of their awesome power. Blagdon's rainbows are renowned for their fighting qualities, but these were to prove twice as strong, twice as active. So perhaps that fish would merely have proved to be my first three-pounder, and not the great trout I imagined.

The next day's pattern was much the same, with John catching a couple of good grayling on the nymph in a delightful stretch of water round some islands, while Peter and I caught numbers of very small rainbows, and one of about a pound, fishing dry fly in the shallow runs near the bank. That evening John had two good rainbows while fishing with a Sedge Pupa before the main rise, much of which Peter spent locked in battle with an immense grayling. We measured that at 63 centimetres or about 25 inches – surely about six pounds and the largest Peter had caught in the Traun.

That was one turning-point for me. Peter took it on a Buck Caddis, and in future I was to fish that dry by day with growing success, as I found the nymph method difficult to master, and for me not as enjoyable as dry fly. Then at dinner Reinhard had a long talk with an immensely tall thin man said to have an unfair advantage in fishing the Traun, since his high chest waders enabled him to go in much deeper than anyone else. He told us of a place close to Gmunden, below the power station, where there was 'super' fishing. We hurried there the following morning and super it was. At the head of the first run my Buck Caddis caught me a grayling of a couple of pounds – 'Tony has a *small* grayling', I heard Reinhard call. Lower down John continued to fish the nymph method, having learnt by now how to trot it down thirty or forty yards without drag. More than a dozen times his red indicator checked, and though the strike still gave him problems he had won battles with seven big grayling and rainbows, before switching to dry fly to catch another five. His three best grayling measured 59, 57 and 56 centimetres as he revelled in this fishing with the bright sunlight and lovely setting.

Meanwhile the Buck Caddis had brought me half a dozen. With few rises to cover it was a question of searching the water, casting now upstream, now across, now floating the fly over areas I had just waded. The grayling took no fright as you waded quietly over them. One rose a few feet from John in water he had just passed and I hooked and lost it by floating the fly down towards him. Traditionally grayling are difficult to hook, but have a reputation of being silly fish that will rise again and again if you miss them. Not so the big ones on the Traun. They gave you one chance and one chance only; and after some of the most confident head-and-tail rises there was inexplicably no touch at all as you lifted the rod in happy expectation.

There was still the evening to enjoy and this time Reinhard and another very experienced Traun angler, his Dutch friend Gerard Tegelaar, undertook to complete our education by standing by us and talking us through the subtleties of the brief sedge rise. The water they had chosen seemed shallow and deserted as we fished it in muted anticipation from six to seven, standing four in a row knee-deep in fast water and casting back to the bank. It was in that period that we had our briefing:

'At seven o'clock you will see the occasional rise, and may take some fish on the Sedge Pupa. Float it down, but fish out the cast letting it drag. With the Sedge Pupa the drag sometimes provokes a fierce take. At 7.25 change to a dark Sedge, while it is still light enough to see. At 7.30 precisely the bats will wheel in, the sedges rise in clouds, the water erupt with rises. By 8 all will be over. Your maximum possibility is four fish [Gerard was in fact to catch five on our final evening in that furious half-hour], because each will take over five minutes to land. Your leader should not be less than 0·20 mm to play them hard enough to give you that chance. You must also cut your cast short, and it is right that you have a white line. For much of that half-hour it will be too dark to see your fly. You must judge its position in relation to the end of your white line and strike whenever you see a rise in that area. Once the rise is on you can wade in close to your fish and it is best to fish only for those within a few yards of you.'

It all happened exactly as described. Nothing stirred for an hour. A couple of swans sailed majestically by. A glider soared noiselessly above our heads. The waters murmured on with unbroken surface, the myriad olives drifting down untouched. A few large sedges began to wing past. Then came the first few rises and my first mistake. I was convinced I could see my pupa drifting towards where a fish had shown and with iron control ignored a rise a few feet away. 'Why do you not strike?' inquired Reinhard. And, when I tightened too late, the rainbow was touched but not hooked. The fly I had thought was mine was in fact a natural floating by, and the trout had indeed taken my small artificial. However, I soon had one nice rainbow, which took me down to the backing twice. A few yards below, John, in even faster water, had even fiercer fights with a couple more, and was then busy for a time with his torch. When a grayling gave up it could be released with ease. But the rainbows never gave up. Even when played out the touch of the hand would send them jumping away again to renew the fight. This one had leaped from John's grasp as he tried to unhook it and broken away with his fly. That was to happen to each one of us over the three nights.

Reinhard stood at my back urging me to fish close. 'Why don't you have a go?' I asked him. 'Look and see,' he replied. Turning round, I found him already fighting a rainbow. 'What did I tell you? It kept rising within a yard of us so I just dibbled my fly over it, and it took it at once.'

The next day belonged to the Buck Caddis. On the same stretch below Gmunden I caught fourteen large fish, several of them rainbows, which took the dry fly with a satisfying swirl. One, hooked in the fast water at the head, ran me all over the river while on the far bank Reinhard, Peter and Gerard, returning from a long, convivial lunch, gave raucous support. In the evening we were given our second sedge lesson before both being passed as competent. During the pupa stage, with Gerard now as mentor, I caught one and lost two, then, as the hatch developed, had two more, though the main sedge rise was not as intense as before.

With seventeen in the day, for once I narrowly outscored John, who had a couple less owing to missing many rises and losing several fish. 'Catch and release' is relatively new to me, and I view it with mixed feelings. It is certainly wrong for small stocked stillwaters, where released fish may be caught again and again. In wide rivers, or with migratory fish, it is a different matter and excellent for conservation. Yet it does take *something* away. So many of the dramatic passages of fishing literature relate to the final moments of loss of capture. But with 'catch and release' it is of no significance whether the fish gets off at the end or not – a more relaxed, but much less exciting and challenging situation. Again the bag at the end of the day has been for me the definitive statement of what you have caught. Unless you are fishing together in a party, you hesitate with 'catch and release' to state the numbers you have taken on a good day, in case of disbelief. John was particularly struck with this difference when we fished for salmon together the following week on Ireland's Erriff River. He hooked one salmon from a high bank then realized that his net was unreachable. The fish's tail would not come up so he tried to lift it out. The first time it exploded into action and nearly broke his cast. The next there was an unusual sense of triumph as he lifted it high at last. Another salmon, hooked on the middle dropper, swirled away as he was netting it and the tail fly caught in the mesh. The cast broke – but happily half an inch below the dropper, so that he was given another chance and landed the second salmon. Both fish gave him rare moments of excitement, with disaster or triumph still in the balance. With 'catch and release' both fish would have been 'caught', no matter which way that final flurry had gone. Something inevitably is lost. But in the cause of conservation that is a fair sacrifice to which it is easy to adjust. Provided, that is, we aren't asked to go the step further, as was recently suggested by a correspondent of *Plaisirs de la Pêche* who proposed hookless flies and the sole aim of *rising* fish.

It is legal to keep a few on the Traun, but the practice is frowned on by the regulars, with Reinhard and Gerard making caustic comment when an Italian killed a large rainbow he had taken on a streamer. The Traun proved the perfect example of the difference between just fishing and fishing in the right place with the right method. In our first two learning days John and I caught five between us on each. Thereafter, Reinhard and

Gerard's instruction, and their choice of water, allowed us a joint average of thirty a day, with John's ability to fish both methods giving him four to every three of mine. It was on the leaded nymph, too, that he caught a magnificent *bachforelle*, a river brown trout, of over two pounds. The tail had a reddish hue, the large red spots on the body were luminously bright, and the underbelly was as yellow as any Leven trout's. The brown trout is surely nature's most beautiful fish and this was the most beautiful specimen either of us had seen. In comparison a *seeforelle*, or lake trout, he caught later was drab of colour – but only in comparison.

Our final day still had a thing or two to teach us about the Traun. The special size 10 to 16 nymphs we used were weighted with bright brass beads at the head and had black and silver bodies, or brown with a few strands of colourful flashabou. As usual John heavily outscored my Buck Caddis with these at the start of the day, taking four large fish in the first forty minutes. The river's flow is controlled by a dam and as the water was higher than before it took longer before my dry fly began to score. Wading deep I then noticed a growing number of branches and bottles floating down the Traun. Just in time I noticed too that the water was now lapping close to the top of my chest waders and made hastily for shore. The clear water of the Traun is deceptive with the bottom often far deeper than appears from the bank. Below me John plunged unconcerned into water he knew to be shallow only to find it now trickling over the top of his waders. The dam had opened without warning and for a couple of hours all débris and all anglers were washed clear from the river. Once the level began to drop we noticed that a number of fish we had seen daily, lying in fixed positions close to the bank, were now cruising purposefully over a wide area. At once John was back in action with the nymph and had two rainbows and a grayling from his first three casts. It was not quite so easy for the nymph thereafter, and even harder than before for the dry fly for the next few hours.

On our last night the sedge rise was again very productive and gave us a splendid demonstration of the awesome power of the Traun's wild rainbows. With five of us fishing a few yards apart, hovering over the main hot spot, Reinhard waded off to another some three hundred yards upstream. Before leaving he commented that in June the whole of this area would boil with trout from bank to bank, and the rise would last a full hour – 'but the fishing then is too easy, the river too crowded'. He was back looking disconsolate before the rise was half over. 'None moving up there?' I asked. In reply he pointed to his Ross reel, which no longer had a line. The first rainbow he hooked had taken him down to the backing and broken it. 'Was it a monster?' I inquired. 'Probably just average,' said Reinhard. Next morning he recovered his new line which the fish had tangled round overhanging bushes in a final contemptuous gesture. The rest of us all caught two or more and were perhaps in a better mood for the special dinner the generous Reinhard had laid on. 'Ritteressen' at the Wirt Am Bach was quite an experience. Instead of the normal crockery one large wooden platter and one sharp knife were laid at each place. Various salad bowls were then brought in followed by a huge board, almost the size of the table, loaded with all types of meat from pieces of fried chicken to chops to steaks and sausages. With only the bones left at the end it was generally voted to be 'fingerlicking good', to steal an appropriate catch phrase.

'It is O.K., yes?' was one of Reinhard's favourite phrases. Yes, indeed, to John and myself the Traun had been O.K. But it is not always so kind to casual visitors. You need guidance, or you need time to get to know it. For a first untutored expedition the 'five rivers tour' might prove a happier experience, with its mixture of large and small streams, hard and easy fishing, wild and stocked trout. Roman Moser of Kuferzeile 19, Gmunden, the great Traun expert renowned for his casting and catching, and with a tackle wholesale business which includes all the Traun specialities, arranges such trips.

The other four rivers include the Koppen-Traun, some fifty miles away past Bad Ischl. There Herbert Grill of Bad Aussee runs the hatchery and dispenses permits, apart from the official general licence required. The Koppen-Traun rules follow much the same pattern as those on the Gmundner Traun: 'You are only allowed to fish with artificial flies. All trout caught must be returned immediately.' No mention of barbless hooks or single fly nymph, though both are customary. The other large river is the Steyer, with its wild trout and similarities to the Gmundner Traun. The small streams close to Gmunden are the Teichl, with a good head of wild trout, and the Volckla, stocked by a Mr Kottl, who only issues some half-dozen permits a day for five hours' fishing. The stocked rivers particularly are easy compared with the Traun, but heavy rain may make the smaller ones unfishable, which the Traun never is. But certainly another of the Dutch contingent at Wirt Am Bach had sampled the 'five rivers' and thoroughly enjoyed his experience.

There is no need for non-angling wives or girl-friends to languish as fishing widows in this area. Close by is the delightful city of Salzburg, overlooked, like Edinburgh, by its hilltop castle; Gmunden's Traunsee is a beautiful lake, shimmering amid towering mountains, whose craggy peaks can be reached by cable-car, and the town itself is well equipped for tourists. The Traunsee provides a variety of water sports and sightseers can match the 'five rivers' fishing tour with the 'five lakes' coach tour. There is indeed plenty to amuse those uninterested in angling. For a family holiday a touch of luxury could be added at some expense by booking in at any of the Gmunden's lakeside hotels, like the Schwan or the

Austria. For those who go for the fishing, however, the Wirt Am Bach and its equivalents provide all the comforts required.

The information sheet from the Forestry Office Traunstein of the Austrian Federal Forests (A-4810 Gmunden, Klosterplatz 1 – telephone 07612/4529) concludes with the Austrian greeting to fishermen – Petri Heil! After a week fishing the Traun we were happy to give the traditional response – Petri Dank! – glad to return thanks for some exceptional trout and grayling fishing.

Yugoslavia

With such fine trout fishing in Austria it is no surprise that neighbouring Yugoslavia also has much to offer. The Yugoslav Tourist Boards will provide maps and pamphlets on the fishing throughout the country, but some of the best is in Slovenia. Another fishing friend, Taff Price, was especially impressed by the trout fishing there on a recent visit. As he found, full details of Slovenian trout and grayling fishing can be obtained from Joze Ocvirk at the Institute of Fisheries Research, 6100 Ljubljana, Zupanciceva 9, Slovenia, Yugoslavia. The cost of the fishing is in keeping with its excellence. The better rivers are charged at 30 US dollars a day, with cheaper ones available. The prime waters, like the Unec, which Taff rates with the River Test, may cost 40 US dollars at 1986 prices, though that is reduced for a three-day or a one-week ticket. It is advisable to take US dollars as the best means of payment. If the fishing is relatively expensive, the rest is relatively very cheap with good pension accommodation costing as little as £10 a day for full board. So there is cash to spare for enjoying the best fishing. Size limits vary from water to water, and barbless hooks are the rule on some rivers. But 'catch and release' is normal for touring anglers anywhere away from home since there is little point keeping fish abroad, unless there are exceptional circumstances. Chest waders are desirable for many rivers. Taff's experience there when fishing with his fiancée, Madeleine, also underlines a safety precaution always desirable when fishing deep waters, particularly unknown ones. Having myself had to be artificially revived after nearly drowning – appropriately on All Fools' day – I am very aware that however experienced you may be you are wise to wear one of the slimline floatation jackets. Swimming and angling rate as two of the most dangerous sports because of the number of deaths from drowning – so don't think, as I did, that it can never happen to you. Remember always the three essential safety rules. All fly-fishing beginners should wear glasses to protect their eyes; floatation jackets are a wise precaution; and be careful with carbon fibre rods which are good electricity conductors, lethal if lightning strikes or if they touch live wires. So be safe and enjoy your fishing, as Taff Price so clearly did in Yugoslavia:

'There are fine rivers in many parts of Yugoslavia, but it is in Slovenia that the best of the trout and grayling fishing is to be found. Careful control of their rivers and their fish stocks ensures good sport for local and visiting angler alike.

'In Yugoslavia the rivers belong to the people and the administration of them is in the hands of various fishing clubs. These clubs issue tickets and husband the water, keeping an eye on the fish stocks. All revenues from the fishing tickets are ploughed back into the rivers in order to maintain the high quality of the fish and the fishing.

'During my 1986 visit we fished the waters of the club R. D. Tolmin and also waters managed by the Institute of Fisheries Research based at Ljubljana. The rivers of Slovenia can be divided into two types. First are the wild crystal-clear Alpine limestone rivers tumbling out of the mountains and usually flanked by natural forests which abound with game. Bear, boar, lynx, wildcat, wolf and various deer are to be found in these green forests of Slovenia. The other type of river is typical chalk stream. These wind through lush watermeadows, filled with every imaginable wild flower providing carpets of colour, a real rainbow of hues to delight the eye. During my brief stay I was to enjoy fishing both types of water.

'Of the rivers of the Institute of Fisheries Research, the River Lapena was a fascinating start point. This small river is one of the feeders of the Soca River. It is a clear stream of fast runs and deep pools and the day we fished it the fierce sun beat down, reflecting off the white limestone boulders with a dazzling brilliance which made sunglasses a must. The surrounding scenery was breathtaking, with tall snow-capped peaks fringing the skyline all around. The sheer majesty of the scenery so distracted me that I found it difficult to concentrate on the fish. There was so much to see, so much to take in all at once. In a deep pool beneath a bridge, I watched about eight large trout cruise round and round, obviously on the lookout for food. There were insects in the air enough to satisfy the most ardent of entomologists, but which insect was going to satisfy the trout? Then I found the answer. The largest stonefly I had ever seen (*Perla maxima*), about two inches in length, fluttered down to the surface of the pool. It had barely twitched its wings when a trout streaked up from the depths and ended its watery struggle. With shaking hands I took off the size 14 dry fly I had intended to use and put on the largest fly I had in my box, a large red sedge. The fly alighted on the water and sure enough a determined trout shot to the surface and seized it. The fish remained on for about half a second and was gone. I had lost my chance of a fish of about two pounds. That was the pattern of the day. The big fish eluded me as they proved too clever. Small browns and rainbows were to be my only reward, but what did it matter? I was fishing in such beautiful surroundings, the most memorable of my experience, and that was reward in itself. Another unusual sensation in fishing there was to be baking and sunburnt from the waist up, whilst from the waist down it was icy cold, for the water temperature was barely over 40°F, due to the snow melt in the water.

'The River Soca itself was a revelation to me. This river must be classed as one of the most beautiful in the world. It is sky blue in colour, gushing through deep gorges channelled out over thousands of years. It is a symbol to the Slovenian people, a natural work of art, and to my mind one of the wonders of the world. The important fish of the Soca is without doubt the marbled trout (*Salmo marmoratus cuvier*), a beautifully marked fish quite different from a brown trout. This was the only trout found in the Soca system of rivers until about 1906, when brown trout were introduced.

'The day allotted for fishing the Institute's stretch of the Soca proved disappointing, for the river itself was clouded by snow melt. This factor combined with a blazing bright sun was not conducive to good fishing. My fiancée, Madeleine, who came with me on this trip, managed to tempt a marbled trout of about a pound to take a small dry sedge. This beautifully marked fish looked more like a brook trout than a brown.

'Looking into a pool on the River Tolminka, a feeder stream of the Soca, we saw marbled trout finning in the current and the consensus put the largest at eight pounds. A number of six-pounders had already been taken on the Soca this season, but the record remains with a fish caught in 1928 at Most Na Soci. It weighed 20 kilograms, a massive fish.

'The Unec provided my next experience and this was unique for me. For some anglers the River Test is the trout-fishing Utopia, for others it may be the Austrian Traun, but for many Europeans it is the River Unec of Slovenia. If the trout is the prince of fish, in Slovenia the grayling wears the crown, and the grayling of the Unec attract fly fishermen from all over Europe, such is their fame.

'The Unec is a magical river. One source gushes out of a giant cave in the hillside, the other bubbles up out of the ground almost under the keeper's house and within a few yards has enough power to drive a sawmill. The river abounds with trout and grayling for about 18 kilometres and then disappears underground only to reappear 10 kilometres further on as a new river, this time full of coarse fish.

'It was a mixed blessing to be fishing during a hatch of mayfly. Never have I seen so many *Ephemera danica* on the wing as I did on the Unec. They floated in vast clouds and I suspect that the fish had had a surfeit by the time we came to try and tempt them. On the trophy section of the river barbless hooks are used. Flies like the Grayling Witch, and other similar patterns, seem to be the most popular during the day and the Slovenian Sedges of Dr Volje work well during the evening rise. The grayling we caught on this stretch were close to the 40 centimetre mark, with Madeleine taking one of 42 centimetres, which is the minimum takable size for this stretch of the Unec.

'Our guide for the first half of the trip had been Marjan Fratnik who had returned now to Most Na Soci for a well earned rest after looking after us so well. He left us in the capable hands of Jose Ocvirk, the Director of the Fisheries Research Institute, and we were indebted to both of them for setting up so entertaining a fishing trip. For our second session on the Unec we chose to fish near the source, where the river tumbles through cool woods. Now this was my sort of fishing for, though a chalk river, at this spot it had the feel of a rough stream. Nowhere in Slovenia was I more at home.

'I decided to fish with one of Marjan Fratnik's Dormouse Nymphs, a sombre grey nymph made from the tail of a dormouse. The dormouse is a pest of the fruit crops in Yugoslavia and many thousands are trapped each year. The fur has no commercial value and is only used by fly dressers to create a number of nymphs, shrimps and dry flies. Within a minute of starting I had tumbled in, complete with my camera. I managed to stay vertical, but was carried down a deep gulley by water that was moving a lot faster than it appeared on the surface. I bobbed down the current not unlike an olive float until my feet touched a gravel bank and I was able to get out of the deceptive maelstrom. On the stretch the fish came fast and free. Whilst I was taking grayling on the weighted nymph, Madeleine was having sport with brown trout using a small dry fly tied with the feathers from a duck's preen gland. Some of the brown trout were beautifully marked, many having two bright red spots on the adipose fin and a belly of golden butter yellow.

'We moved on to yet another delightful river, the Sava Bohinjka. This is another beautiful limestone river cared for by the Fisheries Research Institute. It flows from the picturesque Lake Bohinj and runs through a wooded valley until it reaches Radovljica, where it links up with the Sava Dolinka to form the major Sava River. Heavy thunderstorms had just capped the surrounding mountain peaks with fresh snow, but down on our level the rain caused the lake to rise and the river to flood. Even in flooding it never lost its green crystal colour, but it was moving too fast for comfortable fishing. We contented ourselves by trying the quiet eddies away from the swirling rough and tumble of the stream. We did this by creeping up the bank and short casting upstream with a small white-winged Royal Coachman. This tempted a number of fish to come out of their sanctuaries and both browns and rainbows succumbed to this fly. The best was a rainbow of about a pound and a half. We were interested to hear that the Sava Bohinjka has a run of Danubian salmon (*Hucho hucho*) in the autumn. To add further variety we rounded off our visit to the Bohinj area by deep jigging for red-bellied char in the lake itself and paid a visit to a grayling hatchery on the shores of the lake.

'The institute administers many other waters, but now we explored some belonging to the club R. D. Tomlin. This club has a number of waters under its jurisdiction, including part of the Soca River, as well as Soca Lake, which is situated at Most Na Soci. The lake is formed by a dam across the river and fast-sinking lines and big nymphs and lures can bring you a number of different species of fish – for example, rainbows of five pounds or more, large browns, lake trout, marbled trout, crosses between marble and brown, marble and lake and brown and lake, and, of course, large grayling.

'The River Idrijca was the first of the club's streams we fished. This is another of the clear green limestone rivers which abound in this area. It has some good fast runs, productive smooth glides and some very deep pools in which good-sized fish can clearly be seen. Our first stretch was flanked by thick woods which gave us some relief from the heat of the sun. Stoneflies of various species, including the bright yellow sally, fluttered up from the water seeking the shade of the surrounding greenery. Within five minutes of fishing, Madeleine had her first ducking. The river bed was extremely treacherous and the water ran very fast. She floated off downstream buoyed up by the air in her chest waders. With the stoicism of a true angler it did not stop her fishing and a couple of glasses of the local firewater soon restored her chilled spirits.

'Browns to just over a pound and wild river-bred rainbows provided the pattern of this day's fishing, with one or two grayling to add to the magic. But on the River Baca the grayling was dominant. We fished a stretch of water that descended in minature waterfalls – a pool, a waterfall, a pool, a waterfall, and so on. In each pool grayling of up to 50 centimetres could be seen, some on the feed, others lying quietly in the clear cool pools, perhaps waiting for the sun to go away before they too would rise to take a fluttering water-trapped stonefly or sedge. We all had good grayling that morning. The most effective fly was a small grey-bodied, grey-hackled size 14. The only trout caught were small, but we were assured that good-size fish were also taken on this river.

'Our week in Slovenia had been a magical experience. We had sampled only a small fraction of the trout fishing since there are almost two thousand rivers to choose from in Yugoslavia. But certainly we had been on some of the best.'

The problem in planning where to fish in Yugoslavia is the pleasant one of too much choice. Taff Price was fortunate enough to be guided to some of the best waters and it is sensible to get proper advice in advance, whether from tourist offices or local contacts. For those who read German an excellent guidebook to the country's fishing is Franz Hackstock-Schellenberg's *Salmoniden- anden Schonsten Strecken Jugoslawiens*. All Taff's rivers have pride of place, but from other regions are included equally beautiful streams such as the Rizana, the Una and Unac, the Krka, the Savinga, and the Gacka. Illustrated successful fly patterns range from the Grey Palmer to the Goldie, the Light Cahill and the Fuzzy Wuzzy streamer. There is a special Gacka Nymph, but that river is itself rather special.

From the wide choice in Yugoslavia many pick on the Gacka for preference. Alastair Drew is typical of these, having been attracted there recently by an article in *The Field* which told of massive fish and beautiful countryside. The punch line for him ran: 'Once you have discovered the Gacka you will never want to fish anywhere else.' That was a pardonable exaggeration, but certainly Alastair Drew was keen enough to return once he had sampled this delightful river. For, as he himself recorded in *The Field*, he was drawn back by 'the possibility of catching a 14-pound trout and the certainty of entertaining company'.

His description of the Gacka gives a good picture of this Yugoslavian chalk stream:

'The Gacka rises from springs in the side of a mountain in the Lika district of Yugoslavia, 80 miles south of Zagreb and 20 miles from the Adriatic. Within 300 yards it is a substantial river, similar to the Test at Stockbridge. It flows for only 15 miles before entering a lake from where, until 1964, the water drained away through its bottom. Now the water is used in a hydroelectric scheme.

'Its temperature is normally 50°F and, since the water spends less than a day travelling from source to finish, the maximum fluctuation from midwinter to midsummer is 2°F. The valley is limestone, but the Gacka can properly be described as a chalk stream. The alkaline water and constant temperature provide what may be the world's finest breeding ground for trout food. The average number of insects in a cubic yard of English trout stream is 400; the Gacka holds 13,500

'So the fish get fat. The adult brown trout put on an average 1¾ pounds a year while rainbows, which were introduced in 1937, gain some 2½ pounds (roughly three times as much as an Itchen fish). In other words the "fertile" Gacka water yields a harvest of surplus fish flesh of about 600 pounds per acre per annum – about 2 pounds per yard. The management is long-term and scientific, and the stocking programme extensive; 9,000 ¾-pound rainbows and 26,000 ¼-pound brown trout are being put in during this year – a similar number to last year. But the fish grow big in the wild, and it is anything but a "put and take" system. Putting is easy, taking can be difficult.

'The fish are plump and plentiful, but they are also extremely choosy.'

The most productive method of the locals is to fish nymphs, sedges, or mayflies downstream – and the most productive time can be the famed mayfly hatch in late May. Alastair was helped to master the technique by a local expert, Milan Stefanac, whose father bought half the Gacka in 1934 and who still lives on its banks despite the changes in property laws in Yugoslavia. But, as Alastair put it, the trout may not be easy even at mayfly time: 'Fish rose in profusion, but the river hissed with expletives from frustrated Austrian, German, French, Danish, Italian, Yugoslav and English fishermen. The majority of us could not provoke even a short rise to the artificial, wet or dry, upstream or down. On other days, however, people can catch thirty or more (all but a brace are returned).'

Jean Zender from Luxemburg has been fishing the Gacka for more than twenty years and is so entranced by it that he expects to go on taking an annual holiday there at the Gacka Hotel. On his first trip he could see the large trout in the clear water, but for nearly a week could catch nothing. To add to his bewilderment, a Bavarian visitor at the hotel was taking large numbers of big trout:

'I had been told that it was fly water, I had come with my traditional wet and dry flies, so why was I not catching trout? Finally I had to ask how he did it. Kindly he showed me his fly box. These aren't flies, I thought to myself and said aloud: "What are these called?" "Nymphs." "Nymphs? What are nymphs?" I asked in my ignorance. Once I learnt about nymphs, the Gacka became a very productive river for me too. But the big trout are never easy. One year I spent every evening in vain pursuit of a large trout, which would always rise a couple of times to natural flies then take no further interest. God made the world in a shorter time than it took me to catch this nine-pounder, but on the seventh day he finally came to the net.

'In mayfly time there are intriguing rises on the Gacka. In a 300-yard stretch you can see three different rise forms: trout in the first half show their tails as they busy themselves with nymphs; next a group concentrates on emerging nymphs; and then a group happily sups on hatched flies. You have no hope unless you pick the right fly for the hundred yards you fish.

'It is more important to learn things like that about the Gacka than to be a brilliant caster. Once several of us fished there at the same time as a proud Englishman. We had some very good fishing with many large trout caught – I had eight over five pounds myself – and several lost. But he never caught. Each day he would stride past us, never speaking, never smiling, never watching even if one of us was playing a big fish. On the last day he stopped for once and watched us for a time. Finally he spoke his first words to us: "Your casting technique is very poor," he said before striding off.'

There is indeed more to fishing than catching fish, and more to catching fish than casting. But even if you catch nothing you should enjoy Yugoslavia.

7

Italian Ingenuity and Eastern Promise

From Italy to the Eastern Bloc

Italian trout fishing has some special memories for me. Some of the unpleasantest weeks of my life were spent on banks of the Rapido river overlooked by the indomitable German defenders of the Monte Cassino stronghold and listening to the fortifications of Sant' Angelo village being steadily improved in an area where we would soon have to force a crossing. So it was a pleasure to return years later and catch a trout in its clear fast waters that had once held such threat.

Italian fishing for trout can still embrace methods the fly fisherman would regard as somewhat unusual. In 1986, for instance, they planned to hold their first 'International Trout Fishing Meeting' in the city of Subiaco. The published information included the following on method: 'According to the Regional Laws and regulations applicable to the place where the meeting will be held only the following bait will be allowed: earth and water worms, honey and flour worms, fliganae, insects and larvae, with the exception of the meat fly larvae, seeds and fruit in their natural state, and natural salmon eggs.' So if you fish with artificial flies be sure to check the regulations where you intend to fish.

This can best be done through the main body concerned, the Federazione Italiana della Pesca Sportiva. Most of the rivers and lakes suitable for fishing are administered by the Italian Angling Federation, with only about 10 per cent in private ownership. A government licence issued by the provincial administration is required for all fishing, is easily obtainable and costs only about £2 per year. For private water the owner's consent is obviously needed; for all other waters it is necessary to have a FIPS membership card costing about the same small sum and obtainable from all provincial sections or through the head office, Viale Tiziano, 70 Rome.

Naturally the trout fishing will be concentrated in the more mountainous regions from 2,000 feet upwards. Apart from wild brown trout, grayling and char, Italian waters have a very special species of trout, the *marmorata*, or marbled trout, which runs to great size. One of the best rivers for the *marmorata*, and for other trout, is the Sesia. It was in the Borgo Sesia area that Italy staged the World Fly Fishing Championship in 1983. The wild browns were not easy to catch, but the stocked rainbows came easily enough to well hackled flies or leaded nymphs. My memories of this happy international affair were summed up in two experiences. Even in the high mountain area that summer the heat was oppressive, relieved on practice day by a spectacular thunderstorm which had the prudent hurrying to drop their carbon rods as the lightning fired a nearby building. Perhaps because it was around 100°F, the following day the lunch interval was so extended that the final session started two hours late. My controller was meant only to see that the rules were observed and to record any fish taken from a lovely long pool with even flow and interesting eddies near the stony bank. For an hour and a half I missed nearly every trout that rose and then got broken by a *marmorata*. As I sat down to tie on a new cast the now much involved 'judge' proffered his own recipe for success – two well hackled flies tied as in Walton's day and joined by cast of some 10-pound breaking strain. Reasoning that it would keep him happy, and that I could do no worse, and that local knowledge is often superior, I added it as a leader. After an ineffective quarter of an hour I was about to revert to more traditional flies when a rainbow seized hold. The spade hooks were slightly offset and went on hooking firmly as another seven came to land. With two minutes left I hooked a large rainbow of some 2½ pounds, compared with the pounders previously netted. My net was unfortunately absent without leave, left where I had landed the last one. So I was carefully beaching the fish when my 'judge', unasked and unwanted, weighed in to help, grabbing the cast to haul the trout to land. Alas the rest of the cast was only 4-pound maxima not the thickness to which he was accustomed. So his flies and my fish disappeared back into the Sesia, with the judge looking somewhat anxious. We had a good laugh and went in search of a drink after the weigh-in, with me reckoning that his weird flies had caught me more than his peculiar action had lost. Late that night as the speeches droned on in the main dining-room a small party of English flyfishers were surrounded by locals on the verandah outside busily tying each other flies of varied pattern under the faint and flickering lights. That exactly expressed the spirit of a championship which has as its only two aims the spread of international friendship and the international exchange of ideas.

The Italians won on their home water and, as they won four out of the first six world championships, it was a very fair result; they were equally at home from Spanish to Belgian waters. Chance counts for a lot in fishing, skill for much more. Perhaps the key to the international success of the Italians is the wide variety of skills and techniques called for by their home waters.

An Italian fishing friend, Roby Colombero, gives this description of trout fishing in Italy, where, as usual, the best of the fishing is in the mountainous regions:

'Of the sport fishermen in Italy about a quarter are concerned with trout fishing, and only a quarter of those with fly fishing, though this more skilful technique is rapidly gaining supporters. Both wet and dry fly are used, but predominantly wet fly and sinking line since this is both easier and more effective in our fast streams.

'Our main area for trout covers the hundreds and hundreds of small and large valleys in the Alps and in the Appenines as far south as the Abruzze. All the rivers there (in fact most are torrents rather than rivers) have trout in them. In Piedmont the largest river is the Sesia. It is also the easiest for fly fishing as the banks are clear of vegetation and have few trees. Most of the torrent-type streams have thick cover on the banks, with bushes or trees making casting difficult, demanding special skill on the part of the fly fisher.

'In my home region of Piedmont the most important rivers and torrents are the Sesia, the Orco, the Stura di Lanzo, the Chisone, the Po, the Varaita, the Maira, the Grana Stura di Demonte, the Gesse, the Pesie, the Ellero, the Corsaglia and the Bormida. There are other good rivers in Tuscany and Emilia and also in the north-eastern region close to the Alps. In the Veneto around Venice there are also quiet rivers in the plain which look similar to chalk streams, with much weed in the water.

'There are trout in all the major lakes in Italy, but most of the fishing is for the great variety of other species, and the trout are usually caught only by chance, rather than being specially fished for. The larger lakes holding trout are Maggiore, Orta, Isco and Garda. There are also many small Alpine lakes, some of them manmade to serve power stations. Even these artificial waters are usually set in beautiful scenery and pleasant to fish.

'Fishing in the torrent-type streams depends largely on the season. Early on, while the ice and snow are melting on the high peaks, spinning is the norm, with the water very high and coloured. A short telescopic rod of 1·5 to 2 metres, a good spinning reel and Mepps or Martin artificials in sizes 2 and 3 provide the best equipment. The trout will usually range between 20 and 35 centimetres. If you catch something bigger you will certainly want to take it round to show your friends.

'For fly fishing the best hook sizes are 10 to 14, and size 8 for streamers. Of the three varieties of trout, the rainbow – cheap to produce commercially for stocking – is the commonest, while the *fario* is typical of the torrent streams in which brown trout thrive. The *marmorata*, which can run up to very large weights as its maximum size is 130 centimetres, is much the rarest as it is not produced in fish farms and there is no restocking. The central fishing federation and many clubs stock with rainbows.

'The national federation, FIPS, is the main authority, but every region has its own laws. In principle fishing is allowed from the end of February to 1 October. In my district of Cuneo the overseas visitor may obtain a three-month permit for a fee of about £4. The best waters are private, but the visitor can buy a half-day or day permit with a limit of from five to seven trout. In the beats where the price is highest the trout are mostly browns, which are especially prized, and they will be of reasonable size, probably 350 grams on average. Information in English can be obtained at the local tourist office in all large towns. Tackle shops are even better sources of information and can often provide tickets for private waters.'

Carlo Malvasio of the Club Azzuro is one of several outstanding Italian trout fishermen who are involved in the severe selection tests for the national team. He avoids the rivers of northern Italy, which he considers over-popular and over-crowded:

'If I want to catch a few nice fish I go to central Italy, which is less well known and wilder, and where the costs are also lower. The rivers, or torrents, I prefer, and which are recommended to me by friends who live in those parts, are the Turano, the Velino, the Nera, the Sangro, the Aterno and the Pescara, which flow in the provinces of Terni, Rieti, Aquila and Pescara. To be able to fly fish there all that is required is to hold a government licence, which costs 22,000 lire and to keep to the days which are Thursday, Saturday and Sunday. The cost of accommodation is also very low, from 25,000 to 40,000 lire a day.

'These watercourses are completely different from those in the north, where the water runs faster and where nymph and wet fly work better. The rivers in central Italy flow slowly and are narrower, often screened by vegetation. A dry fly or a light nymph can, however, make some good fish rise, especially if a fine leader is used with flies in size 12 or 14 or even smaller.

'The river which has given me the most satisfaction is the Sangro at Castel di Sangro in the province of Aquila, between Rome and Pescara. This river, which is similar to a chalk stream, but rather narrow and at times very wooded, holds trout of up to two kilograms. These take nymphs as eagerly as small trout, and you can also deceive them with a lightly hackled dry fly. To fish here a FIPS card (25,000 lire) is required in addition to the government licence. Alternatively, you can buy daily permits at a cost of 10,000 lire for a limit of six trout. The best period for fly fishing is from 15 May to 31 July.

'The people of Castel di Sangro are very hospitable and are all true fly fishermen who take a real pride in their river. I was certainly made to feel very much at home there.

'Finally I turn to a river which has enabled me to learn and gain experience in dry-fly, wet-fly and nymph fishing. This is the Aveto torrent in the province of Genoa, and in particular the stretch which runs through the commune of Rezzoaglio. The only trouble with this river is that it does not hold many big fish – the brown trout and grayling average between 25 and 30 centimetres. The reason for this is that in summer the water runs very low and all fish bigger than half a kilogram take refuge in very deep holes which cannot be reached with fly tackle.'

Switzerland and Liechtenstein

Switzerland has beautiful waters and beautiful scenery, but the trout fishing there is more expensive and more limited than you might expect of a mountainous region with such clear, clean water. There are very large trout and char in some of the lakes but they are not taken on fly and can only be caught by trolling very deep. The great rivers of Rhine and Rhône hold some very big trout too, which can sometimes be taken by spinning with a 2½-inch Devon or with a silver-bodied salmon fly. The Rhône above Lake Geneva can be good for trout, but for much of the season the snow melt ruins the fishing.

The various cantons provide a variety of fishing for trout and grayling, though much of it is private. Rules and arrangements differ from canton to canton and it is impossible to generalize. Detailed information can be had from district tourist offices (*verkehrsbüro*), where licences can usually be bought as well, from district government offices, and from the national association, the Schweizer Sportfischerverband Carl Straub, Spiserstrasse 3, 8047 Zurich. A useful contact is the HRH Fly Fishing Club, of Schaffhauserstrasse 514, 8052 Zurich. This is run by H. R. Hebeisen, who organizes a number of fishing classes in Zurich and elsewhere. The club's broadsheet newsletter includes the annual programme of fishing classes, as well as special fly-fishing weeks abroad, from Ireland to the Traun.

The only constant in Switzerland is that you will fish clear waters in impressive surroundings – there are 20,000 miles of rivers and many lakes, most of which hold trout. It is certainly a fishing country to explore, though the snow water does not clear in the lower valleys until late May and in the higher areas until July. Some small hill torrents hide big trout, so you may have interesting fishing off the beaten track.

Liechtenstein
There is only limited trout fishing in Liechtenstein – mainly in the Rhine areas for rainbow, brown and lake trout, as well as grayling. The Vaduz

district is the best centre and information can be had from Landesver-kehrsbüro Vaduz, 9490 Vaduz.

Germany

German trout fishing is of a standard to attract anglers from neighbouring countries, with many regular visitors from across the borders. Two of Belgium's best, Eddy Arnauts and rodmaker and tackle expert Ladislav Elnetti, choose the Ahr as one of the pleasantest rivers to fish, well stocked with trout and grayling, not to mention big barbel. In their view:

'The Ahr is an easy river to fish, varying between 12 and 25 metres in width with alternating runs and glides. There are good fly hatches and some exciting evening sedge rises. While it is best to match the hatch, small Blue Duns or little Grey Palmer dry flies are usually effective. The best method is to fish the dry fly across and down, but nymphs upstream. Unless the water is very high unweighted nymphs are to be used as the water is clear and rarely deep. There is a fly-fishing school at Rech-on-Ahr and much good water in the 40 kilometres from Altenahr down to Ahrweller. There are many hotels where you can get permits to fish and every variety of accommodation, including bed and breakfast. The Pension Marita at Rech-on-Ahr is a comfortable one for fishermen. Another good area is Mayschoss-on-Ahr, where two brothers own most of the water rights. The river here is faster and deeper and you get good trout up to six pounds. Another attraction of the Ahr is that it runs through a beautiful valley with vineyards that are the source of a fine red wine.'

A good river close to the Dutch border is the Lenne, which has many grayling and brown and rainbow trout averaging 1½ pounds. Finnentrop area is a popular centre for fly fishermen, and the Im Stillen Winkel hotel makes a good base. Another knowledgeable Belgian angler, Paul Veke-mans, homes in on the River Kyll, close to the Luxemburg border, as an ideal river to visit:

'This is a very popular river and you may have to stay several days if you want to qualify for a permit. Kyllberg and Hillesheim are the best centres from which to fish this stream, which is a fantastic grayling river as well as having trout. There are many good hotels and bed-and-breakfast accommodation in this area. The river itself is a nice mixture of long flats and fast streams with excellent fly hatches. In the best periods for grayling you will catch well with small dry flies in sizes 18 and 20. Early-season fishing is very good and so is the back end.

'The Loisach River near Garmisch Partenkirchen in Bavaria is a nice trout stream. The trout are small and the river would not merit a visit purely for the fishing, but this is a beautiful area, and the Loisach is a delight to fish as part of a family holiday. For bigger fish the upper Danube is very good, though expensive. It holds rainbows up to double figures, but fishing will cost you £30 or more a day. I have enjoyed some splendid days here, particularly on the fishery of Herr K. Thies in Rothenacker. Nymph and dry-fly fishing are both effective, as they are also on the Weisser Traun between Munich and Salzburg, which is another pleasant river. But if you go that far why not go a little further to the Gmundner Traun in Austria? The Weisser Traun is smaller and not so good – but then few rivers are as good as the Traun near Gmunden.'

For a German's choice I turned to a fishing companion of mine on the Traun, Joachim Bujok, who selected his homeland rivers of Franconia, the 'Frankische Schweiz'. This is the triangle of land between Nuremberg, Bamberg and Bayreuth, with the River Wiesent and its tributaries providing chalkstream fishing of quality. It is an area easily reached by car down motorway E5 past Wurzberg and Forchheim.

Franconia had a particular appeal to artists and academicians in the Romantic era, with its wild and picturesque landscape fitting the ideals of the time. Its famous stalactite caves also attracted scientists and tourists, many of them British, who soon appreciated the fly-fishing possibilities and helped develop the art. H. J. Whitling's *Pictures of Nuremberg and Rambles in the Hills and Valleys of Franconia*, published in 1858, gave a glowing account of the remarkable trout fishing.

The area has retained much of its natural charm, with varied cliff formations dominating the lush river valleys, mysterious ruined castles on the skyline, idyllic millponds with waterwheels in attractive villages. The fishing, too, is of high quality still, though preserved by put-and-take stocking.

The Wiesent is noted for an incredible mayfly hatch, which attracted famous anglers like Charles Ritz and Dr Duncan. For Joachim, however, it is the smaller, faster, clearer tributary streams, the Aufsess and Putlach, which most appeal. This is his overall view of the fishing there:

'The Wiesent flows for 75 kilometres running south at first past Waischen-feld and Beringersmühle as it carves out a romantically beautiful valley. At Beringersmühle it is joined by the Putlach and wends its way westward to enter the River Regnitz at Forchheim. The meadowland round the river is rich in wild flowers, many of them, such as the European orchids, rare in central Europe.

'The river is mostly between 15 and 20 metres wide with a maximum depth of 2 metres. The bed has weeds in profusion – elodea, ranunculus, watercress, and *potamotogeton crispus* and *perfoliatus*. These are never cut from June onwards and can cause problems for anglers; for the trout, however, they provide a store of food with shrimps and the like and many types of ephemeropterans. The blue-winged olive is the most important, except, perhaps, in the mayfly period of late May and June. There are also many varieties of *baetis* and chironomids, with sedges later in the season.

'For a disabled angler this is ideal water, as the road runs beside the Wiesent and Pütlach for their whole length and the meadowland by their banks is firm and level. All along the Wiesent there are nice inns which reserve stretches of the river for their guests. The management of these waters is variable, but two hotels greatly impress me. Each has 3-kilometre beats of river where the fishing for guests is always good. The first is the Hotel Henlein, D–8551 Doos, just north of Beringersmühle. Their water is well stocked with fingerlings, which are acclimatized enough to be "wild" trout when caught at an average weight of about 350 grams. Then there is the Hotel Café Eberhard, Bayroither Strasse 2, D–8551 Muggendorf, Wiesenttal. It was here that Charles Ritz often stayed, and the water is still well worth fishing. It is stocked with sizeable trout so the average is larger than at Doos.

'The Wiesent has slightly clouded water throughout the season so you can only spot rising fish. Because of that, and the plague of boats which paddle down it, my preference is for the Pütlach and Aufsess, where the water is clear and the boats rare. You can fish in peace there in a way that is only possible on the Wiesent after 6 p.m., when boats are banned.

'There are many grayling in the Wiesent, but the Pütlach and Aufsess have more numerous, if smaller, trout. The trout also tend to be more wary in these streams, needing to be stalked and fished for fine. An interesting stretch of the Aufsess, 5–10 metres wide but deep-running, is reserved for guests of the Backmanns, of the Gasthof Neumuhle, a pleasant inn in the village of Neumuhle. The season runs from March to 15 December as in all Franconia, though the fishing is not good until May. The trout average 30 centimetres but there are a number of three-pounders to be had in the Aufsess.

'The Pütlach is a delightful meadowland chalk stream only 5 to 7 metres wide and flowing through a lovely valley, which includes the most famous of many stalactite caves in the area, the Devil's Cavern. The Pütlach is also a put-and-take river and you are allowed to use a spinner, though fly is more effective as well as more interesting. You can get permits for the upper water in Pottenstein and for another good beat from Herr Jakob Schrufer at the Tuscherfeld petrol station.

'The best of the fishing is in the lower part down to the junction with the Wiesent. You can catch good brown and rainbow trout up to two pounds here. The Gasthaus Marita, 8556 Beringersmühle, is an ideal place to stay and has fishing rights.

'On the Pütlach the mayfly hatch is more irregular and less important than on the Wiesent. The trout are wary of the natural and easily scared by the artificial. Often a BWO hatch coincides with a mayfly hatch and as both spinners drift down in the film the trout will sip the BWOs nine times out of ten. I have fished evening rises when every trout in the river seems to be up near the surface feeding greedily, yet I have still struggled to rise fish. Then I learnt that the first choice should be a Pheasant Tail Spinner, the second a Lunn's Particular, size 16. If even these fail I go down to size 18.

'It pays to concentrate on the run-ins as well as the quiet water. There the rises are more difficult to spot, the small dry flies harder to follow, so many anglers give them a miss. These trout can therefore be easier to catch. The locals tend to use very small imitations, but there is rarely any need to go below size 16. Indeed, by day a big Sedge fished under the banks or beside thick weedbeds will often attract fish. The English pioneered fly fishing here and the Franconian trout still take a fancy to English-type flies. Greenwell's Glory parachute flies and Skues nymphs are all effective. Before the evening sedge rises, as the pupae drift above the bottom, a pupa imitation, similar to a Grayling Bug, catches many trout. But should you have trouble in rising fish then seek advice from a tackle shop like Der Wiesentfischer, Breitenbacherstrasse 22, D–8553 Ebermannstadt.

'The fisherman who is content to land fish between half a pound and two pounds, and who finds satisfaction in fishing in a varied landscape which bears vivid witness to a long history of development and settlement, will certainly be fascinated by the Frankische Schweiz, and charmed by the modest and friendly people who live there.'

There is good trout fishing in East Germany too, though not comparable with that in nearby Poland. The main body concerned is the Deutscher Anglerwerhand der DDR, zHd des Generalsekretärs, Hausbergstrasse 13, 1034 Berlin, German Democratic Republic, from which information can be sought.

Poland

A Polish fly fisherman with an outstanding European reputation for his ability as multilingual organizer as well as thoughtful angler is Jozef Jelenski. Who better to picture Polish trout fishing and set the present scene?

'Fly fishing has been practised in Poland from the beginning of organized angling, and in 1879 the President of Cracow, Mr Stanislaw Zyblikiewicz, registered the first anglers' society in Poland. Rivers around Cracow were full of trout, grayling and sea trout then – not surprising, therefore, that in 1899 Professor Rozwadowski, a member of that society, wrote the first-ever book on fly fishing in Poland, *A Handbook for Angling – Sports Fans; or the Art of Catching Trout, Grayling and Salmon with the Fishing Rod* in 1899. Since then fly fishing has been a favourite method with Polish anglers, despite wars and the hard economic situation of the country. Some attempts were made even before the Second World War to start national championships, but it was not until 1963 that the Professor Romaniszyn Cup competition was started on the Dunajec river. Up to now this is named the "unofficial national". The first ever national with eliminators was held in 1977, also on the Dunajec, and since then the event has rotated round Poland on such rivers as the Skawa, the Gwda, the Grabow and the San.

'All Polish anglers, about a million of them, are members of the Polish Angling Association and about 50,000 of them fish on trout waters, which total 65,000 hectares out of 150,000 managed by associations. Fisheries are open and members can fish anywhere they want without additional payment. Of course this causes some managing problems, and not all trout waters are good by European standards. The small streams and rivers particularly are quickly fished out, and good sport can be had only on wide rivers in grayling and barbel regions. Natural trout lakes are few and all of them are in national parks as nature reserves. All these factors and the traditional preference of Polish anglers for grayling as a game fish ensures that fly fishing in Poland is directed mainly to grayling and trout, rather than trout and grayling. Grayling have been introduced to many rivers where they were not originally present.

'Trout fishing in Poland falls into two main regions. First, there are the mountainous, shallow, turbulent rivers and streams in the south of Poland. These have rocky or gravelly bottoms and are similar to the rivers of Scotland. Going from east to west the best are the San, Dunajec, Skawa, Sola and Biala Ladecka. No migratory fish arrive there because the lower Odra and Wisla are badly polluted and blocked by dams and weirs.

'Then, in the north of Poland, with its moraineous lakeland, there are many lake-fed rivers with cool water, which run directly into the Baltic Sea. In their lower stretches sea trout and steelhead can enter them, and do so in some profusion. The best are the Lupawa, the Slupia, the Wieprza and the Parseta. In all of them, and additionally in the Radunia, Wda and Gwda, there is good stock of wild trout and grayling. Here rivers are not as fast or as shallow as in the south, and are similar to English chalk streams with their bottoms of silt, sand and fine gravel as well as abundance of water weeds. They are deep and mostly lined with trees, which makes both bank fishing and wading difficult. It is possible to catch good trout here, but they are few and far between. It is agreed that while in the north trout and grayling grow bigger, they are not as numerous as in the south.

'Fly fishing for sea trout and steelhead is not as popular in Poland as worming and spinning for them. The season for sea trout starts early and, because fishing for kelts is legal, most of them are caught in spring. Fresh-run fish called *srebrniak*, or "silvery", are present in the rivers from February. However, the main runs are in June, July and August. Fly fishers use salmon flies for them, such as Black Ranger, Ackroyd, hairwing Jock Scott, Grey Turkey, General Practitioner and Muddler Minnow, tied on 4/0 to 6/0 hooks. Fishing is with fast sinking lines. The across-and-downstream method works on shallows when the water is high. Low water forces fishermen to turn to a special type of fishing, similar to nymphing of the induced-take type, using size 2 to 4/0 salmon flies, streamers or big nymphs on sinking lines in deep currents. In the seventies an experiment began with massive stocking of the Baltic Sea with rainbow trout of 10–12 inches. Most of them are netted directly from the sea, but many still come into the lower stretches of rivers. From October on they can be fished for with the fly and some of them are caught in summer too. This extends the fly-fishing season all the year round.

'Major hatches of flies are the same as in Great Britain, with a tendency for sedges to be more abundant. Dry and wet flies, nymphs, streamers and fully dressed salmon flies used as streamers – all are used throughout the season. Fly fishing for grayling needs more explanation. There are differences between northern and southern rivers and different methods from trout fishing. The most effective method for the grayling of the north is nymph fishing with big and well weighted nymphs such as a Red Tag, a Sawyer Killer Bug or a Goddard Sedge Pupa in sizes 6–10 on a sinking line. The fly should be fished in Sawyer's induced-take style and then kept at the dangle. In these deep rivers this method is really killing, and the dry fly does not seem to be half as good.

'In the south dry fly is the basic method for grayling, but nymphing with weighted nymphs, imitating mainly sedge larvae and pupae, fished short on floating line, is as good as dry fly. Here nymphs and dry flies must be fished without any drag on an extra fine leader and striking must be fast. Grayling usually lie in such spots in a river that the downstream dry fly proves better for them. By contrast, nymphing, especially in "pocket water", is better done up and across. Then the floating line, kept completely loose on the water, drifts freely and acts as the float, indicating a take. Flies used for grayling are imitations of ephemerid nymphs, duns and spinners, midges, and sedge larvae, pupae and adults – no different from those for trout, except that it pays to use small short-shank hooks in sizes 14 to 20, except for dry sedges and weighted nymphs, which can be tied on size 12 and even up to size 8. Wet fly fished across and downstream is useless, which is the basic difference between trout and grayling fishing here. So when you want to fish selectively for trout on a warm summer evening or in the early morning, use a wet spinner imitation or a sedge pupa across and downstream, and you will catch trout lying among a shoal of grayling without any response from the latter. The same flies used as nymphs and fished upstream would catch grayling – perhaps only grayling. And, using any dry fly as a dropper to the streamer in spring, you will surely rise nearly every trout but not one grayling.

'Fly fishing can be practised all the year round in Poland. It starts with grayling, Danube salmon, rainbow trout and steelhead in September, turns into sea trout and brown trout in February, and from the end of May until September all game fish can be taken. The following is an account of our best rivers throughout the year.

'THE DUNAJEC is a rain-fed river, with its lowest flow of crystal-clear water in autumn and winter, and frequent spates of coloured water in spring and summer. While its biggest tributary, the Poprad, is of little use for fly fishing in summer due to coloured water, the Bialka, its most turbulent tributary, is rarely coloured, taking its waters from mountainous lakes and huge forests of the Tatra Mountains. Autumn is the best season for dry fly for grayling, and small flies imitating olives and midges are used. Nymph fishing for grayling means invariably fishing with weighted larvae of non-case-making species of *Hydropsyche* and *Rhyacophila* sedges, of dull green, olive and grey colour. Winter fishing until March is done almost exclusively with those nymphs in all the deeper parts of the river not covered by ice. In March trout fishing starts with dry blue duns and midges fished close to the banks or streamers fished in deeper currents. It is worth trying all the tributaries in spring – later on it would not be easy to catch a good trout there. Late May, June and July are the best months, despite changes in water level and clarity. All methods are used, dry, wet, nymph and streamers, imitating olives, various sedges and big stoneflies. August is not as good and only a black imitation of the nymph of *Oligoneuriella rhenana*, a strictly localized species of mayfly, and a big, grey, dry imitation of the dun in the evening are good. These duns fly late in the evening in dense swarms resembling a snowstorm, and are good especially for grayling. At the end of August it is worth trying salmon flies up to size 4/0 early in the morning, when it is possible to catch big browns migrating from reservoirs to the spawning grounds.

'The Dunajec and Poprad are the only Polish rivers in which Danube salmon live; they were artificially introduced there. These huchen are fish-eaters and hard to catch on fly. Occasionally those who use extra big nymphs in deep and strong currents hook them in summer or autumn. Still better to use spoons, or big wobblers.

'THE SAN is a river where fly fishing has only recently developed. Only after the construction of two dams and the creation of the Solina reservoir, twice as big as Kielder, did the water become cool enough to support salmonids downstream. Since 1975, artificially introduced grayling have created a dense and expanding population. The water level depends on the programme of a hydroelectric power station. Most of the year the water is clear, especially close to dams, because all silt settles in the reservoir.

'The San is a perfect dry-fly water throughout the year, with dense hatches of olives, mayfly, sedges and midges. Even in winter small midges ("black curse") assure good sport for grayling and, from February on, for trout. In its shallow clear water, and wide channel, regular hatches of duns and corresponding falls of spinners maintain good sport in spring and summer. Nymph fishing is not so easy as on other rivers because the water runs too slow. Only in stronger currents is it possible to use a *Hydropsyche* larva or a leech imitation as a weighted nymph fished short without drag. Usually fishermen use a freshwater shrimp or a small sedge pupa fished on a long floating line in a steady, controlled drift.

'The San is probably the only river in Poland where fly fishing with spinner imitations is also important. Early summer morning falls make it possible and profitable to fish with a wet Pheasant Tail at the dangle – and the biggest trout are caught this way. Evening falls are best covered by dry black spinner imitations for grayling.

'Living in Cracow, my visits to northern rivers are limited. Usually I am fishing in the Slupia and Wieprza in March and April for sea-trout kelts. This fishing is at its best when the water level just starts to drop off after the big spring spate caused by the melting of the snows. Then the mayfly hatch, usually in the middle of June, brings me to the Radunia, the Lupawa and the Gwda with its very good tributaries. The Gwda is famous for its big browns, which presumably grow in the series of reservoirs on it. It is a pity that the Gwda is coloured by algae all the summer, taking water from a shallow, eutrophic lake, and is fishable only in spring and autumn.

'Dry fly for trout on the northern rivers is good only during the mayfly hatch. During the rest of the year trout are caught on spoons or big streamers, and only occasionally on big nymphs intended for grayling. Late July and August are good for fresh-run sea trout on the Parseta, Slupia, Wieprza and Reda, but the usually low water conditions and the impossibility of night fishing reduce the chances of catching one. The

Gwda, Drawa and Wda are good grayling rivers in autumn, which with steelhead fishing on the Parseta, Wieprza, Slupia and Reda rounds off the season until the opening day for brown trout and sea trout.

'Except for a few private fisheries, there are no reservoir trout fisheries in Poland. Rainbows are not popular here after years of fruitless stocking of rivers with rainbow trout fingerlings. We are awaiting completion of highland reservoirs under construction, and we are preparing to stock them with trout.

'The visiting angler will require a licence, which covers all trout waters, available at 15 US dollars a week from any bureau de change of Orbis, the Polish travel office. The Polish Angling Association (Polski Zwiazek Wedkarski, ul. Krajowej Rady Narodowej 42, 00831 Warsaw) publishes a list of trout waters, which are divided into three categories according to the bait allowed: any bait; artificial bait only; and fly only. On fly-only waters you may fish two flies but the use of lead is prohibited. On waters where the use of lead is permitted, a single fly only is allowed. Fishing is from one hour before dawn to one hour after sunset and you may not approach to within 75 metres of another angler.

'Close seasons are from 1 September to 31 January for sea trout, brown trout and brook trout and from 1 March to 31 May for rainbows, grayling and huchen. No Atlantic salmon may be taken in fresh water at any time. Minimum takeable sizes are 50 centimetres for sea trout, 30 centimetres for browns, brook trout, rainbows and grayling, and 70 centimetres for huchen. A daily bag limit of two sea trout or five browns, rainbows and grayling applies, and only one huchen may be taken in a week. A combined total of six fish of all these species is the daily maximum.'

Jurek Kowalski, another Polish friend who has fished with me in England, likens the best Polish rivers to Hampshire chalk streams. He rates the Dunajec and the San as top quality fly-fishing rivers by any standard. This is his view of his favourite, the San:

'The best comment on the San was David Swatland's enthusiastic exclamation: "It's a giant chalk stream." The San has fast-flowing water, which is usually very clear. It doesn't freeze however low the temperature, and the weedbeds on its rocky bottom hold a great variety of fly life. Fly hatches last from April to November creating superb fly fishing conditions over some thirty miles of river. The San is quite shallow, mostly between two and four feet deep, but chest waders are desirable. In its deeper holes are the lies of the hucho, the big fish of the salmonid family which grow up to 70 pounds in the Danube, though the largest one caught in Poland is half that size. The San was stocked with hucho alevins about six years ago and at present they only run up to around 10 pounds. Because hucho feed on sizeable fish like barbel or nose-carp they are rarely caught on fly.

'There are large stocks of brown, rainbow, and brook trout with even more numerous and beautiful grayling. These fish are either completely wild or introduced as small fry up to 4 inches long. The largest brown recorded from the river weighed over 7 pounds and the largest grayling was almost 4 pounds. Like nearly all Polish waters the San is open to any angler with a general licence, and so it is overfished. However it is protected to a large degree by its size, the large stocks in the river, and by occasional high water flows as the dams are opened. The grayling grow fast and spread fast so they thrive better than the trout. That is one reason they are held in high esteem. They are also beautifully coloured and very selective in their feeding, sometimes even more so than the trout.

'The trout feed mainly on freshwater shrimp, sedges, olives, stoneflies, and mayflies. So I was not surprised to find my flies and technique worked as well on the Test and the Kennet. In the near future we will also have the first trout reservoir in Poland as we are stocking the tributaries of the lower reservoir on the San, the Myczkowce, with brown trout fry. We also intend to stock this water with rainbows of 10 to 12 inches to provide some easier fish to catch, and with shorter turnover time. In one or two years both the river and the reservoir will form high quality fishing for any visiting angler who enjoys fly fishing.'

Czechoslovakia

Czechoslovakian trout fishing is very similar to Poland's with the best of it in the high Tatra Mountains. Janicek Pavel was captain of his country's team, which came second in the World Flyfishing Championship on the first occasion that the country entered. This is his view of the limited opportunities for visitors:

'Travel is very difficult and it is not easy for a foreigner to get good fishing, unless there is someone like myself to arrange it. But the best of the fishing is *very* good, not only for brown and rainbow trout, but for grayling as well. The grayling run to over 50 centimetres. The outstanding river is the Vah in the Ruzomberok region in the high Tatras.

'There is a dam at the headwaters and for some distance below that there is fine fly fishing. Generally we use light-coloured flies with yellow or apple-green prominent. The methods are much the same as fishing in Poland (nymph fishing), which is why our anglers were so successful on their delightful San river.'

The organizing body for fishing is the Ceskoslovensky Rybarsky, Nove Mesto, Szaz Zitna 13, 110 00 PRAHA 1.

Romania

Iuliu Lungu, living in Tirgu-Mures, gives this account of fishing in Romania:

'Looking at the map you can see that a third of the country is high enough to be suitable for salmonids. The most common are browns and huchen as well as grayling, but in places you can catch brook trout, rainbows, various white fishes, and lake trout. Our fishing waters for trout include rivers and streams, reservoirs and alpine lakes. For river fishing there are about 66 good areas with 400 rivers, of which I mention only those that are a bit special. The first is the valley of the River Mures where game fishermen from my own town usually go. In an area of about 40 kilometres between Deda and Toplita, grayling fishing affords great satisfaction. In the tributaries from the Caliman Mountain side of the Mures, the Bistra, Rastolita and Ilva streams, you can fish for brown trout upstream and for grayling downstream. In the valley of the Gurghiului Mountains the Salard and Gurghiu streams offer the same abundance of fish.

'Another tributary of the Mures, the Riul Mare, is considered to be the most spectacular mountain-type river in Romania. It gathers its waters from the Retezat Mountains and has the greatest flow of all our mountain rivers. Upstream there are many brown trout but power plants make fishing more difficult in the grayling areas downstream. Another district ideal for trout fishing is the region of the Cris and Somes rivers in the Western Carpathians. The best fishing areas are in the valley of the Iad and Somesul Rece streams.

'On the Moldavian side of Romania there are some delightful valleys, especially those of the Putna and the Casin. Of late reservoir fishing has become very popular. Some fine lake trout (*Salmo trutta lacustris*) have been taken from lakes Tarnita (on the Somesul Rece river), Vidaru (on the Lotru river) and Stejaru (on the Bistrita). A lake trout of 34 pounds was taken from Tarnita in 1984.

'Alpine lakes of glacial origin represent a very special experience. Fishing in such places evokes at the same time two extraordinary feelings. First is the sensation of success in having climbed so high, usually above 6,000 feet, and gained such views of remarkable landscapes. Then there is the pleasure of fishing in such remote yet excellent fisheries. In Romania there are over a hundred such alpine lakes, about fifty of which hold salmonids, especially brown and lake trout. Brown trout may reach large size and weigh up to 8 pounds, as with some caught recently in Gilcescu Lake in the Paring Mountains.

'The greatest number of alpine lakes in Romania (and perhaps in Europe) are in the Retezat Mountains – a real pearl of the Alpo-Carpathian chain. Of almost ninety lakes a third have plentiful fish life, some of them from distant times, some stocked in the past thirty years. There are plenty of brown trout and some lake trout. The largest Retezat Lake is Bucura (8·9 hectares). Other large ones are Zanoaga Mare, Slaveiul, and Taul Negru – the most beautiful.

'Fishing methods in Romania are much the same as elsewhere. You cannot fish for salmonids with live bait, and in freshwater may only fish for them with fly fishing techniques. A maximum of two flies is permitted, usually one dry and one wet. Only in reservoirs and alpine lakes is spinning allowed, as is the use of a bubble float, with two flies.

'The rules on trout fishing are very simple. Fishing waters are under the management of the General Association of Anglers and Huntsmen (AGVPS) or the Ministry of Forestry. Any Romanian citizen may be a member of the AGVPS by paying an annual charge. He is then permitted to fish in any water belonging to the association. To fish waters belonging to the Ministry of Forestry you must pay another daily charge, which varies from place to place.

'For the protection of fish stocks in rivers with reduced flow you can only fish there two days a week. For those with a full flow four days a week is allowed. The trout season is from 1 May to 15 September, with the grayling season starting later on 1 June. Minimum keepable size for trout is 20 centimetres, for grayling 25 centimetres and for huchen (for which a special licence is also required) 65 centimetres.

'Precise information on fishing can be had from the Ministry of Forestry, Str. R. Calomfirescu 8, Bucharest, or its district inspectorates of forests; and from the AGVPS in Bucharest or its district branch offices.

'The total length of the mountain streams and rivers containing trout is 11,500 kilometres. In addition there are trout in some seventy-five Alpine lakes and reservoirs such as Retezat, Paring, and Fagaras. As well as *Salmo trutta* there are a number of other species. *Salmo trutta forma lacustris*, which feeds mainly on small fish, is present in numbers in dammed lakes such as Bicaz, Arges, Lotru, Somes and in a few natural lakes such as Lacul Rosu.

'*Salvelinus fontinalis mitsch* is beautifully coloured, with red and orange stars. In the opinion of many it is the loveliest trout in Romania. When it interbreeds with common trout it produces tiger trout which are studded with beautiful black and velvet stars. Such trout are present in a variety of Romanian waters.

'*Coregonus sp* has recently been introduced, especially to a number of reservoirs. The rainbow trout however is seldom found as it is rarely stocked and the natural conditions do not suit its breeding. *Hucho hucho* can be found in rivers such as the Bistrita, Viseu, Tisa, Moldovei, Somesul, Cald, Mures, Crisul, Repede, Riul Mare as well as in reservoirs like Bicaz, Arges, Lotru but you need a special permit to fish for them. The most prized game fish is the grayling which can be found in over sixty mountain streams covering an area of some 1000 kilometres.

'Foreign visitors wishing to fish our mountain rivers can obtain information from the Romanian National Tourism Office in Bucharest, or from its district branch offices. The visitor should however know in advance that you can only use orthodox fly-fishing methods with up to two flies, or in some cases fish with metallic baits such as blinker, popper, wobbler. Fishing is only permitted from sunrise to sunset. The official body is Associatia Generala a Vinatorilor si Pescarilor Sportivi din R.S.R.- Bucharest sector 11, str. Calea Mosilor nr 128.'

Other Eastern Bloc countries have good trout fishing, but the problems of organizing any expedition may take the edge off the enjoyment unless you have a contact there. The Bulgarian Vice-President of the CIPS (Confédération Internationale de la Pêche Sportive), General Rouskov, flew with a party of us on a visit to Spain. Sitting next to the trophy trout man of England, Alan Parson, he held his own in swapping trout stories and announced that he would have Alan's book, *Catching Big Trout*, translated for home consumption in Bulgaria. Fishermen are prone to exaggeration and the Bulgarian trout fishing may not be quite as good as the General indicated (even before he and Alan challenged each other to a drinking contest – which ended level, though happily not horizontal), but it could be worth exploring if you have contacts there.

Hungary is another country with trout fishing, a friendlier internal atmosphere, and a slightly more relaxed approach, though with no special attraction for the trout angler. The main Hungarian fishing organization is the Magyar Orszagos Horgasz Szovetseg 6 utca 20 Leveleim 1373 Budapest PF 611.

It is Russia where the considerable problems may outweigh the considerable opportunities. On its borders, where the rivers flow in from northern Finland and Poland, the trout fishing is especially good. This vast country with every natural resource has many areas where a cold-water species like trout can flourish, but it is the cold-fish approach of the authorities that make it a less than relaxing place for a trout angler. This great country may well become less secretive and hostile to foreigners, but at present it is hardly the most welcoming place for a visiting fly fisherman without connections.

8

Cleaner Waters, Brighter Streams

The American Dream

'Cleaner waters, brighter streams' is the catchphrase of the American Federation of Fly Fishers and nicely expresses the conservation concepts which dominate American angling. This aspect is echoed by other main bodies such as Trout Unlimited (aiming at unlimited stocks of trout in the waters rather than unlimited catches in a country where catch-and-release and catch limitation are widely practised). The Izaak Walton League is another organization dedicated to conservation; indeed, despite its name, it is more concerned with that aspect than with fishing.

This attitude has helped keep the country rich in fine trout waters which can delight the visitor. But, in so vast a country with such vast fishing resources, where to begin? Who better to advise than Dermot Wilson, that most respected of English chalkstream fishermen whose reputation in America matches his knowledge of that country?

'There is so much good trout fishing in America that it would take several lifetimes to fish it all and at least a further lifetime to describe it adequately. No brief account of it, such as this must inevitably be, can ever do it justice.

'It may help visitors, however, if I begin by making just one or two comments about American fly fishing in general and how to set about making the most of it if you're a stranger to the particular area you find yourself in. A few simple guidelines will put you on the right path.

'But what to say next? How does one cover the advantages and disadvantages of so many thousands of different watercourses and lakes? It simply can't be done. So I intend to choose a couple of very contrasting areas – the areas you're perhaps most likely to head for as a fisherman-cum-traveller – and dwell for a little time, really far too short a time, on each of them. They deserve a great deal more.

'The first of these areas can hardly help being Montana and Idaho. It will draw you like a magnet if you have the slightest opportunity to go there, since it's considered by nearly all Americans to offer the most productive and exciting trout fishing in the whole of the United States. Then the second area, I feel, simply must be that of the famous Catskills. It provides some first-class and indeed fabled trout fishing not far from New York itself, so that as well as being a blessing to New Yorkers it gives many newcomers to the USA their very first taste of American fly fishing.

'First of all, though, one or two overall remarks. You are sure to be glad to know, unless of course you know already, that most American fishing is entirely free, providing you purchase an inexpensive state licence. Legally speaking, all waters in America are free so long as there is access to them without trespass on private land. You must also be able to avoid trespass when you wade up them or float down them.

'Even when a mite of trespass is involved, some farmers and landowners may turn a blind eye to fishermen or may alternatively give you permission to cross their land provided you have the courtesy to ask for it. But they tend to be the exception rather than the rule, especially in the more popular areas. There are still a considerable number of "private" waters to which fishermen at large are denied access. They are usually excellent waters so that it's hard to blame the "owners", who may keep the fishing for themselves or rent it to a private club or perhaps charge greater or lesser fee for a day on it. In some areas these private waters are happily few and far between. Nevertheless, it is extremely unwise to assume that any water you see is yours to fish at will. Before you cast a fly on it make sure that you are entitled to do so. You only have to ask.

'Now for the bad news. At any rate on the more remote waters, a paid guide is a *sine qua non* for your first day or two. That is, unless you're fishing with a friend who knows the water well. The services of a guide do constitute a hefty additional expense, but you will be well advised to make the outlay if you can possibly afford it. It can make all the difference. This is because even on the best rivers there are many attractive-looking places which hold few trout or none at all. You can fish them fruitlessly for hours. All too often some 90 per cent of the trout are concentrated in about 10 per cent of the available water. A guide will be able to tell you where trout can be caught, as well as helping you with tactics, choice of fly and so on. Without a guide, on any water you are not familiar with, you can easily have a blank day. With a guide, on exactly the same water, you can have a triumphant one. But here's the rub. A good guide can cost you £100 per day – no small sum. He won't worry about union hours, however. His sole concern will be to see that you catch trout till it's too dark to do so. You're also likely to find him an exceptionally interesting and charming companion.

'Now let's suppose you find yourself in some part of the USA where you have never been before, but where you have heard there is good fishing to be had. You have no idea how to take advantage of it, however. You don't even know where it is. How do you start?

'First let's imagine that you are lucky. If you have a fishing friend in the place, or even a fishing contact, or even a new-found fishing acquaintance whom you've run into in the local bar, your problems are over. With the habitual generosity of the American nation, any of these will put himself out to make sure that you enjoy the best fishing that the district has to offer. If he possibly can, he will probably go fishing with you.

'But what if you're unlucky? You don't know a single soul within miles who fishes, nor do you meet one. What then? Cheer up – all is far from lost. Simply make for a good tackle shop. If you can obtain advice as to the best one around, take that advice.

'Most American tackle shops – often called "outfitters" or "sporting-goods stores" – provide a far wider range of services than their European counterparts do. They supply not only tackle, but plenty of well-informed advice. They supply guides. They supply transport. They supply accommodation if you need it. They are well accustomed, in fact, to supplying almost everything a fisherman could ask for, including the hire of tackle. So put yourself in the hands of one of them. You're most unlikely to be disappointed, especially if the shop has a good reputation, since it will go to great lengths to keep its reputation up. It may even hope for more clients from your country. You will naturally be charged, possibly quite a fair amount, but you will have value for money.

'If you can possibly let such a shop have warning of your arrival, as far in advance as you can manage, it will be able to do all the more for you. The problem, of course, is to know where to write. But this is not always insuperable. If you have any American friend who is a keen fisherman, he may well be able to find out for you the name and address of the best-reputed tackle shop in the place you will be visiting. (American fishermen, despite the size of their country, maintain an intelligence network that MI5 and MI6 must envy.)

'Any prior information you can find out about the fishing will probably save time when you arrive, so it may also be worth your while to write beforehand to the fish and game department of the state you are going to. Since they are busy people, a short letter is best. Tell them when and where you'll be arriving, ask for any printed literature they can send you, and ask finally for the names and addresses of local tackle shops entitled to issue licences. (This is the department's business and will furthermore provide you with a short list of good shops.) You may get a very useful and informative reply, but unfortunately you can't rely on one since departments vary a great deal as regards the details they are prepared or equipped to send and also as regards their willingness to reply at all. In any case, if you write try to do so as early as possible, since the reply will almost certainly come by surface mail and take several weeks to reach you.

'However, most people who visit any part of America to fish will doubtless plan to go, if they possibly can, with a friend who has been there before, in which case there will be no initial problems. You will go with the right tackle. With luck he will know the best places to fish and the best guides – and with even more luck he may be able to act as your unpaid guide himself. He is almost sure to have made friends in the place already, friends who will go out of their way to help you both. Your trip will not only be easier but less expensive as well. Besides, a friend as companion always adds to the fun.

'Again, there are some happy people who have good fishing friends in America itself (I count myself fortunate and extremely privileged to have several). With the outgoing open-handedness that makes most American fishermen so charming, they are very liable to issue an invitation to go over and stay with them to fish. If this happens to you, jump at it. You may well have the best fishing holiday of your life. Your host will know the local ropes backwards and you are almost sure to discover just how fabulous American hospitality can be. If you can reciprocate by offering him some good fishing near your own home, all the better.

'To fish in the USA is always an unforgettable experience. However and wherever you go there to cast a fly, I cannot see how you can fail to enjoy it and be fascinated by the people, the countryside – and of course the fishing itself.

'MONTANA (AND A LITTLE ABOUT IDAHO) When American fly fishermen dream of a fishing holiday, they usually dream of Montana. This beautiful state happens to have a quantity and quality and variety of trout fishing unrivalled in the USA. Other areas can certainly provide superb fishing too, perhaps equally good in certain spots and at certain times, but hardly the amount of it and by no means the incredible variety. Montana has yet another advantage in that it lies next door to Idaho. Idaho has less good fishing than Montana but does possess two of the most notable trout rivers in the West – Silver Creek (near Sun Valley) and the celebrated Henry's Fork of the Snake River. I have fished both and have seldom enjoyed myself more. Silver Creek supports a large and active head of wild rainbows, with a few brown trout and brook trout as well. Hatches of fly can be excellent and you may sometimes find yourself with a dozen rising trout within easy casting distance. You won't catch a dozen, however. These fish can be most intriguingly choosy. Few of the trout are in the trophy class, most of them running between one and two pounds but each can be a fascinating challenge to deceive. The stream itself is comparatively small, but all of it is splendid dry-fly water.

'I am ashamed to say, incidentally, that before I ever fished in America I was rather misled by the word "creek". I had always thought of a creek as a muddy, slow-flowing, mosquito-infested ditch, full of silt and alligators. But not so. In the West and often elsewhere, most medium-sized and small streams are called creeks – or "cricks" in the local patois. Many of them are spring-fed, clear as crystal and in some ways not unlike British chalk streams.

'The Henry's Fork, though a river rather than a creek, is also spring-fed. Its source is a sight well worth visiting, since it consists of the sixth largest spring in the USA. I myself have seen nothing like it. A fully-fledged river emerges direct from the ground, with good trout immediately visible. You are not allowed to catch them, however, since this particular stretch is protected. The mass of insect life in the Henry's Fork is an eye-opener, as it is in so many other Montana waters. There are plenty of ephemeropterans, not very different from common European upwinged flies. But in addition to these there are hosts of sedges – which are always called caddis in the USA. There are hosts of stoneflies too. Good imitations of both caddis flies and stoneflies are far more important in Idaho and Montana (also in the USA) than they usually are with us. A great many terrestrials also fall or are blown onto the water.

'The part of the Henry's Fork that I fished is perhaps the most popular, the stretch at the Railroad Ranch, just outside a village with the delightful name of Last Chance. Here the river is at its broadest, some 100 yards wide at least. Yet throughout most of the summer the entire width of it is nearly everywhere wadable in thigh waders. The custom is to fish a dry fly or nymph downstream on a loose line, to make quite sure that trout catch no glimpse of the leader. Other stretches of Henry's Fork, however, are narrower and very different in character. As with Silver Creek, the river is full of wild rainbows with a lesser number of brown and brook trout. Some of the rainbows grow very large indeed. The average weight of the trout, however, is probably a little less than it is on several other Montana rivers.

'The rules for fishing the Railroad Ranch water proved interesting. Barbless hooks only were allowed and the limit of trout permitted to be taken was four – one only of over 20 inches, and three of under 12 inches. This policy of removing very few large fish and no medium-sized fish does seem to have been most effective in maintaining a good balance among the trout population.

'I was lucky indeed in my companion and mentor on the Henry's Fork. He was Craig Mathews, one of the best fly fishermen and fly tyers in that part of the world. For some time Craig was Chief of Police in West Yellowstone, Montana. After a while, however, he came to the conclusion that on the whole he would far rather catch trout than criminals. So now, helped by his wife Jackie and others, he runs a splendid tackle shop in West Yellowstone, which is within easy reach of the Henry's Fork in

Idaho. West Yellowstone also happens to be within easy reach of many of the very best Montana waters. For this reason it has become by far the most renowned fly-fishing centre in the West. If you should chose to base yourself there, I can offer no better advice than to contact Craig Mathews in advance. Given due notice, he will take marvellous care of all your needs, including the provision of excellent guides. His address is c/o Blue Ribbon Flies, Box 1037, West Yellowstone, Montana 59758, USA.

'There are other good centres too, of course. One of them is Livingston, where you will find Dan Bailey's world-famous fly shop. And another is Dillon. If you go to Dillon you should try to contact a unique and noteworthy character called Al Troth. Among many other achievements, Al has the distinction of having developed the Elk Hair Caddis for America. It is arguably the most popular fly in the USA today. Al guides as well, however, and if you're very fortunate, since he is much in demand, he will take you on a memorable float trip down the Beaverhead river or the Big Hole river. Five-pounders are not uncommon on either and I honestly believe that Al knows the name and whereabouts of every trophy fish in those many miles of water. He can also tell you where they are most likely to take a dry fly, where they're most likely to take a nymph and where they're most likely to take a wet fly or streamer.

'On my first day with Al we decided that we would concentrate on the dry fly. During daylight hours, before the superb evening rise, we floated fourteen miles downstream and stopped at no more than eight places. These were the only places, Al said, where we would see fish feeding on the surface. And so it proved. At each spot we caught or lost trout. Without Al, however, I might never have spotted a rise all day. His address is: Al Troth, PO Box 1307, Dillon, Montana 59725, USA.

'Now for Montana's "spring creeks", or smaller spring-fed streams. These must without doubt rank among the best dry-fly waters in the world. They are naturally much sought after. A number of their characteristics are similar to those of British chalk streams. Their extremely alkaline water, for instance, encourages the plant growth which in turn harbours trout food, and their temperature and flow remain comparatively constant throughout the season. In fact they succeed in surpassing the chalk streams of Southern England in many ways. Their unbelievable clarity makes the phrase "gin-clear chalk streams" seem something of a misnomer. More important, however, the richness and variety of their insect life would give most Test and Itchen fishermen a severe and prolonged bout of jealousy.

'I have already tried to describe the multiple forms of insect life to be found on the Henry's Fork. The same comments apply to Montana's spring creeks, only sometimes even more so. Leaving aside the generous hatches of upwinged flies, caddis abound and are also a major part of the trout's diet. Stoneflies range from fairly small species to the gigantic salmon fly (*Pteronarcys californica*), usually no less than 40 mm in length. The trout may be feeding on any of these, which makes choice of fly difficult – especially since spring-creek trout are notoriously selective. Or again they may be feeding exclusively on terrestrials – beetles or ants or grasshoppers, according to the time of year.

'The first time I saw one of the larger Montana grasshoppers I could scarcely believe my eyes. I had innocently expected something no bigger than common British grasshoppers but there, on the bonnet of our car, sat some kind of prehistoric monster. It looked straight at me through the windscreen, obviously debating whether to have Wilson leg or Wilson breast for supper. Trout, I felt, must find it hard to open their mouths wide enough to engulf such a creature. But they do.

'Most of the spring creeks support enviably massive populations of wild trout, predominantly brown trout. With such a profusion of surface food they rise not only readily but also for long periods, sometimes almost all day. In some of the streams, though not all, they reach very impressive sizes too. Two years ago, on my own favourite creek, my host had a fourteen-pounder – using a small fly on a 6X leader. I myself saw at least one even more prodigious trout in the water – but failed to deceive it.

'One problem for the visitor is the difficulty of getting a day's fishing at short notice on the better-known and most productive spring creeks, such as Armstrong Creek or Nelson Creek. There is no public access to most of the best stretches and, although day tickets can sometimes be booked, they are naturally heavily subscribed for. Nevertheless, your tackle shop may be able to arrange a day or two for you and the longer the notice you can give the better the chances are. Even if you can't have a day on a famous spring creek, however, you will never find yourself short of good fishing in Montana. There is so much of it, so many tempting waters to choose between. Trout seem to be almost everywhere, often in unexpected places. Not far from the Madison river, for instance, there is an old gold-boom town with scores of abandoned pits or diggings nearby. All of these are now full of water, so that they look just like small, ugly and barren ponds. Most of them do indeed contain little enough life. But in just a few of them, a very few, are some extremely large and respectable trout. They are not for visitors, however. The exact location of the very few ponds is a matter of local knowledge only.

'The best time of the season in Montana is from June to October. Then you may very possibly discover, as I did, that in several ways the fishing excels anything you have ever known before. Yet another of Montana's advantages is that whatever sort of flyfishing you prefer, or whatever sort you are used to, you will be able to find it there. If you are a keen stillwater fisherman, for instance, Montana has an abundance of still waters waiting for you, some of them very good indeed. The majority of them have boats or tubes which fishermen can hire, and many of the trout are wild. There are also waters where nymphs or wet flies or streamers are the most effective means of catching trout, as well as waters which offer some of the cream of the world's dry-fly fishing.

'This variety extends to the species and size of the fish as well. In some streams, such as those in Yellowstone Park, you can catch small but exciting cut-throat trout (*Salmo clarki*). Other waters contain slightly larger brook trout (*Salvelinus fontinalis*). Then many of the rivers and spring creeks can give you either medium-sized or very large browns and rainbows. And, finally, there are certain Western reservoirs where a man called Del Canty, specializing in large brown trout, has caught more 25-pounders and 30-pounders than anyone else in the USA. Thirty-pound browns! But you have to be a Del Canty, or at least one of his fellow specialists, to stand much chance of catching one.

'Here are just a couple of little anecdotes which illustrate how two streams, almost next door to each other, can produce entirely different trout.

'The scene of the first was my favourite spring creek, mentioned earlier. One day, when I happened to be fishing fairly close to my host, he saw me catch a brown trout which seemed to take some time to bring in and release. "Was it a good one?" he called to me. And, so help me, I heard myself replying, "No, not really, only about four pounds." Only! I should have been ashamed of myself. I'm not usually blasé.

'The second story concerns a lesser creek only a mile or two away, running through the selfsame ranch. At one point the little stream flows into a swamp and there the beavers have made a series of small ponds, overgrown on all sides. Strangely enough, the swamp had been scarcely visited, and the ponds seldom if ever fished, for the past twenty years. It was almost virgin territory, an exciting prospect. So I asked my host if I could fish there. "Why not?" he said. "You might find one big old brown trout or something." But he made me take with me a dismounted cowboy (in fact one of the ranch managers, who became a great friend of mine) carrying a rifle to protect me from all the black bears reputed to live in the swamp. Black bears are a good deal less aggressive than grizzlies, except sometimes when they have cubs, but even so I was happy enough not to meet one.

'It wasn't very easy to find a place to cast from, but eventually we did. I happened to have a Goddard Caddis on my leader, so without much hope I threw it onto the surface of the beaver pond. The very moment it touched down there was a nice rise and I landed a 12-inch brook trout, probably just under a pound. "That's lucky," I thought as I released the fish, "catching maybe the only trout in the pond at the first cast." Still, I threw the fly out again. History repeated itself exactly. Again a 12-inch brook trout. Bet it won't happen a third time, I told myself, but it did – yet another 12-inch brook trout.

'I should have stopped then. It was too easy. But I did want to find out whether any of the trout grew a trifle larger. Apparently they didn't. After about three-quarters of an hour and thirty casts and twenty 12-inch brook trout – fish that wouldn't have been sneezed at back East – my gun-toting guardian said, "Ain't you a mite bored?" I was. We went back to his home for a barbecued steak – one more of Montana's many delights.

'Here my apologies are due. I only wish that there were more space to describe some of the pleasures of Montana apart from the fishing. The scenery, for instance, most of it mountainous, has a grandeur which makes it positively awe-inspiring. (They say that if you could flatten Montana it would cover the whole of the USA.) The climate in summer is usually marvellously warm. Occasionally the temperature climbs as high as 100°F but the land is so high up and the air so dry that you hardly ever feel uncomfortably hot.

'Then of course there's the wildlife. Montana has far more than its fair share of it. Go to any of the ranges and you are bound to find yourself humming "Where the deer and the antelope play". You will see many fascinating animals, many new and enchanting birds, often wonderfully colourful. And you may see just a few creatures which will add excitement to your trip, such as grizzlies, rattlesnakes and skunks – which have a squirt-range of no less than eleven feet! None of these will worry you, however, unless you treat them foolishly.

'Montana has only one disadvantage that I know of. Certain popular spots are very tourist-ridden at vacation time in summer, and the tourists are as unattractively noisy as they are everywhere, But they are never hard to escape, for Montana is huge. Americans have nicknamed it the "Big Sky" state and no wonder. It is very easy, especially if you are a fisherman, to find places where you feel entirely alone with the golden eagles and other wildlife – and as happy as you have ever felt.

'I suppose I have paid a fair number of fishing trips to various parts of the world, often only to come back thinking that I would probably have had more fun at home. Montana is the supreme exception. I would go there any time, at the drop of a hat.

'THE CATSKILLS   More people must travel to New York, bent either on business or pleasure, than to anywhere else in the United States. So it is well worth saying a little about the best known fishing of really high quality within easy reach of the Big Apple. This is in the delightful streams of the Catskills. Unlike the spring creeks of Montana, the Catskill streams are on the whole rain-fed rather than spring-fed. But since they are stony and gravelly, and run through stony country, it is very seldom that they are too coloured to fish. In times of drought, however, their flows can diminish considerably and their levels become very low. Again, however, this is not a common occurrence.

'Of all the many streams in America, these perhaps most deserve the adjective "classic". To a large extent they were made famous by the writings and experiences and discoveries of that great American fly fisherman Theodore Gordon, who frequently exchanged letters about them with both Halford and Skues. Since Gordon's day the streams have been fished, as have the Test and the Itchen, by countless celebrated fishermen and fishing writers. They are indeed a great and integral part of American fishing history. Their names are household words in every fisherman's home – the Beaverkill, the Willowemoc, the Esopus, the Neversink, the Delaware. Many of America's most famous fishing personalities – including the legendary Lee Wulff and his charming wife Joan – have chosen to set up residence on or near their banks. The Beaverkill and Willowemoc and Delaware, in particular, have prolific insect hatches which take place in regular sequence at the same time year after year. The annual mass hatch of Hendricksons on the Beaverkill, for instance, is world-famous. The Delaware has one further distinction, too, in that all its rainbow trout are wild.

'No streams, however, could provide a greater contrast to those of Montana. First, they are different in character, being "freestone" streams rather than spring-fed streams. And then, whereas Montana is almost all thinly populated space, you will find less space and more people in the Catskills. The fame and quality of the rivers, and also their proximity to New York, inevitably attract large numbers of fishermen, especially at weekends. Yet again, and as a result, while most Montana trout are wild, long stretches of nearly all Catskill streams are liberally stocked.

'There is no need, however, to let any of this discourage you from visiting the Catskills. You will have room enough to fish and there are indeed plenty of compensations. You are bound to like nearly all the fishermen you meet and it is almost a certainty that you will make several good friends among them. You will probably learn a bit from them too, perhaps particularly about fly patterns and fly tying, since the majority of Catskill fishermen are very knowledgeable and also highly interested in the effective representation of natural flies. This is a Catskill tradition, started by Theodore Gordon himself. Some of America's most renowned fly tyers – such as Harry and Elsie Darbee, and also Walt and Winnie Dette – have lived their lives in the Catskills. Sad to say, Harry and Elsie have now passed on. But Walt and Winnie, two of the kindest people ever, are still there. Best of all, however, you will find it far easier than in Montana to get friendly advice, good advice too, on where to fish and how to set about it.

For this reason there may be little need for me to say as much about the Catskills as about Montana.

'Most of the fishing on Catskill streams is dry-fly, but by no means all of it. Especially in the deeper pools, wet flies and heavy nymphs and even streamers are also used, often on a sink-tip line. And, incidentally, if you enjoy still waters, there are some truly excellent ones in the Catskills, though not unnaturally their fame has been somewhat eclipsed by the rivers.

'On most of the Catskills streams the season lasts from 1 April till 30 September, with the best period being from late April till mid-June. The trout are less large than they are in many Montana waters, mature fish normally running from three-quarters of a pound to perhaps two pounds, but they are certainly none the less fun for that. Nor are they at all easy. Just after a stocking, admittedly, a number of the least desirable fishermen may descend on the water in a horde and catch their limits. But very shortly afterwards, partly due to the widespread custom of releasing every trout caught, you are likely to find it hard to deceive many a rising fish. Again, this makes the fishing all the more intriguing.

'Imagine now that you have just arrived in New York, thoughtfully bringing with you an 8-foot or 8½-foot rod and a reel and line to match. What next? How do you put your rod and reel and line to good use in the Catskills? One good idea is to head for the little town of Roscoe, either by car or bus. Roscoe, on the banks of the Beaverkill and some three hours' drive from New York, is probably the most convenient and certainly the most used focal point for Catskill fishing. Unlike Montana yet again, the Catskill streams are close together and within easy reach of each other.

'Here in Roscoe you will find many of the most skilled Catskill fishermen and many of the best outfitters, as well as by far the best accommodation, such as the time-honoured Antrim Lodge. Here too is the comparatively new Catskill Flyfishing Centre, where you can get all the information and advice you will need. Anyone in Roscoe will be able to direct you to it.

'If you stay in New York for a few days before going to the Catskills, however, here is another idea – or perhaps I should call it a privilege. New York is the headquarters of a club called the Theodore Gordon Flyfishers. TGF, as it is usually dubbed, constitutes without doubt the largest and most influential group of fly fishermen and conservationists on the East Coast. They are dedicated to the improvement of fly-fishing waters and have achieved some remarkable successes. I admire them immensely and am lucky enough to be a member.

'The privilege I mentioned is this. The current President of TGF has assured me that any visiting fly fisherman who contacts the club will be made welcome and helped in every possible way. He has promised as well that his presidential successors will follow the same policy. Many TGF members know the Catskills like the backs cf their hands and will be glad not only to tell you about tackle and flies and so on, but also to set you on the right path generally. This is a most generous gesture on the part of some very well-known American fishermen. Obviously, if you take advantage of it, you will wish to do your level best to reciprocate in some way. Here is one thing to remember, however, if you do not yourself practise catch-and-release. Every TGF member does, so it will be far from tactful if you are ever tempted to boast of the number of trout you have killed.

'To contact TGF write to them in advance. The address is Theodore Gordon Flyfishers Inc., 24 East 39th Street, New York, NY 10016, USA. They would prefer a letter to a telephone call and you can rely on a very co-operative reply. The club meets every Tuesday at lunch time. If you are invited to one of these meetings and can attend, I can guarantee that you will be fascinated. Even if you are not around New York on a Tuesday, however, TGF may well be able to depute someone to meet you and give you all the assistance he possibly can.

'Now for one final idea. Lee and Joan Wulff (a spendid fisherwoman and a casting champion in her own right) now run an élite fly-fishing school on the Beaverkill, where they have some excellent private water. Unless you consider yourself as much of a past master as Lee is, and so long as you can afford it, why not book in for a two-day course there before going on to fish elsewhere? First, you will have the best possible introduction to American fly fishing. Second, you will be able to enjoy the company – and I can tell you that it is highly enjoyable – of America's most famous and respected fly-fishing couple. Third, and most important, you will find out exactly how to fish the Catskill streams.

'Lee has told me that you will be very welcome indeed, provided of course that he has room for you. So write well in advance for full details to Lee Wulff, Beaverkill Road, Lew Beach, NY 12753, USA. A two-day course costs about £220.

'I should not forget to mention, finally, that the Catskills themselves are both impressive and beautiful. In a few isolated spots, admittedly, some rather unbeautiful commercial exploitation has taken hold – but any such eyesores, thank goodness, are few and far between. The great thing is that here, within easy reach of New York, you can have access to some lovely countryside and some fascinating fishing.

'NOTE I have not recommended any particular fly patterns to use in either Montana or the Catskills. I must state my defence. First, it would have taken several pages to do so, bearing the many different rivers in mind and also different times of the season. Second, opinions do vary, Third, local advice is always the best.

'POSTSCRIPT ON CATCH-AND-RELEASE   American fishermen are usually regarded as the greatest proponents and supporters of catch-and-release. They are by no means alone, however. Catch-and-release has become popular in plenty of European countries as well – though less so in Britain than in many others. This is no place to discuss the pros and cons of catch-and-release. They have been argued over often enough. But it is certainly the right place to say a word or two about behaviour as regards catch-and-release when fishing in America as a visitor.

'Not all American fishermen have adopted catch-and-release, very far from it. This is why strict limits are always laid down as to how many fish of such-and-such a size may be taken from the water in a day. It is true to say, nevertheless, that the vast majority of experienced, skilled and highly regarded fishermen in the USA do practise catch-and-release. Sometimes this is for reasons of conservation. Sometimes it is simply because they prefer to see a good trout swim happily away than to hit it on the head.

'There is another factor, too. Many American rivers have stretches which have been designated "no-kill" stretches. On these it is actually illegal to kill a fish unless it is so badly hooked that it stands no chance whatsoever of survival. Some of the most famous no-kill stretches of all are in the Catskills, on the Beaverkill and Willowemoc rivers. These stretches, and it can hardly be a coincidence, provide by far the best fishing and are immensely popular. They regularly produce very large trout, many of them wild. Then there is the question of courtesy. On any first-class water you are almost bound to be fishing either with or close to catch-and-release devotees. A very good way of not endearing yourself to them is to kill fish in front of them or have them find out that you have taken trout.

'My wholehearted advice, therefore, is to release all the trout you catch – except perhaps in a few exceptional circumstances. If you are not used to returning large trout, I can assure you that it becomes entirely natural in a surprisingly short time – especially if others are doing so. You can be quite certain, then, that you will give no offence to the sportsmen of your host country. On the contrary, you will be accepted as a fellow spirit by all the best fly fishermen you meet.

9

The North American Experience

Tales from America, Canada and Alaska

The problem of choice in America is only partly eased by the very comprehensive guidebooks for every troutworthy area. They are so comprehensive that indecision may still remain. As example the *Montanan's Guide to East Montana Waters* covers an incredible range, as a few random extracts indicate:

'FISH LAKE   Go by horseback to the Cutaway Pass. Now strap on your climbers and make like a mountain goat up the little tributary over talus and slide rock to the lake, 8,490 feet above sea level. It is impossible to get a horse in here and is not recommended for any but the youthful rugged type. The last recorded visitor searched for this one for 4 years and finally made it on the fifth go-around. Once there the lake is about 18 acres, deep, in a barren ice-scoured cirque with a few trees and fair to good fishing for 10 to 12 inch rainbows. . . .

'HELLROARING CREEK   The Montana Waters here are in a timbered canyon, but the Creek flows south into it from a 4-mile stretch of open mountain meadows at 7,150 feet elevation. Good fishing for 10 to 12 inch cut-throat. . . .

'BIG HOLE RIVER   Big Hole country is a land of beauty, legends and wild trout. Arising in extreme south-western Montana, the Big Hole River flows for 113 miles before it is joined by the Beaverhead River to form Jefferson River near Twin Bridges. Throughout its length the river is undammed, a wild river in the truest sense and one of the most scenic in Montana. Below the valley of a thousand haystacks the fishery of the upper river is essentially comprised of brook trout, grayling, and mountain whitefish. There are scrappy brookies up to 15 inches here, as well as fair numbers of beautiful Arctic grayling. The river has changed a great deal since Lewis and Clark first explored it in 1805. Then the game fish in the river were cut-throat trout, Arctic grayling, and mountain whitefish. Cut-throat trout are nearly gone now, victims of competition from rainbow, brook, and brown trout introduced in the 1920s. Grayling remain in the upper river only, where they represent the last major stream-dwelling population in the United States south of Alaska.'

Wild river or stocked lake, pan-sized cut-throats or big browns – America has them all. So far as big browns go, here is one American's view of what constitutes them, where they are to be found, and how many get caught in the Idaho region:

'The Western spring creeks have a population of large brown trout defined as over 20 inches long. The following statistics give a realistic perspective to the difficulty of catching them. Henry's Fork Anglers of Last Chance, Idaho, has a reputation as one of the best guiding outfits in the north-west. It keeps six experienced guides busy from May through October fishing all the best waters of Idaho and Montana. In 1982 its clients caught 17 trout over 20 inches; in 1983 the total was 19. Whichever way you slice it, this amounts to a lot of well-guided fly fishermen catching very few big trout throughout the season in one of the best areas in America.'

Big trout take in a leisurely way and usually after careful inspection of their food. That makes them difficult to deceive, but also means the lies will be where they don't have to snatch at passing morsels. Instead of the fast streams they will be in the quiet tails of pools, or backwaters, alongside the main current, or in foam patches and other places which make it hard for the fly fisherman. So they are hard to catch, but all the more exciting for that. Americans accept that now, though when brown trout were originally imported they poured scorn on them because they were so much harder to catch than brook or cut-throat trout. Now many of them share the outlook of Bill Humphrey in his delightful book *My Moby Dick*, the tale of a season-long pursuit of one huge trout which is finally hooked and lost.

Even more dedicated to the pursuit of big trout was an English angler whom Hampshire river keeper Ron Wilton met while fishing in Yellowstone. His relentless pursuit of a wily and elusive eight-pound trout was so prolonged that he twice extended his holiday, giving phoney excuses to his boss. He had the trout at last – and the sack. Perhaps he felt it a price worth paying for such a fish – but what if he had lost it?

Dermot Wilson has singled out some of the best of American trout fishing, but there are great riches in many areas. Anywhere from the Mexican border, beyond which there is trout fishing in Mexico's northern mountains, to Alaska, where it is best of all, there is scenery and fishing of infinite variety. That is illustrated by the experience of four visitors to different areas. Ron Wilton himself had sampled that variety before reaching Yellowstone on a trip across the country with the American writer Darrel Martin.

'Darrel started me in a float-tube on a lake near Seattle. It was a pleasant way of fishing and easy for long casting. The snag was when a hooked trout ran towards you. It could tangle the line round your feet and there was no way you could reach down to free it. After I had caught several without any such mishap, the rising wind wafted me far out and paddling with my hands made no progress against the waves. So Darrel had to tow me back.

'When he told me we would be "rafting" down the Yakamar river I imagined a much more solid platform. The "raft", however, turned out to be a rubber dinghy, which often seemed in danger of being punctured by the spearlike branches of dead trees in the water's edge. On occasions, too, you would be drifting quietly down a smooth glide, then round a corner to find yourself in turbulent water frothing white between jagged rocks. That was quite an experience even without the many trout we caught. Our surroundings were often beautiful, sometimes awe-inspiring. One day on Spring Creek we fished in steamy heat with the sun reflecting off the bare rocks. Suddenly a bank of cloud rolled down the hill above like a descending avalanche. The temperature dropped some 20° in a matter of minutes, leaving us shivering instead of sweating.

'Nothing, however, rivalled Yellowstone. The quality and quantity of the fishing there was mind-blowing. You could stop anywhere and find marvellous trout fishing close at hand, and so much of it that there was little crowding. We stayed a dozen miles away at Aspen in a self-catering lodge as a comfortable base. The fishing was always fascinating, but for me there was one especially memorable hour. The trout often gorge themselves on huge stonefly nymphs over two inches long (*Pteromarcys californica*) or the proportionately large stone and sulphur flies. This they were doing in the broad sweep and rush of the Yellowstone River. As I watched I saw that a number of cut-throats were changing diet and coming into a quiet backwater to sip down the smallest flies. In the clear water it was possible to see it all so vividly. But the trout could see movement just as readily and though cut-throats often live up to the reputation of being easy to catch on occasion they can also be shy and choosy. So I waited until I saw a fish angled away from me, then flicked a size 22 Black Gnat in front of it. The trout took at once and there was a lively fight before I was able to admire the brilliant colouring and scarlet slash of a two-pound fish. Using the same tactics I had another seven in an hour.

'The main river was alive with trout and so were the quiet sidestreams.

Exploring up one of them I hooked a good fish, which ran out line. Following it, I suddenly found my feet boiling, the cast nearly melting, and the fish turning white as it had dashed into a hot spring area. Another time I spotted a fine three-pounder in one of the smallest sidestreams, but it darted away as soon as I raised the rod. Creeping back later I spooked it again with the slightest of movements. Next day I waded in some two hundred yards below the fish, taking almost twenty minutes to move up slowly enough to avoid sending small fish rushing ahead in fright. This time I was able to cover the trout from an angle he hadn't experienced before. There was the satisfaction of a confident rise, and a wild fight before I released this beautiful and much-prized trout.'

Peter Cockwill is a fishing companion of mine noted for his ability to catch big trout. Inevitably it was the steelheads which attracted him to the Columbia River and its tributaries:

'The Far West of North America is served by many famous river systems, of which the mighty Columbia River between Oregon and Washington is renowned for its big run of steelheads. To catch these on fly tackle is regarded by many as the ultimate game-angling achievement. The river and its tributaries also receive large runs of Pacific salmon throughout the year. Numerous state-run hatcheries ensure a steady spread of such runs and the licensing system is designed to enhance this. Sections of river are opened for specific periods only so as to allow sensible cropping of the fish. It is essential to check the regulations governing the various rivers, which are designed to provide maximum opportunity for sport subject to protecting the future stock.

'As an example, it is not legal to kill a steelhead with an adipose fin, as this will be a wild fish. All hatchery fish have their adipose fin clipped for identification. Apart from the state licence, it is also necessary to purchase a card on which must be entered the details of any migratory fish that is killed. Failure to have this punch card properly filled when in possession of a dead fish is a serious offence.

'Both states abound with rivers and creeks, mostly fed by snow melt from the mountains, and many of them hold excellent stocks of rainbows, brooks, and browns. Limestone rivers such as the Deschutes in central Oregon are noted for free-rising trout. Lakes and ponds with trout are everywhere, many in the spectacular high timber country. As with all the United States, the area is so vast that it is difficult to comprehend the choice available. Certainly it is essential to obtain local knowledge and we were fortunate to have a guide like Jim Teeny, but sports stores will pass on their extensive knowledge of local facilities. We found wheeled transport essential as the better fishing areas were a long drive away. The arterial roads are first-class, but it is very different off the beaten track in the forestry roads. You need to be alert as everyone seems to drive huge wheeled trucks without too much regard for the blanket 55 m.p.h. speed limit.

'You need to be fit to enjoy it to the full as often a considerable hike is involved, with stiff climbs down into rock-filled valleys. Summer temperatures hover around 100°F, but the waters are surprisingly cold. Lightweight chest waders with felt boots are very necessary. It is often necessary to scramble across rocks as a startled steelhead strips line from the reel at alarming speed. The American vogue is for light rods and no. 8-rated English trout rods proved adequate for us. Everywhere in these states there are rivers with fine trout fishing. Rainbows of four pounds are common, brook trout in lakes run to five pounds and the browns grow to great size. As a tempting example, one of 22 lb 6 oz was taken on fly from Oregon East Lake in 1982.

'My fishing trip with Gary Brooker was spent fishing a number of rivers, but the most memorable was the Wind, a tributary of the Columbia. We caught steelheads up to ten pounds and also chinook salmon up to thirty pounds. The successful fly patterns were Teeny Nymphs – not small ones as the name might suggest, but those specially tied by our mentor, Jim Teeny. They were of varied colours made up of dyed pheasant fibres tied on salmon hooks. The chinook loved them.

'In the upper reaches where we fished, the Wind is only some 15 yards wide and very clear. In the fast water the fights were spectacular on our light trout rods. The leaders, however, had to be powerful enough to cope with the surging strength of these fish, as did the reel. So we used 12-pound BS nylon and large-capacity reels with strong braking systems. Any ordinary reel would have had little chance of holding them. But with this equipment we were able to catch and release a large number in some of the most exciting fishing of my experience.

'There were many good tackle stores in the area where advice could be had for free. Naturally, the Teeny Nymph Co., Gresham, Portland, Oregon, appealed to us.'

Charles Jardine, noted fish painter and expert fly dresser and fishing instructor, found Colorado his dream experience:

'Tumbling from the time-ravaged glacial spine that divides America's West Coast from the eastern plains, the Rocky Mountain rivers possess qualities not to be found anywhere else in the world. They are the quintessence of a wild world which is a vanishing part of the globe. Man has, of course, left his mark but the peripatetic angler would be forgiven if he thought that every turn of the bend would yield a trout, so inviting are the Rocky Mountain streams. Sadly, this was not always the case, for due to heavy mineral excavation great tracts of water had lain devoid of life until, recently, the Colorado chapter of Trout Unlimited re-created an area that rivals that of the established Blue Ribbon waters of neighbouring Montana, Idaho and Wyoming. With a careful catch-and-release policy, they have created a fly-fishing Mecca.

'In an area so rich and diverse in fishable waters it is hard to know exactly where to wet a line. A fly fisherman has a choice of fishing the gin-clear mountain lakes with conventional stillwater tackle, long leaders, pupae, damsel and shrimp imitations, searching out the patrolling rainbows and cut-throats in the margins, or drifting, Colorado-style. This is not, as one would imagine, with a conventional boat, but using a float-tube or "belly boat" powered by the angler's flippered feet. It is a slightly unnerving feeling to see the comparative safety of the weeded shallows slip away from beneath one, giving way to pure indigo-green unfathomable depths with only a tractor's inner tube for support. Or perhaps it might be a day spent afloat the Colorado's cantankerous current, casting with both dry flies and huge black stonefly nymphs. Float tube fishing is one of the best ways to capture the grandeur of the Colorado River's magical scenery, meandering through canyons that have seldom echoed to human voices and where eagles, hawks, deer and the occasional bear will be far more likely companions.

'During a recent visit, I elected to concentrate on some of this state's "Gold Medal" water – by definition "rivers that enjoy the highest quality acquatic habitat for trout that exists in Colorado". There are nine such rivers in Colorado: the Arkansas, the Blue River, the Colorado, Gore Creek, Gunnison, Rio Grande, Roaring Fork, South Platts and the nationally famous Frying Pan. In such an enormous land area one's primary thought is one of distance, necessitating careful planning so that valuable fishing time is not wasted. With the delightful township of Vail as my base camp, two rivers offered possibilities – the Frying Pan and Gore Creek. Gore Creek meandered with an almost Welsh jauntiness some four hundred yards off my hotel, inviting the prospect of a leisurely breakfast followed by a stroll, rod in hand, to flick a fly amidst the boulder-strewn pools. Certainly not a proposition to be missed. So the first morning of my visit saw me chest-wadered, picking my way through the boughs of aspen and breathing the pine-scented thin mountain air before making my first tentative casts in Colorado.

'Local knowledge, as any travelling angler knows, is of the essence and my companion, Gary Bovis, was fortunately a seasoned Colorado fisherman, possessing infinite streamside knowhow. Together, we deduced that due to the lack of waterborne activity (save for the odd caddis) prospecting with a nymph might be a sound tactic. Here I was introduced to the deadly and tactile method known as "pocket" fishing. Gore Creek is a labyrinth of boulder-strewn current deviations, creating small pools and quiet spots which immediately swirl away or become frenzied. There is slack water behind the obstacles, necessitating careful wading. I positioned myself opposite a slack area created by the boulders and, after being advised that the local acquatic inhabitants were mostly caddis and stonefly nymphs, was given a Prince nymph heavily laden with lead. With more lead positioned some six inches from the fly on a twelve-foot leader, I was ready. It was not so much a cast as a decided flick that had my fly twisting and cavorting in the white water. Immediately taking up the slack the little nymph, I imagined, would swing into the quiet water where any self-respecting trout would sit in comparative comfort awaiting the arrival of his chosen fare. Six fruitless pitches were made, then on to another likely holding area, beneath a canopy of spruce once more to send the nymph dancing through currents. This time, however, things were different. There was a straight heaviness between rod and fly – I had missed my first Colorado brown. The rest of the morning was taken up with Gary's tuition and, finally, I felt the weight of my first fish, not big, about 14 inches, but a trout and to a new method.

'The afternoon was spent on a more familiar method – the dry fly – but again in a different guise. Although fished upstream, it was once more pitch and put in the pocket water and eddies. The drift time with both nymph and dry fly is lightning-short, with either drag or current racing it out of effective feeding areas, so accuracy is vital and with the dry fly buoyancy is important too. Deer-hair patterns such as Humpies, Goofer Bugs and Elk Hair Caddis all embody the essential floating qualities. The current's turbulence obviates any great need for exact imitation and the angler is looking to bring fish up rather than fishing to observed trout.

'Together, Gary and I picked our way, casting here and there, through the little river's gurgling narrows and pools, the scene enriched by a background ablaze with colour beneath an azure sky. The odd brown or cut-throat or rainbow splashed noisily at our bobbing flies with an alacrity and gusto that matched their size – very nearly perfection.

'. . . The Frying Pan's majestic, albeit short, length is matched by its surroundings of cathedral-spired towering sandstone valley walls, tar-tanned with spruce, aspen, birch and rowan; the river, an interplaying maze of boulder strewn frenzy that spills and fans out across mozaic-bottomed, sparkling "flats" and pools.

'Every angler searches for his fly-fishing Eldorado and, if he finds it, knows that thereafter anywhere else will be measured against it. The Frying Pan, which we fished the following day, was mine. I lost my fly-fishing heart to it. Not because of the insect multiplicity, nor the trout's eagerness to rise, nor indeed, the difficulty in their capture. These were just part of the sum total. It was simply the atmosphere – wild and unfettered. Many other anglers must think so too, as the river receives a fair amount of angling pressure. Strangely, this does not compromise the river's aura and in talking to fellow fly-fishers you feel they too have fallen under its spell.

'Our visit to this water started with the delights of Taylor Creek's angling shop – a mere weatherboarded shack in the township of Basalt, bulging with every conceivable requirement of the fly fisherman and, more importantly, the source of the local information. So, with our fly boxes rejuvenated, we left the village at the junction where the Frying Pan enters the Roaring Fork and begins its journey to the Mississippi, then ventured upstream to the head waters controlled by the Reudi Dam. Everywhere there were fish rising. It was midday, with temperatures soaring into the eighties, and still in the clear, brilliant mountain sunlight *Baetis* hatched in their thousands, the bankside air a blizzard of tiny ephemeropteran wings. It was obvious that light-line tactics were the order of the day. Fifteen-foot leader to 7X, a no. 4 line and a soft but fast-actioned 9-foot rod.

'Finding fish was not a problem; it was a case of which one to cast to. They were clearly visible, both rainbows and browns, casually lilting up and down in the slack water behind underwater rocks and other watery débris, sipping and webbing down the passing *Baetis bicandatis* with see-sawing regularity. Everywhere, it seemed, trout were enjoying an almost orgiastic feeding spree. I made cast after cast with no-hackles and paraduns of sizes 20 to 24 but got no reaction. Traditional chalkstream fare of Beacon Beige were rejected too. So finally I resorted to an old and trusted bankside friend – my fly-tying wallet. It is a form of river first-aid kit containing all the bare essentials. Having caught one of the naturals, I then made a passable facsimile in colour, size and wing (which I noted were substantially larger than those found on its English counterpart). Off went my artificial and as it gyrated in the twisting current a rainbow of about sixteen inches eased itself up on its fin, opened its mouth and blipped the surface film, and my little *Baetis* was no more. Instead a dour and sullen rainbow sought sanctuary amidst the riverbed. It proved to be a short-lived success as subsequent trout rejected my innovation and reassessment was necessary.

'As in most heavy hatches of fly, trout can become infatuated with one form or another. This can be the hatched fly, the emergent fly or even the nymph. On closer inspection, I felt a nymph might just tilt the balance so up went a diminutive, feather-fibred size 20 Olive Nymph. The upstream nymph worked and proved to be not only a method unknown in Colorado but one certainly relished by the trout. The remainder of the time was a happy mixture of fish caught, lessons learned and occasional frustration through my local fly-fishing ignorance. Throughout it all there were the hatches, droves of mayfly giving way to a multitude of caddis and stonefly then on to the returning spinner – a seemingly never-ending stream of insect activity. It was all so fascinating, but perhaps one area stood out above all others.

'Upstream from a bridge a large pool was formed by a torrent of white water. To its right ran a little stickle which produced an agitated lane of rippled water about twenty yards long. Throughout its length was a column of trout – easily fifteen fish, perhaps more. In their eagerness to rise, they rose over each other giving the impression of a coiling mass of feeding rainbows fused into one. For two hours I cast at those fish with not even the briefest of contacts. It seemed impossible, frustrating and a decided dent to my fly-fishing pride. But, try as I might, I could not get an offer. Sufficiently chastened, I sat to ponder this almost ludicrous situation. I looked and looked but saw nothing, no tell-tale wings, no sign of fly at all. However, at my feet lay some *Baetis* in a very bad state of disrepair, cripples really. Some had been unable to hatch and were caught between adulthood and nymph; others had a wing missing. Could it be that these trout were feeding so selectively that they were in fact only feeding on still-born and injured insects? Anything by this time was worth a try. So, tearing a wing off one of my painstakingly fashioned spinner patterns, I once more waded into position and off went the dishevelled pattern into the continuing rise forms. It vanished. The dismembered pattern had actually been sucked in and went on to deceive five more fish following that first hapless trout, leaving me to reassess many old values.

'My parting gift from the Frying Pan, however, was one I shall always remember. It in many ways epitomizes the character of the Rocky Mountains. Gary and I were just tackling down when I decided to spend a few quiet moments by the river, drinking in its unique atmosphere. From my position on a sandstone rock I could see the river sparkling, a silver thread through dark spruces. Suddenly, a red-tail hawk swung across the river not twenty yards from where I sat, seized a small bird and alighted on a gnarled spruce branch opposite. In some ways a cruel sight, but in another way breathtakingly beautiful – a scene of wild, untamed nature, which is how I shall always remember Colorado's rivers.'

You can always enjoy casual unplanned trout fishing in many areas of America so it is worth taking a rod on a random visit, as Francis Lodge, a former president of the Flyfishers' Club, discovered:

'A long-standing invitation to visit the United States was finally accepted by my wife and myself in September 1985, as guests of an old friend living in Berkeley, California.

'Prior to our departure, I wrote to a young nephew living in San

Francisco, asking him to obtain any information that he could about trout and steelhead fishing in California. Rather to my surprise, a large parcel arrived by air mail at a cost of some $25 containing a number of excellent monographs on the fishing in various areas. So I decided to take a minimum of equipment to cover any chance of fishing. The kit comprised one Shakespeare Sigma 8½-foot rod, a very ancient French 6½-foot split-cane spinning rod in two pieces, and a long handled Y folding net (Hardy, *circa* 1900). These were packed together in a five-foot length of rainwater pipe. In a canvas fishing bag I packed one Hardy Viscount reel with a no. 6 DT floating line, a Japanese spinning reel (never before used), and my fishing waistcoat containing a selection of flies, spoons, minnows and spools of monofilament in various weights.

'With a kind hostess prepared to drive us anywhere we wished, we were soon headed for a look at Yosemite National Park, with a view to going on to Lake Tahoe. Up to that point the weather had been glorious and we looked forward to seeing the mountain scenery. However, as we approached the Yosemite area the clouds descended and our first view of the valley was one of rain and thick mist.

'At our motel at El Portal we learned that the Tioga Pass to Tahoe was blocked by snow. The following morning we woke to a perfect early fall morning with clear skies, brilliant sun and the trees beginning to turn red and gold. We set off up the spectacular valley stopping from time to time to take photographs.

'We stopped almost at the foot of the famed El Capitan Rockface. The Merced River at this point runs through stands of timber and open tussocky meadows and has a good sandy gravel bottom. Fallen trees everywhere made fishing difficult, but the greatest problem was the lack of water for, alas, the river was shrunk to a series of still pools and very shallow runs. It was also a popular place for canoeists and other travellers in inflatable boats, who portaged from pool to pool.

'I was able to find one or two pools so totally unsuitable for canoeing that they were undisturbed, with small fish rising under the steep far bank, just reachable without waders. It was not easy to drift a fly over them as I was using, on local advice, a tip of one-pound breaking strain which, I find, curls up like a watch-spring on reaching the water. I was rewarded by two or three very small rainbows which were returned to grow to a more respectable size.

'One of the books that I had received describes the Merced as a fine trout river where good fish can be caught in the fast water and deep wading was advised to reach those fish which had not become wary of artificial flies. But for me, no waders, no fast water, no big fish.

'The next day we left El Portal for our journey back to Berkeley via route 49, as the passes to Tahoe were still blocked despite the warmth and sunshine of the valley. The road follows the river and some five or six miles downstream I saw a long pool below the road with some reasonable fast water at its head. Imagine my surprise when looking down from the road I saw several very large fish cross from the tail of the fast water and head upstream in the slack water below me. Too tempting! I got out my little spinning rod and tackled up – here were monsters for the catching. But in deference to my hostess I promised to limit my fishing to one hour. I clambered down to a smooth projecting rock and cast my small spoon across to the far bank. There was a whirr and a click from the Japanese reel and I found I had a bird's nest of some considerable size. Knowing that time was short, and unwilling to climb back to the car for my fly rod, I quickly took off the offending knitting-machine and substituted my fly reel with a leader and a large Woolly Worm fly. I had cast a fly with this rod before, in France in 1944, and, although the overhanging bank behind me was a mass of willow saplings and dead branches, I managed to get out a reasonable line. I was not, however, prepared for the lightning speed of a rainbow trout of about one pound that came up from nowhere to take my fly, and came unstuck at once. This should have set the adrenalin flowing to speed my reactions but, alas, this was not so, and rise after rise was missed. The short rod, wide rings and well greased line sent every cast landing in the water like a corrugated snake. With so much slack line between me and any fish a firm strike was impossible. One hour had been allotted and one hour can seem unbelievably short in such circumstances. I left the Merced River with a prayer that I might be spared to return again one day when the river should be in fine fettle and I would have the time and equipment to sort out those gleaming fish.'

For a fishing trip to Canada there is an equal embarrassment of choice. British Columbia, with Vancouver as starting-point, is perhaps the best. Close by is every type of game fishing that the heart can desire. Five species of pacific salmon shoal in the waters round Vancouver and Vancouver Island. Sockeye, chum, pink, coho and chinook are there for the taking, with most of the fishing in the sea or at river mouths, and with the largest chinook, the tyees, running to huge size. When I was last there the capture of a seventy-pound salmon, some six pounds above the UK record, was worth just a paragraph in the local paper. The world record rod-caught salmon of 92 pounds was taken in the Skeena river up the coast north of Vancouver.

From a tributary of that river, the Babine, came the record steelhead of 37 pounds, and there are prolific runs of this gamest of all trout. After his first experience of steelhead fishing in this area, the angling author John Goddard commented that he had caught every kind of fish from marlin to the superfast bonefish, from trout to salmon, but nothing, not even salmon, could compare with the fighting ability of a steelhead. Writing in *Country Life*, John recounted being flown out with three friends to a river in the north of the province, where they lived in a tented camp beside the stream made high and coloured by late August rain. This is his account of that initiation:

'I had never fished for steelhead before and decided to use a no. 8 slow-sink shooting head on a 9½ foot carbon rod. This was the ideal combination for the first few days, although later in the week, as the water fined down, a floating line could be used with flies fished just below or on the surface. This proved to be the most exciting way of taking these fish. Choice of fly did not appear to be critical, and during the trip we used only three or four different patterns.

'The river was very fast, cold and boulder-strewn, making wading difficult if not dangerous, and during the week we were all to receive at least one ducking. In the beginning a lot of flies were lost on the rocky bottom until the technique of avoiding too much slack line was mastered. My initiation came on the first morning with a magnificent fresh-run steelhead of a little over fourteen pounds. The sheer power of this fish was astonishing. Its first run took most of my backing, and after several magnificent jumps it was off again. Ten minutes later I succeeded in beaching it. As it lay at my feet, a shimmering bar of silver, I marvelled at the perfect streamlined shape and great broad tail.

'During six days' fishing the four of us hooked 139 steelhead, and all but one were released to fight another day. The unlucky one provided a magnificent meal on our last evening in camp. The average size of steelhead in most rivers is 7–10 pounds, but our average on this river was much higher; the smallest caught was over nine pounds and we had a lot of fish between sixteen and eighteen pounds. My largest weighed twenty pounds but another member of my group bettered this by two pounds on the last day.

'Fishing for steelhead is physically very demanding, and even the most experienced anglers, after several days' fishing, cannot avoid bruised and cut fingers from the line and handle of the fly reel, which revolves at an unbelievable speed on the fish's first savage run.'

The angling author and broadcaster Rafe Mair gave me this summary of the opportunities in British Columbia:

'British Columbia is 366,000 square miles and every area, from the populated to the sparse, has good fishing – not as good as we often would like, but pretty good nevertheless. There is good steelhead fishing accessible by road from Vancouver and plenty on Vancouver Island which can easily be reached by ferry and car from Vancouver. There is excellent steelheading, which is more remote in the sense that one must fly in and, unless one is familiar with local conditions, stay at a camp and be guided. In this regard I am thinking of places like the Dean, the Babine, the Stikine, the Kispiox and countless others.

'I happen to be that rare breed, a lake fisherman. There the possibilities range from lakes very accessible indeed – with large trout – to privately controlled waters. Some of the private waters are not all that remote – an expatriate Londoner, Peter McVeigh, runs a camp near Merritt (about 3 hours by car) which has access to lakes with very large trout indeed. I recently took a couple of seven-pounders from one of his lakes. Other high-quality lakes are more remote, fly-in situations.

'For steelhead – summer variety – I choose the Dean River, where there are two camps, Robbie Stewart's and Darrell Hodgson's. They are good friends and have this river sewn up. It is a fly-in situation for fly fishing only in spectacular scenery with unbelievable fishing.

'For winter steelhead I would suggest the Babine Lodge. However, there are plenty of alternatives. For a lake I would suggest either Peter McVeith, Corbett Lake, or my old friend Bob Hearn of Skitchine Resort – a fly-in, very private, high-quality. You can get addresses and information from the British Columbia Wildlife Federation or the Interior Fishing Camp Operators, or the traditional source of the Ministry of Tourism.'

The Fish and Wildlife branch of the Ministry of the Environment is based in Parliament Buildings, Victoria, British Columbia, and is a useful source of information along with tourist offices. The ministry is well aware of the special nature of steelheads and has taken special steps to preserve them. One cheap licence, costing only about £15, entitles you to fish anywhere in British Columbia's teeming waters, subject to the sport-fishing regulations for non-tidal waters (there is a similar fee and different rules for tidal waters). But for steelhead another licence is required, an annual retained catch of ten steelhead is the maximum permitted and the catch card has to be filled out each time one is kept.

The regulations are themselves a useful guide to fishing. The synopsis of them runs to over thirty pages and contains information and maps covering the fishing in the eight regions. They point also to some of the best fishing since the other special extra licences are required for waters providing exceptional angling, which have been designated as special lakes or special rivers. Much of the angling in British Columbia is indeed exceptional. The balance of trout and other species is well illustrated in the statistics compiled every ten years of estimated catch (not counting the much higher 'releases'). This was the 1980 record, and bear in mind that most salmon are caught at sea. The kokanee are the prolific landlocked salmon, second only to rainbow trout as a freshwater fishing resource in British Columbia.

9   Graham Swanson out early at Brumby's Creek, one of Tasmania's most popular and prolific waters.

10   The author fishes Little Plains river, a peat stream in Australia's Monaro area, watched by Australian expert John Sautelle Senior.

11   The Soča river in Yugoslavia which Taff Price describes as one of the most beautiful in the world and which holds the indigenous marbled trout (*Salmo marmoratus cuvier*).

12   The big browns cruise in a few inches of water in the shallow margins of Tasmania's London Lakes and John Sautelle Senior makes sure this four pounder doesn't run into the tangle of dead gum trees.

13 One of Poland's best rivers, the Dunajec, has the Tatra mountains as an inspiring background.

14   The Pütlach chalkstream meanders through a quiet valley in the Frankische Schweiz on its way to join the Wiesent, another famed trout river.

15   The author dry fly fishing on the Porma, one of the five Spanish trout rivers in the Leon region.

16   A different style of fishing hat for a Japanese fly fisherman on one of the fast, clear trout
streams which are becoming ever more popular in this land of twenty million anglers.

17   In New Zealand even the small streams can hold large trout and the crystal clear water and exotic background scenery enhances the pleasure of catching them.

18, 19   The delights of 'catch and release' in Colorado's beautiful rivers. An angler plays and exhibits a brown trout before returning it.

20   Jay Rowland with an eighteen pound steelhead from the British Columbian river graphically described by John Goddard.

21 Melting snow can rapidly alter fishing conditions on Kashmir's rivers but the majestic mountain scenery is an unchanging delight.

22 Graham Swanson, out early to fish on the Horton Plains in Sri Lanka, watched by the ever-present game guard.

1980 CATCH STATISTICS
FROM THE BC FRESHWATER ANGLING SURVEY
Estimated total number kept by species

Rainbow trout	4,292,000
Kokanee	1,320,000
Cut-throat trout	611,000
Brook trout	430,000
Dolly Varden	302,000
Whitefish	279,000
Lake trout	195,000
Salmon	187,000
Grayling	48,000
Bass	41,000
Burbot (ling)	25,000
Other gamefish	95,000
Coarse fish	161,000
Total	7,986,000

Estimated effort and catch by freshwater anglers in British Columbia

Licence Sales	1960	1970	1980
BC Residents	139,383	203,376	341,125
Other Canadians	8,862	22,662	56,527
Non-Canadians	26,958	69,098	52,673
Total	175,203	295,136	450,325
Average days fished per year			
BC Residents	13·5	15·0	17·4
Other Canadians	6·4	6·4	7·9
Non-Canadians	5·3	5·3	6·0
Total angler days (millions)	2·1	3·2	5·2
Average catch per angler day	3·8	2·7	1·5
Total fish catch (millions)	8·0	8·6	8·0

Catch-and-release is a splendid conservation tool, and is becoming more widely appreciated by fishermen. What is not so widely appreciated is the need to do it with care, otherwise you merely condemn the fish to a cruel death or return damaged fish which may well spread disease. British Columbia very sensibly sets out the rules you should follow, which ought to be universally trumpeted to catch-and-release enthusiasts.

RELEASING FISH

There is a growing trend among anglers to release, unharmed, a portion of their allowable catch. The Fish and Wildlife Branch heartily endorses this philosophy of voluntary 'catch and release'. The release of certain species is also mandatory in some waters where fish stocks are depleted. By following a few simple rules you can be certain that released fish will live to spawn and/or be caught again.

Remember that a fish that appears unharmed when released may not survive if not carefully handled:

1 **Time is of the essence.** Play and release fish as rapidly as possible. A fish played gently for too long may be too exhausted to recover.
2 **Keep the fish in the water** as much as possible. A fish out of water is suffocating and, in addition, is twice as heavy. He may pound himself fatally if allowed to flop on beach or rocks. Even a few inches of water under a threshing fish acts as a protective cushion.
3 **Gentleness in handling is essential.** Keep your fingers out of the gills. Do not squeeze small fish . . . they can be held easily by holding them by the lower lip. Nets may be helpful provided the mesh does not become entangled in the gills. Hooks and lines catching in nets may delay release, so keep the net in the water.
4 **Unhooking.** Remove the hook as rapidly as possible with long-nose pliers. IF THE FISH IS DEEPLY HOOKED, cut the leader and leave the hook in. Be quick but gentle – do not roughly tear out hooks. Small fish are particularly susceptible to the shock of a torn-out hook.
5 **Reviving.** Some fish, especially after a long struggle, may lose consciousness and float belly up. Always hold the fish in the water, heading upstream. Propel it back and forth, pumping water through its gills. When it revives, begins to struggle and can swim normally, let it go to survive and challenge another fisherman.

There are special regulations too about boat and raft fishing, which is banned in many areas.

Resident trout, char, grayling and whitefish in stream fisheries attract about a quarter of the angling in the province. There are some 300 such streams covering 20,000 km but accounting for only a fraction of the total freshwater resource.

My own first experience of trout fishing in the Vancouver area was in the Cheakamus River. The single-track railway running up from Vancouver past Howe Sound climbs into the mountains close to the Cheakamus as it froths and boils through canyons below. The river runs quieter in the upper reaches near Whistler. There is steelhead fishing in the lower parts but here, below the Daisy Lake dam, rainbows and Dolly Varden are the fish in great profusion. When the dam was closed down the river immediately below shrunk to the size of a Scottish burn with a blue glacial look to the water. It was then that traditional wet flies proved most successful for my son and myself. The rainbows were not large, but the intriguing aspect was that those spawning turned red in colour, looking like goldfish when you saw them swimming in the stream. Close by was a small stream called the River of Golden Dreams, which seemed to sum up the waters of British Columbia.

On the other side of the Rockies there are adventurous types of trout fishing on offer. The *Alberta Adventure Guide* lists a wide range of trail riding to fish, as well as fly-in and float-fishing trips. The surrounding scenery can be breathtaking as you view the bare majestic peaks of the Rockies, the forests, the lush meadows of the valleys, the sparkling glacial streams full of trout. Typical providers of the horse riding and trout fishing expeditions are Amethyst Lakes Pack Trips Ltd and the Jasper Wilderness and Tonquin Valley Pack Trips. At Amethyst, Wald and Lavene Olson invite their guests to mount up and ride to the colourful lake of that name, where double-figure rainbows can be caught. With expert trail guide supervision you can ride down the inspiring Tonquin Valley to Amethyst. If you go in from the Mount Edith Cavell route you can fish your way along the Astoria River enjoying also the alpine flowers and the clear mountain air. At the trail's end pleasant rustic cabins await you at the lakeside. You can book such adventure fishing trips through the Olsons, PO Box 508, Jasper, Alberta (winter address: General Delivery Brule, Alberta T0E 0C0).

Gord and Dorothy Dixon run the Jasper Wilderness trips, some of which also go through the Tonquin Valley to Amethyst. Additionally there are the seven-day trips along the boundaries of Jasper National Park. The northern trip embraces the easiest riding and most varied fishing, taking in the delightfully named Little Heaven, Topaz, and Caribou lakes along the Ancient Wall, and Twintree and Smoky lakes near Mount Robson, with the southern trip taking in Brazeau and South Esk lakes. On these wilderness trips brook trout up to double figures may be taken as well as many sizeable rainbows. For full information, the Dixons' mailing address is PO Box 550, Jasper, Alberta T0E 1E0. But get the *Alberta Adventure Guide* for the description and addresses of many others. This includes Panther Valley Pack Trips, who arrange remarkable rides to alpine lakes past canyons of tumbling waters, and sulphur springs.

Float-fishing trips include those to the Bow River, which provides some of the finest trout fishing in North America. The lower Bow River is reckoned to have 400 rainbows and 500 browns per kilometre of river with small dry flies very effective and trout over five pounds frequently taken on dry or wet flies in a river where nymphs and streamers will also catch well. A typical day involves 8 hours on the river with some 10 kilometres covered in a comfortable Lavro drift boat. Two companies organizing such trips are the Bow River Company, Box 15, Site 9, RRI, De Winton, Alberta T0L 0X0, and the Barry White Float Fishing Service 14515 – 61A Street, Edmonton, Alberta T5A 2A4 (June to September: PO Box 8451, Postal Station F, Calgary, Alberta). There are good air services to Calgary with some of the best Bow River fishing just below the town.

For fly-in fishing, what better than Andrew Lake Lodge 1084, Haythorne Road, Sherwood Park, Alberta T8A 3ZA? From Fort Chipewyan or Fort Smith guests are transferred to the lodge by chartered float plane or helicopter. The main lodge and the log cabins provide a comfortable base to fish a trophy lake. Of the hundreds of Alberta fishing lakes only some half-dozen are designated as trophy lakes by the government of Alberta. Lake Andrew easily qualifies because of the huge lake trout running up to thirty pounds, as well as its great northern pike. These are only a small sample of the adventure trips available, with more than forty listed in the guide, including the Rocky Mountain Cycle Tours for the fit fisherman uncluttered with the usual excess of tackle.

Canada's Saskatchewan province also provides a range of trout fishing from the wilderness waters of the north to the easily accessible streams and lakes of the south. Full information can be had from tourist offices, or direct from Saskatchewan Tourism and Renewable Resources, 3211 Albert Street, Regina, Saskatchewan (where the Lands and Surveys Branch will provide maps and air facilities maps for flying to remoter areas), or the Department of Northern Saskatchewan, La Ronge. A complete list of fishing camps, resorts and accommodation is available in the *Saskatchewan Travel Guide*. There is also the *Outfitters Guide*, listing the camps or services supplied by 'outfitters licenced by the provincial government to provide accommodation and/or rent equipment and guide services for fishing'.

As a sample, Choomo Lodge Ltd, Uranium City, Saskatchewan SOJ 2WO, is ten minutes' walk from Tswaler Lake, with only short portage to Thluicho Lake. Close by is Tarzin Lake with 300 square kilometres of water. Trophy lake trout are in all three lakes. Then there is Rainbow Lodge, PO Box 40, Meath Park, Saskatchewan SOJ 1TO, a resort located on the shores of a small rainbow trout lake with many big rainbows from ten to fifteen pounds. Or Little Bear Lake with 'varied bodies of water and six species of trout'. Or Jackson's Lodge, London, Ontario, boasting that it 'still yields the best lake trout fishing in North Saskatchewan. Portage lakes and stream fishing for grayling'. Or Johnson's resort, which features 'fishing derbys, fish frys, hay rides and honest fishing information' – that last is always worth having! Some of the best fishing is in four main areas. In the Hanson Lake Road–Hudson Bay area the lake road provides easy access to much good trout fishing with lake trout in Little Bear, rainbows in Piproll, Zeden and many small lakes, brook trout in many streams and in Dorothy and Nipawin lakes. Zeden also has kokanee salmon and Dorothy Lake brown trout, which are also present in numbers in Opal.

In the Meadow Lake–La Loche area the Meadow Lake Park is rated the largest and most beautiful in the province. Lake trout are in Gold Lake, rainbows and brooks in many others in or near the park. For lake trout try Lac La Plonge; for rainbows, lakes Vivian, Atchison, Shirley and Shamrock.

Prince Albert–the Far North is another good area for trout and grayling with lake trout in Lac La Ronge and the Albert National Park lakes of Kingsmere and Crean. For Arctic grayling the Cree and Fond du Lac rivers provide excellent fishing, as do Althouse, Lusier and West Naniskak lakes for brook trout, and East Naniskak and Mekewap for rainbows. In the southern areas of Saskatchewan there is a wealth of trout fishing, especially for rainbows in the Frenchman River, Battle Creek, and Loch Leven; for brook trout in Sucker, Boiler and Belanger Creeks; for browns also in Belanger and in Conglomerate and Bone.

For detailed information of the northern fishing you can contact Northern Saskatchewan Outfitters Association at PO Box 2016, Prince Albert, Saskatchewan S6V 6K1. They even have 'Fish Line' (1–306–763–5434) to deal with telephone queries. As two unusual aspects of fishing in Saskatchewan there are some waters designated as 'fish for fun' areas, where it is unwise to eat your catch because mercury has been discovered to be present in some fish. The Department of Health, 3475 Albert Street, Regina, can give up-to-date details of the few areas where this applies. And in the unlikely event that you want to fish with a bow and arrow you must get authorization from a conservation officer and have it entered on your licence.

Like America, Canada offers limitless trout-fishing opportunities and this sample can only point to some of the best and indicate the range. Other provinces also supply full information in their guides, notably Manitoba in its very detailed *Fishing Guide*, listing, star-rating and picturing more than a hundred fishing lodges and providing a map and chart of the best areas for particular types of fish. There are also details of the provinces' 'master angler awards' for catching large fish – 1.8 kilograms or over in the case of trout.

At the geographic centre of North America, Manitoba extends north to Hudson Bay and south to Minnesota. Three-fifths of its 647,500 square kilometres consists of verdant forest and crystal-clear waters. In many fishing areas you can combine the feel of the wilderness with the home comforts of luxury lodges. Everything is big about the fishing there. North America's indigenous species of trout, the lake trout, run to thirty pounds or more. There are sturgeon running to 200 pounds or so and, as in most areas of Canada, walleye, which run large and are rated the best eating of all. Many of those looking for their fishing heaven find it in God's Lake or God's River. The river is outstanding for brook-trout fishing, with brook trout up to ten pounds being taken from it. The vast lake, 65 miles long and 20 miles wide, is ringed with fishing lodges and holds huge lake trout as a favourite quarry for anglers. You can fly direct from Winnipeg to Elk Island Lodge on God's Lake, an ideal centre from which to fish the lake. The lodge's advice on method is to use Daredevils, KB or Red Eye spoons for lake trout, small Daredevils, Paul Bunyon '66' jigs, Mepps, flies, or streamers for brook trout.

With Ontario, first stocked in 1913, another trout fishing centre, the angling pressure in Canada is widely enough spread for the quality of fishing stocks to be maintained naturally, but in several provinces, especially Manitoba, anglers are urged to catch and release to maintain the stocks. The Maritime provinces as well as Newfoundland and Labrador are also well endowed with trout. In general, the quantity and quality of the trout fishing in Labrador and the island of Newfoundland is indicated by the bag limit of 24 per day, or the number of trout totalling ten pounds plus one trout. The trout season runs from 18 January to 15 September, but for rainbows only from 1 June. The *Outdoor Guide to Newfoundland and Labrador* gives full details of the fishing, with the salmon fishing more outstanding than the trout.

The Federation Department of Fisheries and Oceans, Information Bureaux, PO Box 5667, St John's, Newfoundland, can add more up-to-date and specific information. In Ontario the strong Izaak Walton Fly Fishermen's Club, centred on Toronto, is a helpful source of information.

If catching fish is your prime concern, if adventurous fishing in remote areas is a challenge you enjoy, then there is nothing to rival Alaska. The one that got away is of no consequence there as another will so quickly follow. Typical is the experience of Michael Green, whose business card describes him as Sportsman Extraordinaire and part-time optician. Another man with the proper priorities in life:

'Alaska is one of the most unexplored and underpopulated areas of the world – a place where it is quite possible to cast a fly where no one has ever previously fished. For the angler, the natural resources are seemingly limitless, and fish-farming and artifical stocking are unknown and unnecessary.

'Travelling to Alaska involves an eight-hour flight from London to Anchorage, usually followed by a further short charter flight to the lodge, camp or destination of your choice. Weekly fishing permits are readily available at a cost of approximately $15, and these entitle the holder to fish almost anywhere in the whole state. Because of the weather, the angling season extends from June until the end of September, and during this period, contrary to what you may expect, it is usually quite mild and pleasant. I have generally found a woollen shirt, sweater and (Bob Church) quilted waistcoat perfectly comfortable, with a waterproof coat always at hand. (From October to May much of the state is, of course, frozen up.)

'Away from the populated areas, roads are practically non-existent, and the universal mode of transport is light aircraft, usually a Cessna, sporting either wheels, or, more commonly, floats, which enable them to land almost anywhere on the rivers and lakes which abound. (Incidentally, I hold the dubious distinction of being the only Rainbow King Lodge guest to have initiated two unscheduled landings to spend a rather large penny.)

'A fishing trip to these parts can take many different forms, depending on taste and size of wallet. At one end of the scale, you can arrange to be dropped (not literally) by float plane on a remote lake, complete with guide, camping equipment, etc., then float down one of the many river systems, fishing as you go. After a predetermined period, you are then picked up by plane, again from an agreed location. This type of holiday will suit the more adventurous angler, who will appreciate the isolation, proximity to nature, and, incidentally, *considerably* lower cost.

'For those who prefer the hot shower, gin and tonic and four-course meal, followed by a post-mortem of the day's events, and a good sleep in a warm and comfortable bed, there are numerous comprehensively equipped lodges, providing five-star food and accommodation, and running up to a dozen aircraft for ferrying guests to rivers and fishing of their choice.

'As to the fish themselves, the native trout is the wild rainbow – basically the same as our own "tame" ones, but more streamlined and brightly coloured with a pronounced red strip. (I have also caught wild rainbows of a similar shape and colour on the Derbyshire Wye.) They are very hard fighting, and can run large, especially in the latter part of the season, when 12–15 pound fish are numerous, and 18–20 pounders are not unknown. In rivers like the Copper, Newhalen and Dream Creek, and, in fact, most of the streams which run into Lake Iliamna in central Alaska, there is an invasion of sockeye or red salmon; starting during the first week of July, 13 million were recorded running the Kwichak River in 1984. These wonderful sporting fish swarm up the stream until they reach the headwaters, which turn bright red when viewed from the air – a breathtaking sight!

'Needless to say, the rainbow fishing is temporarily ruined by the salmon run, but the bonus is that the sockeye are usually followed by shoals of large rainbow feeding avidly on the carpet of roe. Although I have not personally experienced angling during this phase, I am assured that it is pretty incredible, and, naturally, the only fly worth using is one which imitates the salmon egg. These are always readily available from the Lodge or guide.

'Prior to the appearance of the red salmon (which, incidentally, all die within four weeks of entering the fresh water), the rainbows respond to both wet and dry-fly techniques, and daily catches of up to twenty fish in the 2–7 pound bracket can be expected for a competent fly fisherman. Though local patterns like Bitch-Creek Bugs, Woolly Worms and Skyomish Sunrise are recommended, I scored very heavily with Black Marabou lures and even better with a size 10 wet Wickham (especially during sedge rises). The water in these beautiful streams is invariably fast-running and gin-clear, so presentation and concealment are, as ever, of great importance.

'Other species of interest are Arctic grayling, which are huge compared with our own, between 1½ and 4½ pounds. Dolly Varden, beautiful silver-grey fish with pale pink spots, and very similar in appearance to the closely-related Arctic char, which also abound in some of the rivers, particularly in the Ugashik area. The latter species run to 14 pounds, with an average of between 2 and 4½ pounds, and fight like sea trout. If they have a drawback, it is that they are so easy to catch, suicidal at times, taking wet or dry flies and lures. I well remember one occasion when I wandered half a mile or so upstream, finding shoals of between 50 and 150 char in every gin-clear pool. As an experiment in one pool, I kept changing flies and caught about a dozen fish on everything from a size 6 Black Lure to a size 18 dry Grey Duster. I then waded through the shoal with chest waders on, straight up the middle of the pool, and having reached the head, tied on a 4-inch rubber eel and caught a char first cast out of the same shoal.

'On another occasion, fishing with Roy Thomas, I stripped all the dressing off a size 12 Greenwell, and cast down and across with a bare hook. On my second cast a three-pound Arctic char was firmly hooked, and landed for the cine camera. We had about three hundred fish between four of us that day (though I must say that another party from our Lodge visited the same stream the following day and only had seventeen – what sort of anglers they were I dread to think).

'In short, the fishing in Alaska is simply superb, and well worth the journey and expense (I once caught 100 red salmon to my own single-handed rod in one day, all between six and ten pounds, and never cast further than eight yards to do it). There are three other species of salmon, including the chinook, or giant king salmon, running to over sixty pounds, and large numbers of pike and lake trout, which no one ever seems to bother with.

'Incidentally, brown bears, moose and caribou are present in some areas, but despite their considerable size the danger aspect should not be exaggerated. The rule is, if a bear decides to share your pool, leave him to it – there are *very few* incidents of bear attacks during any year.

'Please give it a try – you will not be disappointed.'

Rainbow King Lodge is outstanding in the fishing it provides and in its facilities for the 36 guests, matched 1 to 1 by a crew of 36 to ensure that they get the best of the fishing in remote areas. As the owner, Ray Loesche, puts it: 'We don't like to take our guests where there are other people as it detracts so from the quality of the experience.' While there is a shortage of intrusive humans there is no shortage of fish – too many almost to make the fishing really enjoyable. In his report on the 1985 fishing out of the lodge, Loesche commented regretfully that many caught so many silver salmon on their first day they didn't want to go back for another day of fishing for silvers: 'On days when a person has to work hard to catch ten silvers it is much better for us as they will want to return for that species. Days of 200 or 300 silver salmon were not uncommon, as were days of 150 to 200 char. Earlier in the season we had days when we would take 300 or more sockeye. We also had days when we would take well over 200 rainbow, but I won't say that is common, as they are always a bit smarter than the other species.'

That season there were two special additions to the lodge's fishing schedule. Close by was the previously ignored Willow Creek, which was fished when an aircraft was diverted by bad weather. 'We found it a really beautiful stream, with lots of nice gravel bars to fish from and really loaded with grayling. Everyone thinks grayling are so plentiful in Alaska, but that is not necessarily true. At times we have more trouble finding grayling than most other species.' The main addition of the year, however, was the Iliamna River. 'All the land in that area is owned by natives of Pedro Bay. Some years ago they asked us to keep off their lands and not fish that stream. We honoured that request and now they have granted permission to us and one other lodge. We have two jet boats on this lovely stream and we took a lot of char up to fifteen pounds. There were also a lot of rainbow, but no big ones, nothing much over ten pounds anyway.'

The Alaska Peninsular Corporation and Rainbow King Lodge have an agreement which gives the lodge special rights to some of the best waters in the Kokhanok area. The Copper River, Dream Creek and Gibraltar River are three of the best rainbow streams anywhere in the world. They have fishing too on the Talarik and Newhalen rivers to complete the access to a range of remarkable trout rivers where rainbow proliferate. For detailed information, the summer address of the lodge is PO Box 106, Iliamna, AK 99606; in winter, PO Box 3446, Spokane, WA 99220. They can provide, at a price, some of the cream of Alaskan fishing in which the only worry is whether a surfeit of fish may stale the appetite.

10

Trophy Trout

South America

Argentina

Trout were never indigenous in the southern hemisphere, but once transported to and established in some regions of the far south they have multiplied and grown to an extent that few places in their original habitats can match. The fabulous trout fishing to be found in New Zealand and Tasmania is equalled in many respects by what Argentina, Chile and, indeed, the Falkland Islands have to offer. Wild rainbows and brown trout grow to prodigious sizes, but some of the finest fishing in these areas is for sea-run brown trout or, as some would say, for sea trout. Brown trout and sea trout are in fact the same species, and there is no anatomical or taxonomic distinction between the two. They can interbreed with fertile offspring, a sea trout confined to fresh water reverts to being a brown trout, and browns which by some quirk of nature or local conditions have, or acquire, a more strongly developed migratory urge go to sea and become sea trout. As in South America, brown trout introduced to some parts of New Zealand have gone to sea and become anadromous, as also did brown trout brought from Loch Leven to Newfoundland in 1884, to the Maritime provinces of Canada in 1921, and to Vancouver Island. Rainbows can also thrive in salt or brackish water, and the rainbows indigenous to the West Coast of North America have produced the magnificent and much-prized anadromous steelheads, although this transition does not seem to have been repeated in other parts of the world. Strangely, perhaps, attempts to acclimatize Atlantic salmon in southern seas around Tasmania, New Zealand, South Africa and South America have met with little success, but landlocked salmon introduced from the USA to Argentina and New Zealand have thrived and there are some runs of Pacific Quinnot salmon in New Zealand's South Island.

The magnificent trout fishing available in parts of South America is not widely publicized. The *South American Handbook*, for example, makes only a brief passing reference to trout fishing in Argentina: 'The trout and salmon have been introduced from abroad. The Limay has good trout fishing and other rivers – such as the Malleu, Chimehuin, Collon Cura, Hermose, Melequina, Calenfu – are less good. The season is early November to end of March. The lakes are full of fish in November and December.' Lakes such as Traful, Futulaufquen, Huechulaufquen and various others from Quillen in the north to Argentino in the south are then listed. The handbook makes no mention at all of trout fishing in Chile, or the other Andean states such as Bolivia, Peru, Ecuador, Colombia and Venezuela, in all of which trout have been stocked, although it professes to cover every aspect of life and tourism in these places.

Brown trout from England were first introduced to Argentina on various occasions between 1904 and 1910. They have done best in the more southerly waters, including streams in Tierra del Fuego, where a strain of sea-run browns developed that grew to enormous size. Further north the rainbows which were introduced later have proved generally more successful. Also in competition are the landlocked salmon, *Salmo salar sebago*, which are of the same species as Atlantic salmon. These fish live in freshwater lakes and do not migrate to sea, but run up the rivers to spawn. Introduced early this century from their original habitat in the Rangeley Lakes section of Maine, USA, to Lake Traful, they are now to be found in other lakes and rivers of Argentina, for instance in the Nahuel Huapi, Lanin and Futulaufquen national parks.

The American angler and author, Joe Brooks, caught many great brown trout, rainbows and 'sea-run browns' in the rivers of Argentina, as well as landlocked salmon, and in his book *Fly Fishing* he tells us how he did it. Fishing the Chimehuin river, below where it flows out of Lake Huachulaufquen, with two Argentinian friends, he suggested trying a big multi-winged streamer tied to a 1/0 hook, a fly he had sometimes found successful elsewhere for big fish in both fresh and salt water. His friends, fishing small traditional flies, scoffed at the idea. Using a 9-foot rod with a WF–8–F line, he cast a 1/0 'Platinum Blonde', a white bucktail with 3½-inch wings, across the current and almost immediately hooked and caught a ten-pound brown trout. Thereafter he took many double-figure browns up to eighteen pounds from the Chimehuin on a Platinum Blonde, and one of his friends – soon converted – using a 'Honey Blonde', landed a 24-pound brown. The streamers also proved effective for big rainbows, landlocked salmon and sea-run browns. Another fly that did well in Argentina was a Marabou Muddler tied on hook sizes 4, 2 and 1/0 in various colours – black proved best for browns and rainbows in the Chimehuin, grey for sea-run browns in Tierra del Fuego. In a subsequent year, having caught several trout of 'only' 6–10 pounds in the Chimehuin, and having been told by one of his Argentine friends of a 26-pound brown caught earlier on a spoon, he decided to try a large Popper Bug. On that he took a brown of 18½ pounds and, a day or two later, one of fifteen pounds.

Another angling writer experienced great difficulty in landing large fish from the Chimehuin, Limay, and other big Andean rivers, rocky and fast-flowing, with a 9-foot rod and trout reel, mainly because his line got snagged and frayed round rocks, or he was unable to keep close enough to his fish as it set off downstream. His solution was to develop a shooting head consisting of some 8 yards of floating line spliced to 150 yards of nylon backing greased to float. This did not fray so easily, the reel held a much greater length of backing than was otherwise possible, and a long cast could be made from a very short back cast to avoid the bushes lining the banks. These thorny bushes also snagged a net or gaff, so he dispensed with these accessories and had no difficulty in finding places to beach his fish. But he always carried a good strong wading-stick with a heavy iron point to carry it quickly down to the bottom in the fast-flowing current, enabling him to follow his fish down more easily.

Some of the rivers of Argentina hold not only big rainbows and browns, but also landlocked salmon, which can be fished in the same manner as the trout. Although of the same species as sea-going Atlantic salmon, they do not in general grow as large, 3 to 12 pounds being their normal size range. The Traful river is perhaps the best landlocked salmon river in the world and has also produced the largest, a few fish of over 24 pounds having been recorded. They can be fished for with ordinary salmon flies, or with large nymphs, or dry flies. Fishing the Traful river, Joe Brooks and his friends caught many 'landlockeds' averaging around 7½ pounds with a best fish of 12½, caught on a 1/0 platinum blonde streamer.

In a 1986 issue of *The Field* Bozo Ivanovic described a fishing trip with a friend to the southernmost tip of South America to fish the Rio Grande for its legendary 'sea trout'. In six days each had four averaging 10½ pounds and some forty resident browns or rainbows averaging 1½ pounds. His largest sea trout of 15½ pounds took a size 8 Mrs Simpson, but he watched a local catch one of 19 pounds on a fuzzy Woolly Worm. Ivanovic advised flying to Buenos Aires and then to the Rio Grande by Airolineas Argentinas and booking accommodation through Mrs Carreras, Estambo 1650, Buenos Aires 1430, in the Kau-tapen lodge in Rio Grande. An even more recent visitor was my fishing friend from Spain, Rafael de Madariaga Giraldo, who gives the following description:

'After a long trip from Madrid to Buenos Aires, three further hours of flight landed us at 2.00 a.m. in Rio Grande, the capital of the Argentinian part of the big island of Tierra del Fuego, located between the Strait of Magellan and the Beagle Channel, and divided from north to south between Chile and Argentina. Rain, wind and cold were waiting for us, as well as a guide who had come from Buenos Aires and who fishes every year at that southern edge of Argentina. A few sleeping hours at a nice hotel and then our group of seven people started to prepare all the necessary tackle for the fishing. Another local guide joined us, and both were of the opinion that almost all the equipment we were carrying was inadequate for fishing on the Rio Grande for its enormous sea trout.

'The only item which aroused admiration was our braided copper-nylon sinking leaders, which later on proved to be very efficient, to the point that by the third day every local fisherman asked us for some, and we had to promise to send a big quantity for the next season.

'The sky was overcast and the wind was horrendous, though we were told it was only average wind. The day before there had been a big storm in the mountains of the Chilean part of the river, which besides raising the level had melted the snow. So the water was brown in colour and very cold. Anyhow, we decided to go to the river and try.

'The Rio Grande is very big, a slow-flowing river surrounded by a bare landscape with some tufa herbs to feed the sheep, but very few trees, since most of them were cut by the beavers decades ago. The river meanders lazily through the plain. Its bed is gravel, very comfortable to wade. There is a succession of pools, not very deep, long flats and few streams. It is hard to read the river and without the aid of an experienced guide you can lose many days fishing the water without any possibility of finding big fish. The huge sea trout come into the river between November and March, and slowly ascend to the spawning areas, either on the main river, 80 kilometres away from the sea on the Chilean side, or up any tributary with enough water. The weight of these trout is considered as acceptable from seven pounds to thirty-three, which is the record of the river. The average is between ten and seventeen pounds.

'Straight from the sea they are wonderfully silver, but since they travel very slowly, at twenty miles away from the sea they have already lost their brightness, and revert to brown-trout colouring. The river also holds non-migratory brown and rainbow trout up to eight pounds, but these are scorned by the locals.

'We went to the river in two cars, with the two guides. In fact, the water was one metre above its normal level, with a chocolate colour, and we looked for a part where the river divided in various arms to find less water. The fishing technique consisted in looking for a pool then casting a streamer from the shallow water bank to land six inches from the opposite side at right angles to the river. It was assumed that the sea trout hover near the opposite bank (no matter where the fisherman is) and take the lure when it turns into the stream. The best places are the heads and tails of the pools, but the flies are often seized in the current or close to the fisherman's bank.

'That afternoon, the wind, like the water, ran from right to left, moderate according to the guides (that is some 40 m.p.h.) and it was raining slightly. We, usually dry fly fishermen, realized that with such a wind we were not capable of casting our streamers the necessary 25 yards without hooking ourselves or our clothing. As I was the only left-handed angler in the group, and fishing with a favourable wind, I got many offers to buy my left arm.

'We did not catch anything that afternoon, but we did realize that the majority of our fishing rods were too soft for such hard conditions. We were also all using hollow braided nylon backing, which tangled frequently in the wind. At the end of this delightful afternoon it rained hard – moderately, according to the locals – and we were horrified at the thought of fishing in a 60 m.p.h. wind, driving rain and freezing cold.

'The waters in Argentina are all free, though access is not. In some places there are estates from 25,000 to 150,000 acres in extent surrounding the streams up to forty miles. All the land is divided into fenced plots, and if you do not know the owners it is practically impossible to reach the Rio Grande. Fortunately, our native guide knew all the owners.

'On the following day it continued impossible to fish the big water, and we decided to make a trip to a small river called Fuego, some thirty miles away from the city of Rio Grande and famous for the quantity of fish, though without sea trout. By unmetalled roads and tracks, we eventually reached the Fuego river. It was small in size and flowed through such a level plain that the river was a continuous succession of meanders.

'We fished the upper section in the morning. The brown and rainbow trout took quite well at the heads of the pools, mostly a leaded sedge nymph, and were caught one after another. In the streams however we had no success. In the afternoon we went down the lower part of the river, and there we had to fish with chenille streamers and yellow Dog Nobblers, as well as white and orange. We caught well, even in broad sunlight.

'Late in the afternoon, there was a sparse hatch of small sedges, and the two of us who put on a dry fly enjoyed ourselves very much. All of us got an average of some thirty trout between 3/4 and 5 pounds, but they were not very strong fighters.

'Another day we went to the Rio Grande again, in two cars as a breakdown or two punctures could mean a fifteen mile walk. The level of the river had gone down a foot and it was clearer. Nothing in the morning, but in the afternoon my companions, Isabel and Kelly, and with the local guide, fished a pleasant slow pool and my friend caught our first big trout at the inflow. The playing took seventeen minutes since the fish – a bright twelve-pound sea trout – took full advantage of the current. We had left the video camera in the car and Isabel ran half a mile to fetch it, crossing a small river arm. When she came back with it, the trout had run 300 yards downriver and she had to cross a pond with the camera on her head and the water up to her neck. You call that loving a husband!

'The next day on the Rio Grande, the water had gone down a little, and late in the afternoon we caught four sea trout between ten and fourteen pounds. It was very cold, the sky was dark and all our woollies seemed thin to us. We had a storm, and rain was announced for the following day, so we decided to fish the smaller San Pablo river, 90 miles to the south of the Rio Grande, where we were assured that big sea trout also ran. After 30 miles of metalled road, we did the rest through an horrendous track to reach the river, with a very nice landscape full of oak woods. When we reached it we discovered that a boat had closed the mouth of the river with its nets and was taking – totally illegally – all the sea trout trying to run the river. Therefore we concentrated on the river trout without much success.

'The return journey was a nightmare, as one car punctured twice and we were left on the track with the prospect of sleeping in the cars and spending a cold night when the petrol for the heaters ran out. Fortunately, the guide remembered that a few miles away there was a farm owned by the son of Spanish Basques who, he believed, had a Falcon car like one of ours. They welcomed us like brothers, lent us spares and eventually we reached Rio Grande at 4.00 a.m.

'We spent three more days on the Rio Grande river, each time with less water and with better fishing. We were lucky not to have big winds and even one sunny day, when at half past twelve there was a hatch of upwinged flies which were taken on the surface by the river trout. Fishing a dry fly with a light rod and four-pound point I took trout between two and five pounds. The heavier rainbows almost always broke the leader after jumping four or five times six feet into the air. On those three days we caught some fifteen sea trout, the two biggest weighing sixteen and seventeen pounds.

'Our most successful flies were streamers, especially the locally tied ones of 3–5 inches in length tied on large (2–1/0) hooks in yellow, orange, red and white. Tandem hooks would have been effective but they are prohibited by law.

'The locals were very welcoming, and hotels cost about £20 a day for bed, breakfast and dinner. The cost of local guides, with car, was £15 per person per day.

'An additional bonus is the wildlife – I have never seen so many wild geese and ducks of all kinds, not to mention eagles and albatrosses. The rivers abound in beavers, muskrat and mink. Blue foxes and their relatives the *culpeos* are countless.'

Another river which produces equally large sea-run browns is the Rio Gallegos across the Magellan straits in the southernmost tip of the mainland. But according to one local guide the largest trout of all in that river were 'resident' browns, which fattened near the source in Lago Blanco in Chile, one of 23 pounds having recently been caught there.

'Back again to Buenos Aires at dawn and another three-hour flight to San Carlos de Bariloche. The splendid morning soon presented the magnificent range of the Andes ahead, with its giant peaks over 20,000 feet covered with perpetual snow emerging from a circle of clouds.

'Bariloche is mostly known as a winter tourist centre with an incredibly beautiful landscape above the huge lake Nahuel Huapí. It is a perfect place for a honeymoon and though it has many trout and of very big size the only way to catch them is by deep trolling – not a pleasant method of fishing. Every river in the range – only the southern part of the Andes range has trout – runs through one or more lakes before reaching the eastern plains. The places where the streams flow out of the lakes are called "mouths". In general trolling is not allowed near these "mouths". Fish of any size concentrate in these mouths to feed on fry and they take mostly at dawn and dusk. The problem is that an average "mouth" is about 80 yards wide and is difficult to cover. Fish are always circling around the mouths and to hook a very big one is a matter of chance. It is sometimes possible to find big fish a couple of miles downstream of the mouth, but then again you need the permission of the owner of the land to cross it, except when the mouth and part of the river belongs to a public park.

'From Bariloche we can divide this zone of the range into three areas: one around 50 miles from the town; the northern one 100 miles or more; and the southern one 200 miles away. We had not enough time to fish the three areas and we opted for the northern district. All the rivers there have brown and rainbow trout, some lakes and their outflowing stream have sebago salmon, and brook trout occur often in many waters. All the fish are extraordinarily strong. They take freely and any lure seems to work. We had the best results with Chenilles, black, white or yellow, Dog Nobblers, Woolly Worms, Matukas, and Muddlers, but anything was taken by the rainbows, the brownies being more selective. The sebagos liked bigger lures and a kind of fry imitation or something with long marabou feathers. Brook trout in lakes liked very much one-inch-long streamers with purple or yellow and orange marabou feathers, with long strips of silver tinsel mixed with the feathers along the hook.

'Trout were much more selective with dry flies. When there was a hatch – which only happened in calm weather – we had to match the naturals as closely as possible. A nice medium-size sedge proved to be good even without a hatch. The rises were superb and the fight was unbelievable. Unfortunately, most of the rivers we fished had few places suitable for a dry fly.

'The nearest river to Bariloche is the Limay, which in fact is the outflow of the Nahuel Huapí lake. The mouth is narrow, perhaps 60 yards wide, but the water flow is enormous and much too fast and deep.

Downstream the river widens, but due to the gradient it has always too much flow, clean and clear water but too deep even to be fished with extra-fast sinking lines. It has big trout, probably not many but certainly the strongest we ever found. We did not stop long there as the wind was too strong to allow us to cast properly. Even so, we hooked half a dozen two-pounders. It must be absolutely certain that the Limay holds trout of over twenty pounds, the problem being how to catch them. Sometimes a big one is hooked with a very heavy spoon. The river runs for about 50 miles and ends in an artificial lake which also holds the water of the River Traful. We arrived on the lower beats of the Traful a couple of hours before dusk; the water level was excellent and we started fishing a stretch of very fast streams, with a stony bed with some boulders but wadable with the help of a wading stick. We had tied leaded sedge nymphs to 6-pound points and sinking leaders and it seemed that all the river's rainbows were waiting for them, taking in the strongest of the current and fighting like devils. Kelly and I hooked some twenty each in one hour from half a pound to five pounds. They fought like ten-pounders. The two others, fishing quieter water, were not so lucky. We left the Traful with sorrow but had to drive 60 miles to sleep in Junín. The last three days of our trip were to be spent in the higher beats of Traful with trout and sebagos. There is another small river called the Calefú which we had no time to fish this year, though it is close by. There trout take dry flies and nymphs very well, but are much smaller.

'Junín de los Andes is a small village with a nice hotel, the Alejandro 1, owned by a Lebanese lady and open only for the fishing season. Accommodation and food are cheap to our standards. As always, the number of American fishermen and hunters – there is very good red-deer stalking in the area – exceeded by far all the other guests, and all looking for records.

'Record fish may be caught in the mouth of river Chimehuin. It is the most famous mouth, very large and fished only at dawn, when the trout come down from the lake to feed in the stream. Perhaps an average of one fish from ten to twenty pounds is killed per day and there are always a lot of anglers. We went to fish some twenty miles downriver. This was not free fishing, but the owner of the estate was very kind and showed us the best places. The Chimehuin is a medium-to-large river and we had to cast streamers or dries depending on the water. We did not hook many, but the average was close to two pounds with some over four. Streamers with some red paid best, and small olives for the dries.

'In the evening we paid a visit to "Bebe" Anchorena who with Jorge Donovan made up the most legendary Argentina fishing team in more than forty years. He has a beautiful country house and spends the whole summer fishing every day, still very strong in his late sixties. Whilst Isabel and the charming Mrs Anchorena had a chat, the "Bebe" showed us his collection of dry and salmon flies of superb quality. He knew the whole river inch by inch and had a key for every gate in every fence. We agreed to fish together in two days. The River Malleu was our next target. It is a medium-sized stony river, very suitable for dry fly. It flows from a lake with plenty of large brook trout which we had fished in earlier years. You need to drive 60 miles over a very bad track, pushing the car sometimes and carrying a boat, to reach the good areas and fish the late afternoon and evening rise. It is worth it if you camp there and spend a couple of days. Instead we went to the very lower beats of the river and "Bebe" arrived after breakfast and, with the help of a magic key, we reached the best beats of the river Ouilquihue, very close to the village of Junín. A small river, good for dry fly but a very windy day. Even so, trout moved by midday and we were catching them, especially with a size 14 brown sedge, till five o'clock when they stopped rising. A couple of three-pounders among twenty smaller ones was my tally. Big fish did not move that day, probably because of the wind. What astonished us was the number of hares, as big as dogs, that hid in every bush – I dreamed of having a horse and some greyhounds. We left Junín de los Andes in the evening and drove 70 miles back to a very small but nice inn next to lake Traful. We spent the next two days fishing the higher beats of the river. It seems the water was too warm for the sebago salmon to come down out of the lake. The trout fishing was excellent, mostly with black streamers size 6 long shank. Again the rainbows were taking in the strongest of the current and fighting hard. The biggest fish were about six pounds, and the average was over two pounds. I had some thirty in a single afternoon. The Traful is probably the best river at that time of year (March, late summer) though not very suitable for dry fly.

'There is certainly very good trout fishing in Argentina, but probably not as good as it was twenty years ago. The experience of the big sea trout of Tierra del Fuego is unique, but you should only go when the river is in good condition. Inquire first at Buenos Aires, and if conditions are poor on the Rio Grande fish the Junín first. The best solution is to spend a minimum of three weeks there, preferably in February or March, which will give you the best chance of fishing for sea trout, trout and sebago. Food and lodging are cheap and as all waters are free a general permit (quite cheap) will allow you to fish everywhere. In general, the owners of the estates are kind and will allow you access through their land, especially if you tell them that you release fish.'

Chile

Neighbouring Chile provides as good trout fishing as Argentina, but Rafael found on an earlier trip that the central lakes were not so productive of big fish. Without expert advice and guidance it was also difficult for him to locate the best areas.

It was in 1905 that brown trout from England were first introduced to the rivers of Chile and, as in Argentina, sea-run browns are to be found in the far south of Chilean Patagonia and Tierra del Fuego, but it is perhaps the rainbows which provide the major attraction for trout fishers. First imported some ten years after the browns by an Irishman who had settled in Santiago, they have colonized the rivers and lakes from there down to Patagonia in the far south, fattening on the crayfish which abound in the rivers.

In his incomparable book *Going Fishing* Negley Farson tells of a great battle he had with a rainbow hooked on his very first cast in Chile. He was fishing the Laja river which swirls down from Lake Laja high in the far Andes in long, flat sweeps or crashing over rocks, some 50 miles south of Chillan. He was fishing with a light trout rod and insufficient backing, but finally landed a fish of over six pounds. On that day and the next he and his companions had several more rainbows of from three to six pounds. Thereafter on his way across the Andes further south to Argentina he stopped to fish Lake Llanquihue, which lies directly opposite Lake Nahuel Huapi on the Argentine side of the Andes. There he caught some strange fish, said to be peculiar to that lake, which slightly resembled a rainbow, but were not of the salmonid family.

Further south still, 30 miles south-east of the small coastal town of Chaiten, opposite Chiloe Island is Lake Yelcho. In the *Flyfisher's Journal* L. K. Leach records how in February 1982 he and his wife fished the lake and the Rio Yelcho which flows from its north-west corner, a fast-flowing turbulent river which pours down to the sea through forest and farmland. There are shingle banks and open places from which the river can be fished, but the big fish, both browns and rainbows, tend to lie beneath sunken logs submerged in the forest sections of the river. He saw one brown of nine pounds caught on a plug, but preferred to stick to fly himself. They stayed at a small pension in the tiny hamlet of Puerto Cardenas, arriving by air from Puerto Montt, and were very well looked after. There and elsewhere they received a warm welcome and great kindness. They took with them an expert guide and did most of their fishing on the lake, a beautiful place set amid imposing and magnificent mountain peaks. In ten days fishing on river and lake they caught more than 60 fish averaging well over three pounds. A few were kept for the table, the rest put back. Their best fish was a rainbow of 6¾ pounds, caught by their guide, who had earlier hooked and lost a bigger one. They fished mostly with a deer-hair Tom Thumb or Massey Muddler on the surface, or a large nymph or Grey Ghost on a sunken leader. The lake fish fed heavily on snail that live on weeds around the edge, one big rainbow they kept being found to have 120 snails in its stomach. The fish they hooked gave a tremendous fight, strong and deep, and often threatened to take all the backing off the reel.

In the far south at Punta Arenas the hotel Los Navegantes advertises a high standard of accommodation and cuisine, and a variety of tourist attractions in the Magellanes district, including abundant sporting fish in the numerous lakes and rivers. One of these is the Rio Serrano, a few hours' drive from Punta Arenas, which has a good run of sea-run browns.

Other Andean countries like Peru, Ecuador and Colombia have good trout fishing, but you have to leave the mainland and cross to a disputed island for anything comparable to Argentina and Chile's.

Falkland Islands

It was not until after the Second World War that brown trout were first introduced to the Falkland Islands. In 1948, and thereafter annually, consignments of ova were sent out from Britian, but for some years, although a few small brownies were to be found in some streams, the results were not encouraging. However, in February 1954 a trout of 4¼ pounds was caught on fly in a tiny stream, but it was not until February 1956, when a trout of 3½ pounds was caught in the Murrell River near Stanley, that it was realized that the earlier stocking of brown trout from Britain had produced a strain of sea-run browns, as had happened two decades earlier in southern Argentina and Tierra del Fuego.

The two Falkland islands, East and West, are not large, their combined area being roughly the size of Wales, nor are their mountains high, a little over 2,000 feet for the highest peaks. There are no trees or bushes and the country is mainly rolling peat bogs, interspersed with rocky outcrops, across which a strong, often violent, wind blows almost constantly from the west. The rivers course through the peat bogs, swelling rapidly as they go, but are for the most part short, shallow and fast-flowing. Because of the boggy nature of the ground and the changeable weather even in summer, they tend to stay at a fairly constant level, with occasional floods after heavy rain. The longest and best are the San Carlos River, which flows west across East Falkland and by the time it reaches San Carlos Bay is a wide, vigorous river that is ideal for fly fishing, and the Malo River, some 30 miles from Stanley. On West Falkland two of the best rivers, but shorter and more remote than those on the eastern island, reach the sea at Roy Cove and Pebble Island. Virtually all the rivers and streams on both islands have runs of sea trout which are mostly from two to nine or ten pounds in weight. It is recorded that in the two years after the first sea trout was taken in the Murrell River between three and four hundred trout were caught in that river alone, ranging up to twelve pounds, but bigger fish than that are sometimes caught, the recognized record being a trout of 23½ pounds from the Malo River.

The brown trout that first elected to go to sea and produced such a large and prolific strain evidently fattened on the dense concentrations of krill, on which whales grow to such a vast size, and immense schools of small smelt-like fish that abound in the surrounding seas. When first caught the sea-run browns are bright silvery fish, resembling Atlantic salmon, but soon lose their silvery sheen and indeed some have reverted to the darker, gold colour of trout before they leave salt water.

There are two separate runs of these sea-run browns, the spring run in October–November which provides most of the larger fish, and the Autumn run in February–March. The best place for fishing is normally in the brackish water where the river meets the sea, but the larger rivers offer good opportunities for fishing higher up. When a run is really on, the trout arrive in considerable numbers and positively boil up through the river entrance, feeding hungrily on any suitable offering. But it is not always easy to judge the right moment and local advice should be sought as individual rivers vary. In the San Carlos River, for example, the main run comes in at high tide, while the Roy Cove River run occurs as the ebb turns. Spinning is the locally favoured method of fishing the estuaries, though muddlers or large, brightly coloured or silver flies also do well. Higher up, smaller dark flies such as Connemara Black and Zulu or Mallard and Claret are effective.

Once each run is over the sea trout disappear and the lower stretches of the rivers become virtually empty of fish, but higher up in the winding moorland streams are 'resident' half-pound brownies that never developed the sea-going urge, and the hill lochs, though often dour, can provide exciting sport with finely-coloured trout of up to one, or even two, pounds. Before the coming of brown trout, the rivers were well supplied with an indigenous fish which, although not of the salmonid family, is known as 'local trout' or 'zebra trout'. Reaching a maximum weight of two pounds, these fish were once prolific, easy to catch and good to eat, but have now been displaced by the browns and are found only in remote streams or hill lochs.

In the vicinity of Stanley the Murrell River offers good fishing during the seasonal runs and there are fishing huts where one can stay, or hotels in the town. Further afield is the prolific Malo River, an arduous three- or four-hour journey by Land-Rover from Stanley, which also has a fishing hut. For access to other rivers, however, it would be necessary to arrange accommodation on farms, but there are no roads and transport is by foot, horse, Land-Rover, a farm tractor or – for the lucky ones – military helicopter. Once on a river there are no restrictions as the land is communal and used for sheep grazing. But it is wise to seek local advice over routes and locations, and to take precautions against bad weather and the possibility of a night out. Much of the land is remote, desolate and inhospitable, and the weather, even in summer, changeable and unreliable, with dense fog, and rain or even snow storms arriving suddenly with little warning.

Towards the end of 1983 my nephew Richard was posted to the Falkland Islands in command of a squadron of Royal Engineers to do a construction job on the west island. Having recently read an article in *The Field* magazine about sea-trout fishing in the Falklands, he took a rod and tackle with him. He arrived too late for the November run and had little time to spare the following February–March, but the captain of a ship that brought them supplies, a keen and experienced angler, managed to get away more often and borrowed Richard's rod. On one occasion they were able to go together in a Chinook helicopter to the Roy Cove River. Two hours later, when they had caught two 2-pound trout, the Chinook unexpectedly reappeared and signalled them urgently to get back on board – fog was closing in and soon they saw it ahead, a thick white blanket that blotted everything out. At zero feet they hover-taxied back along the coast using the beaches as markers until they judged they were opposite the ship 500 yards out in the bay. With visibility down to ten yards, half the length of the aircraft, finding the ship was a hazardous, but eventually successful, operation. On other ventures the captain was more successful, returning with trout up to six pounds, and once the tale of one that got away because it was too big for the net.

But a tale that Richard heard from an army colleague had a different ending. Three soldiers were fishing from an army assault boat in the San Carlos estuary for mullet, which often appear in enormous numbers and reach a few pounds in weight. They had little fishing experience and were using the battalion rod, a hefty weapon with a heavy sea-line, wire trace and spoon. Suddenly there was a tremendous pull, the boat nearly capsized and all three struggled with the rod and line. When they had calmed down they pulled for shore and finally capsized the boat as they struggled with the fish in the shallows. Eventually they got it ashore, but had no idea what it was and took it back to the army cooks, who weighed it and then set about it with carving knife and meat axe. Meanwhile two experienced fishermen had been called who examined the dissected fish and said it was unquestionably a sea trout. Whatever it weighed – the cook reputedly said 27 pounds – it was clearly a very exceptional trout. And in the first weekend of the current 1986–7 fishing season another exceptional trout of twenty pounds was landed from the Malo River by Mr Terry Spruce, secretary of the local angling club in Stanley.

Another soldier, Major Tim Glass, who was in the Falklands the year before Richard, gives this account of a March morning's fishing in East Falkland:

'We were three rods in all; Mark Conroy, a keen fisherman and wildlife expert, Sergeant-Major Jake Sutton, who had fished only once before, and myself. For some time we had been hoping to get a chance to fish a stretch of river called Swan Inlet, not too far from Bluff Cove, even though it involved a tortuous five-hour cross-country drive from Goose Green. When we arrived at an empty rancher's cottage near the Inlet late one evening in the midst of a heavy storm the river was in spate and the prospect did not seem very good.

'At first light Jake Sutton headed off for a pool a mile upriver, which he'd heard about from the locals. Mark and I emerged an hour later and looked at the water without much enthusiasm. Although the river had dropped a foot or more from the previous evening it was still very murky and flowing fast. Nonetheless we started fishing a hundred yards apart leap-frogging upstream in turn to cover the most likely holding places. We were both spinning downstream using bright silver Mepps or two-inch Tobys. Within half an hour Mark took his first fish, a bright silver sea trout of over 4 pounds, which deepened our concentration.

'Over the next hour we had four more fish of similar size and were then just short of the pool to which Jake had headed two hours earlier. He came to meet us and astonished us by emptying from his pack five magnificent fish, all taken from the same pool with the largest weighing 8½ pounds. We continued fishing on up to the pool and before noon had killed another eight sea trout. By then it was time to drive back to Goose Green. There were several unusual aspects of this morning's catch of 18 trout weighing some 70 pounds, which provided a feast for a company of soldiers later that day. First was the way the fish managed to take in such muddied water. Then there was the surprising variety of markings on the fish. Some had the classic brown trout look, others were mixed silver and brown, some pure silver. We headed home reluctantly, wondering what might have been possible had fishing conditions improved. Sadly we never got another opportunity to find out.'

A few weeks earlier in February Major Glass had had his first oportunity to try for Falklands sea trout after a helicopter trip to Fox Bay to fish Sand Pond estuary. Fishing late one afternoon, bivouacking overnight, then fishing again briefly next morning before being picked up again he had some twenty sea trout. They were taken on a silver Mepps and were mainly small fish of up to a pound, with three larger ones from 1½ to 3 pounds. He described them as 'a beautiful mottled brown, bronze and silver with small, pointed mouths'. They also fought like demons, harder than any he had hooked elsewhere. At one point he hooked a much larger sea trout, but 'the sudden speed and ferocity of its run just after the take' broke his ten pound leader. In the shallow sandy water of the estuary he could see great shoals of mullet, including large fish of up to 8 pounds. Indeed one mullet which took a Mepps was also large enough and strong enough to break him. Of the larger trout he kept, one was found to have a 4½ inch sprat in its stomach and others were full of whitebait, at least 17 in one case, illustrating the prolific feed which produces such exceptional sea trout. Mark Conroy had further confirmation of that with a friend detailing for him the catching of ten sea-run trout on a Viva fly, fishing between midnight and 5 a.m. on a flat calm pool lit by a brilliant full moon.

Information about fishing in the Falkland Islands can be obtained from the London Office of the Falkland Islands Government (29 Tufton Street, London SW1), who will also advise on travel arrangements – currently possible only on transport provided by the Ministry of Defence (Tristar from Brize Norton). They will also supply the address of the secretary of the local angling club in Stanley, if more detailed information about fishing is required; fishing holidays are occasionally advertised in *Trout and Salmon*, and recently a new company, Falkland Islands Tourism Ltd, has been established in Stanley (PO Box 13, Stanley, Falkland Islands – Manager, Mr Dave Morgan).

11

As Nature Never Intended

Lebanon, Sudan, Ethiopia, Uganda and Kenya

The start of my fishing career was in Africa, and from the beginning I was able to outdo any other tall fishing story with a true one of my own. Not many people can claim the first fish they hooked was so large that it caught them! Aged four, I was asked to hold a fisherman's tackle as he went in search of his lunch. The bait was still in the Nile and a monster fish chose that moment to seize hold. Losing the tug-of-war, I was dragged into the water and rescued with some difficulty. No wonder I settled later that year for worming a Scottish burn and yanking small trout over my head into the heather. The fish that nearly caught me was a Nile perch, or Aigel, which can grow to an immense size and is delicious to eat, if not to be eaten by. Two hundred pounds is not uncommon and my brother Philip when he was stationed in Khartoum in the early 1950s recalls an occasion when he and a friend set off one morning before dawn to go sandgrouse shooting in the desert west of the White Nile. As they drove towards the Omdurman bridge, along the embankment beside the Blue Nile, they saw a great white object gleaming in the dark across the road ahead and stopped to examine it. It was a Nile perch, just hauled ashore from a night-line, which they roughly measured at nearly 8 feet in length and guessed must have weighed some 300 pounds or more. Its captor had gone off to hire a taxi to take it to the Khartoum fish market. If anyone dismisses that as the usual fisherman's exaggeration, let him reflect on what happened to A. L. Allen, not in the great River Nile, but in a small river of Wales, the Towy, on the night of 25 September 1933. He and a friend had set off from the local pub for a night's sea-trout fishing in White Mill Pool, some 3 or 4 miles upstream of Carmarthen. In the dark something seized hold of his line, surged off down the pool and came to a crunching stop. His friend went to investigate, but soon returned, shaken and incredulous. Together they went back to the bottom of the pool and found, stranded on a shingle bank, what turned out to be a sturgeon, 9 feet 3 inches long and weighing 388 pounds. Had they returned to the pub with a true tale of 'one that got away', how many would have believed them? But it did not get away. They offered it to the King, who declined, and so they sold it in Carmarthen market for £5.

Mine was only a brief acquaintance with Africa. Philip knows it far better from serving, like my father, in the Sudan Civil Service. So the African chapters which follow are left mainly to him. His starting-point, however, is the Lebanon, that beautiful land which only the reckless would visit now in pursuit of trout. This is his story:

'Trout sometimes turn up in unlikely places, so when I travel abroad I take a rod with me, if at all possible. In 1941, when my field artillery regiment was sent overseas to an undisclosed destination, I found space to pack an old split-cane trout rod, and an assortment of flies and casts among my limited belongings. We travelled, in some luxury for those days, by P. & O. liner round the Cape to the Middle East. When we joined 8th Army in the Western Desert, my trout rod was clearly superfluous and was dumped with most of my kit at base depot. I did not expect to see it again, whatever might be the outcome of the desert fighting. In 1943, however, the armoured division to which we were attached had lost most of its tanks and equipment at Alamein and in the subsequent pursuit of Rommel's army, so we were sent back to be re-equipped. This took longer than expected, as priority for new equipment was given to forces at the front, and in the late summer we found ourselves encamped near Baalbek in Lebanon. While there I learnt there were trout in the Orontes, but a wireless aerial with the traditional bent pin on a length of string produced no result. We returned later to Cairo where, surprisingly, I was able to trace and recover my belongings intact. Then in March 1944 I was granted a few days' local leave, so I set off by train for Beirut, together with another officer who was no fisherman but had somehow acquired a shotgun.

'From Beirut, we hitch-hiked across the mountains and down to the Bekaa valley, then north past Baalbek to a point not far from the Syrian border. From there a small side-road leads down to the Orontes, across a bridge and thence to the small village of Hermel, a mile or two up in the foothills. Below the bridge, beside the river, there was a small mud hut where I hoped we could stay, and this was duly arranged. The only furniture in the hut was a bench and a thick wooden rectangular table, carved into the side of which were three notches, said to measure, successively, the length of the largest trout caught in the river. We had some camp equipment with us, and acquired a few provisions in Hermel.

'The valley of the Orontes (*Al-Aasi* to the Arabs) lies between two mountain ranges rising to some 10,000 feet, and throughout the summer is extremely hot and dusty – not a likely environment for trout. How they came there in the first place is a mystery. Some say the Romans introduced them, others that a migrating duck, with trout spawn on its webbed feet, passed that way. Possibly the French introduced them in the early days of their mandate. Certainly in the post-war years at the luxury hotels of Beirut you could order fresh rainbow trout (à la Française) farmed in ponds or streams high above Beirut. But the trout of the Orontes are brown trout in origin and long-established, and there is no doubt about why they thrive there. The source of the Orontes lies a mile or two upstream of Hermel bridge, a deep cavern in the rocks from which a full-grown river wells up, fed through underground channels by melting snows and springs high up in the mountains – a fascinating place. There the waters are always ice-cold and crystal-clear, downstream there are plenty of weeds to encourage insect life, and the waters remain cold enough for trout to live and breed for some distance below Hermel bridge, perhaps as far as Homs lake into which it flows. For the rest of its journey to the coast near Antioch it becomes totally unsuitable for trout. Perhaps the true explanation of their origin is that they arrived during the ice ages and, as in the Atlas mountains of North Africa, were left there when the ice finally receded.

'We spent three full days in the hut below the bridge. The nights in March were cool, the days unbroken sunshine, clear after recent rain, crisp in the mornings and evenings but hot in the middle of the day. On the first day I caught three or four trout averaging around three-quarters of a pound – pink fleshed and delicious – while my friend searched for some suitable bird or rabbit to shoot. The early morning had proved unproductive, the middle of the day was too bright and clear, and the trout mostly came towards sunset. I had taken on as a gillie a small boy called Ali. His principal duty was to keep all the other small boys as far away as possible, but he also delighted in netting my trout with a small net I had acquired in Beirut. On the evening of the second day, just before dusk, I was fishing a long, deep pool a mile or so below the bridge when my sunken fly was seized by a trout that was clearly far bigger than anything else I had seen. It fought well but eventually Ali, with not a little skill, got it into the net. We went back to the hut where, without much hope, I laid it out on the table. As I expected, it fell well short of the shortest of the notches, and I do not know what it weighed, around three pounds I thought. The next day was our last and I arranged my fishing to arrive at the same pool at the same time as the previous evening. What happened there I described as follows in a letter to my brother:

I had put on a 2X cast and a small sea-trout fly with a silver body, yellow tail and grey-brown wings. Half way down the pool I caught a fish of three-quarters of a pound in lovely condition. That was the only rise I had till I got near the end of the pool, well past the place where I caught my large trout the previous evening. It was now about 6 p.m. and the sun had set.

Suddenly there was an enormous swirl like the rise of a salmon and I knew that I had hold of something out of the ordinary. For some minutes the fish played deep and I was in two minds whether to play it from where I stood and risk getting caught in the rushes in front of me (I had been casting over them with some difficulty) or to go straight down the bank as far as I could to a spot where there was a break in the rushes and a shelving bank – an ideal place from which to play and land a fish. The danger was that the fish would make off downstream where various obstacles made it impossible to follow – I had only fifty yards of line, including backing, and my cast though strong had seen much service in pre-war days. I decided to go down. As I went the line kept just catching the rushes and I couldn't see what the fish was doing. However, it followed down willingly enough and even came quietly into about a foot and half of water not more than a yard from where I was now standing. I realized then how large it was. The little boy – Ali – was all in favour of trying to net it then and there, but I told him to keep well away. As I expected, the trout came suddenly to life and sailed majestically off downstream for thirty or forty yards before I could stop it. I held it there for some minutes with difficulty and began to wonder how I could ever get it back. The river at that point is about twenty-five yards wide, fairly deep and with an even flow of water. To hold the fish against the current seemed about all the strain my tackle could take. Slowly I started to reel it back, occasionally losing a little line, till it was again at my feet.

The time for the kill hadn't yet come as with my small net I wanted to exhaust the fish completely before attempting to land it. By this time it was getting dark. The fish made a few short runs and then started off downstream again taking twenty yards of line and then another twenty and jumping once in the gathering gloom. This time it came back more easily and the moment for landing seemed to have come. It was too dark now to distinguish line from cast and netting was impossible, but the spot was ideal for beaching. I got it on to some pebbles half in and half out of the water, but there it stuck – the strain was too much for the hold and the fly came away. But I had played it for nearly half an hour and the fish was too exhausted to move. I threw down my rod and shovelled it high on the bank with my hands.

'Afterwards, as we hurried back to the hut, I reflected that this time a new notch would surely be carved in the table, and so it was. I also determined that, one way or another, I must find a means of weighing it. So I set off up the track to the lights of Hermel village and succeeded in borrowing a set of balance scales and two 1 kilo weights. Back at the hut I weighed out one more kilo of potatoes which, with the weights added and half a small potato removed, just balanced the trout – 6½ pounds. Next morning before we left I took it up to the bridge for my friend to photograph. While we were there a car drove down and a British army major got out. "Samek kwaiyis," said the major. In those days I knew no Arabic but his meaning was obvious. "Yes, not a bad one," I replied. The major looked again at my sunburnt face and tattered clothes. "Good Heavens," he said after a pause, "I thought you were a native." Heaven had indeed been good to us. Cars were few and far between in that wild and remote area, and we had not been relishing the prospect of lugging our kit a few miles up to the main road. Having rewarded Ali for his help and sent him back to Hermel with the scales, I donated the trout to the major's mess and he gave us a lift to somewhere near Baalbek, from where hitch-hiking to Beirut was no problem.

'Many years later, in 1971, my wife and I drove from Beirut to the Hermel bridge. The hut had disappeared and so had the notched table. As we walked along the river towards the source and watched a shepherd driving his flock of sheep, the bells tinkling round their necks, my wife remarked that little had changed since biblical times. We had no rod with us and saw no fish. At the source we sat down to eat some sandwiches and were soon joined by a small party of local peasants who invited us to share their wine. By then I could speak Arabic and asked if there were any fish in the river. A few, they said, but small. I told them I had once caught a fish of three kilograms below the bridge. One of them promptly claimed that a fish of four kilograms had been caught in the past, but, since the war, hand-grenades and other post-biblical weapons had taken their toll. More recently, no doubt, these have been kept for sterner purposes and perhaps, when peace returns to Lebanon, large trout will again be found to flourish in the Orontes.

'Of all the African countries where the British have been involved, one of the least likely to have trout is the Sudan. Nonetheless, in November 1945, when I was able to get a release from the army and fulfil my pre-war ambition of joining the Sudan Political Service, I took a trout rod with me.

'Those who do not know the Sudan well may think of it as a country of hot and arid conditions, largely desert, in the north, changing to a tropical and humid African climate in the south. But it is a vast country, almost one million square miles, and contains many types of landscape. In the far south, on the border of Uganda, lie the Imatong Mountains, of which Mount Kinyeti, rising to nearly 10,500 feet, is the highest. In 1948 a young forestry official, J. K. Jackson, successfully stocked the Ngairigi stream with rainbow trout from Kenya, but later it was found that its temperature rarely dropped low enough to allow the trout to breed. Consequently, towards the end of 1949 he introduced more trout to the headwaters of the Kinyeti river at about 8,500 feet.

'At that time I was stationed some 300 miles due north of the Imatongs, more or less in the middle of nowhere, an endless, flat, low-lying grass plain, hot and humid, most of which floods annually when the rains come and the Nile rises, where the Nuer tribesmen herd their cattle – no place for trout. But in 1951, having been transferred to Khartoum, I had to make a business trip to Torit, headquarters of the district in which the Imatongs lie. To get there meant catching the weekly Dove service to Juba, headquarters of Equatoria province, some 800 miles south of Khartoum, and thence by road (so-called) to Torit, a further 100 miles south-east of Juba.

'Having concluded my business in Torit, I had a couple of days to spare before catching my return flight to Khartoum. With this possibility in mind, and having heard of the trout in the Imatongs, I had brought my trout rod with me. I went by car to Katire, a forestry station some 50 miles away up a mountain track, then on up the track to Gilo, and stayed the night there in a rest-house. Next morning I set off early with a guide up Mount Kinyeti. Several hours later we came to a small tumbling stream, with clear cold waters and little pools among the rocks and boulders, and I wondered, as I started fishing, if the rainbows had survived. They had, and I caught a few, around half to three-quarters of a pound, and two of them I kept for the evening meal and breakfast next morning. Soon it was time to start back and we arrived at the rest-house as night was falling. My dinner that evening was an unusual one for the Sudan – freshly caught rainbow trout, followed by strawberries grown in the garden by the rest-house keeper, together with cream from his herd of cows.

'Since the Sudan became independent in 1956, the south has been a troubled, often rebellious, part of the country and even at the best of times the headwaters of the Kinyeti river are extremely remote and difficult of access. I wonder how many fishermen, before or after me, have had the opportunity to fish for trout there – or will do in the future.'

But Africa has a habit of producing the unexpected. Someone I met by chance in Devon, on leave from Tanzania, gave me an introduction to an intrepid tea planter, Jonathan Niblett, an expert and knowledgeable fisherman who has fished extensively in Africa and to whom I am indebted for much of what follows. He had been tea planting in the Acholi Hills, part of the Imatong range, and was shortly going back again. Much of the country there is wild and unexplored; Gilo was more than four hours' walking distance away and just as long by road. There were still small rainbows to be caught in the Kinyeti stream, but he normally found it more profitable to spend his spare time shooting game for the pot, as I had done many years earlier among the Nuer, or fishing the Nile with fly or spinner for bigger quarry.

Two other countries which border the Southern Sudan are Ethiopia and Uganda. Parts of both have been stocked with trout, but in neither of them in present-day circumstances is fishing any more practical than it is in Sudan.

Ethiopia with its extensive ranges of high mountains, lakes and great rivers probably has the potential to become the best of all the East African countries for trout fishing. In the post-war years rivers in the mountains of southern Ethiopia were stocked from Kenya, a fishing club was constructed to which those who could afford it were able to fly, and Jonathan Niblett recalls seeing photographs of great rivers and big trout averaging five pounds or more. No doubt some are still there.

Recent events have given Ethiopia an unfortunate reputation and fishing holidays there would seem an irrelevance with its famine and other problems. Some of the trout fishing may still be adequate, however, particularly in the area of the Bale Mountains National Park. The high altitudes of this region made it ideal for the original stockings from Kenya, and initially trout flourished there. At its best trout could be caught there in numbers, with some topping seven pounds. Indeed, the fishing there was good enough to attract England's big trout man, Alan Pearson, to visit and add to his records of large bags. The Shiya river is noted for having produced weighty trout, though the easy fishing for an abundance of small browns and rainbows was in rivers like the Webbe (or Uebi), which rises in the Mendebo mountain range and provided all too easy fishing. Traditional flies were found to be effective, small spinners even more so, but it is doubtful if quality trout fishing has survived intact.

Attempts to stock trout in Uganda were first made in 1930 led by the Governor, Sir William Gowers. These failed, but in 1932 the Surrey Trout Farm supplied 50,000 ova. After various vicissitudes a tenth of these survived as healthy fry, some of which were successfully liberated at Kikuchu in the Ruwenzori range at a height of 10,000 feet. But Uganda too has seen so much turmoil of late that there is little to encourage a visit by peaceful anglers. The trout fishing there was never good and has suffered further in the recent unrest. Certainly there is no trout fishing of a quality to make anyone contemplate a visit to that troubled country for fishing alone.

Yet in Africa in general there is still a surprising variety of fine trout fishing. Only in the Atlas range of mountains in Morocco are the trout indigenous; elsewhere man has made up for nature's oversight. Most of Africa consists of deserts or low-lying plains, swamps or tropical jungles. There the climate is far too hot or dry for trout to live and breed. Trout on the Equator seems a contradiction anyway for a cold-water fish. But there are areas where the mountains are high enough and the climate cool enough, even on the Equator itself, to provide ideal conditions. Beginning at the end of the nineteenth century many of these places were stocked by British pioneers with browns and rainbows, usually at their own expense. Countries like Tanzania, Kenya, and South Africa have enjoyed, and still enjoy, fine trout fishing as a result of their efforts. If the description of present opportunities encourages a visit bear in mind always that rapid changes can take place as administrative outlooks change or political situations alter.

Jonathan Niblett has listed a dozen flies which serve him well fishing in Tanzania, Kenya and Natal. This African collection starts with dragonfly nymphs as a safe bet for all dams and rivers in sizes 8 to 12. For sunny days a Barbus to imitate *barbus kerstenii*; for warm evenings a Yellow Nymph. Another standby is the Black and Peacock Spider for all times and waters in sizes 8 to 12, leaded and unleaded, with copper rib. For times of indecision he has the Nusu-Nusu fly. That is Kiswahili for 'half-'n-half' and the fly is a mixture of Mallard and Claret, Black and Peacock Spider, and Tup's mixture on 6 or 8 hooks. The plain Mallard and Claret is his best bet for the evening from 6.30 on. In autumn or winter in the dams the Coleon Spinner is effective. On cold grey days or in flat calm a lure-type Ghost is a needed addition. Two varieties of leaded freshwater crab may be productive on waterfall pools, but not in dams. Other essentials are White Ants, with the body tied from yellow-dyed Klipspringer hair – the Klipspringer being the only antelope with hollow hair. Finally he ties Hopplers – Muddler grasshoppers – from Klipspringer hair plus a great grey goose wing, which are apt to catch big trout in dams. In addition to these the Coachman is a very effective fly for East African trout.

These flies will also do well enough in Kenya, which had a great reputation for trout fishing and still offers much choice. In 1905 Major Grogan, at his own expense, imported Loch Leven brown and rainbow ova from Howietoun Fisheries of Stirling, which he stocked in the Gura river, high up in the Aberdare range. In 1907 he imported a further consignment from the same hatchery, but all were lost. In 1909, trout were seen spawning and some large ones caught. In 1910 Commander Barry imported browns and rainbows from South Africa. Further importations were made in 1921 from South Africa and subsequently from England. A friend of mine who was born in Kenya and spent the first thirteen years of his life there tells me that in the mid-1920s he used to go trout fishing with his father. On one occasion, after a close encounter with a black rhino, they came to a pool where his father had heard tell of a large trout. His father fished for it and caught it – seven pounds – but in doing so disturbed another large trout. So he continued fishing and, in due course, caught that one too – eight pounds. In those days, he told me, the local tribesmen of Kenya, partly because of their animistic beliefs, had no taste for river fish and thought little of those who caught them. But in the days of the

Mau Mau troubles many of the tribesmen involved had to forage for themselves in the bush, tried out the river trout and found them good to eat. Thereafter poaching became a popular pastime, and difficult to control. A book published in 1932 refers to large trout being caught up to eight pounds but nowadays such fish are few and far between, a result perhaps of the widespread poaching that goes on.

Visitors to Kenya, on holiday or business, can obtain help and guidance from the Kenya Fly Fishers Club in Nairobi and there are a few hotels that cater for anglers. The main areas in which trout are found are the Aberdare mountain range and Mount Kenya. The Outspan Hotel at Nyeri, nearly 100 miles north of Nairobi by road, is well known by safari visitors on their way to Treetops or The Ark game-viewing lodges in the Aberdare National Park, and is an excellent base for fishing the Gura, Chania and other streams. The hotel's game and fishing book provides an interesting record of fish caught there in the past, including many large browns in earlier days. Or continue on to Mweiga and stay at the Aberdare Country Club. At Naro Moru, some thirty miles north of Nyeri, the Naro Moru River Lodge provides a centre from which that and other streams running off Mount Kenya can be fished. And in the west of the country, not far from Lake Victoria, Kericho is another trout-fishing centre, mainly dam fishing, staying at the Mid West Hotel.

Fishing is at heights of over 5,000 feet, which provides an ideal climate in exciting surroundings. Being virtually on the Equator the seasons do not vary greatly and the trout are in condition the year round. There is, however, a rainy season in March and April, and again between late October and early December, which can lead to very sudden rises of water. The rivers often flow through thick vegetation and the angler must bear in mind that wild animals can sometimes be encountered, and that the transition from daylight to total darkness can be very sudden.

There is a government trout hatchery at Sagana but only a few rivers are stocked, and those infrequently. Both rainbows and browns breed naturally at heights of 5,000 to 6,000 feet but nowadays brown trout are seldom found, and most of the streams hold only rainbows. These too are not easy to catch and the fisherman will probably have to work hard to get a decent basket. The streams are generally fast-flowing, with tumbling rapids and some deep pools. Although wet-fly fishing is the norm, either up or downstream, dry-fly fishing is possible on many rivers for about half an hour at dusk when there is a definite rise; also on rivers on the moorlands at 10,000 feet, where there can be a hatch of fly at any time.

Kenya's fishing reputation was high after the war and many have enjoyed catching trout there. A Sudan friend of mine spent a leave there staying at the Tulaga farm, the home of one of the original settlers. From the bush he had created a prosperous farm at the back of the plateau above

Naivasha, nestling against the wooded foothills to the west of the Aberdare range.

Just below this house flows the Tulaga river, a small stream tumbling down from the hills into the Rift Valley. A dam had been built not far from the house and formed a small lake of perhaps half an acre. This was used for the farm and had been stocked with brown trout. During the war years maintenance was difficult and the dam finally burst, releasing the trout into the river. The largest recorded fish in the lake had been one of three pounds and a few of that size escaped. My friend told me of an evening's fishing there shortly after:

'I borrowed a light rod, some flies and a net and went down to the little river shortly after tea. A little below the original site of the dam was a deep rock-girt pool under a small waterfall, which measured perhaps seven or eight metres long and a mere four metres across. I tied on a medium-sized wet fly and let it drift down and round with the current. On my third cast I thought I had snagged the bottom, but it appeared to be moving and I realized I had hooked an unusually large trout for that small river. I never saw him until the final moments, but his main tactic was to skulk on the bottom – difficult to cope with on such a light rod. Luckily he seemed to tire fairly quickly as a result of continual pressure, and when he finally surfaced I realized his size and was able to net him quickly in the small area of the pool. With this fish safely in the bag I went downstream to the next pool, of the same type but larger and somewhat shallower. Soon I had hooked another large trout which put up a better fight but proved a mere tiddler compared with the first one. By now I was feeling in need of a whisky and soda so carried my trophies up to the house. I had been away for not much more than an hour, having enjoyed one of those truly magical evenings. The two fish weighed 2¾ and 1½ pounds – the former the second largest trout ever caught in the Tulaga river up to that time.'

Typical of past fishing experience in Kenya is this account by David Porter, chairman of the Southern Confederation of English Fly Fishers, who served there a few years ago with the King's African Rifles, based at Nanyuki, a town 6,000 feet up on the slopes of Mount Kenya and precisely on the Equator:

'The impact of a beautiful, fertile and colourful country, together with abundant wildlife and fabulous climate, to a soldier fresh from tactical exercises on the North German plain was remarkable, exciting and challenging. Kenya consists of a tropical coastal strip a few miles wide. The hinterland then rises gradually for 300 miles until the central plateau is reached, which is itself bounded by Mount Kenya to the north, Mount Kilimanjaro to the south (across the border with Tanzania) and with Mount Elgon to the west, on the border with Uganda. These mountains rise to great heights – Mount Kenya over 17,000 and Mount Kilimanjaro over 19,000 feet. The summits are covered with perpetual snow, and the air is so clear and rarefied that those of a weaker constitution have great difficulty in breathing at any height over 15,000 feet. Naturally enough, the snow and ice melts during the daytime and over the years the rivers and streams have carved deep valleys through the rock strata.

'The first reports of snow-covered mountains by early explorers were discounted by the Royal Geographical Society, who could not accept that snow fell on the Equator. Various explanations were propounded, that finding most acceptability being that bird droppings or guano caused the "white" deposits, and it was not until the first explorer climbed Mount Kilimanjaro and made a snowball that this quaint theory was disproved!

'These rivers which flow to the north and west of Mount Kenya and the Aberdares link into one vast and turgid stream which flows north, then due east off the central plateau into the semi-arid Northern Frontier District. The river, known as the Ewaso Ngiro, eventually disappears into the Lorian Swamp. Running from snowfield or glacier to swamp, these rivers flow through high-altitude moorland, dense bamboo and cedar forest, the haunt of buffalo, rhino, elephant, leopard and the very rare bongo, before finally reaching the agricultural and ranching areas of the plain. Those that flow south from the Aberdares and Mount Kenya form the great Tana river which flows out to sea between Malindi and Lamu.

'There is no natural stock of fish in the upper reaches of these rivers (although there are catfish further downstream), very little fly life, and a type of freshwater crab as the only creature of any size. A diet of crab may be monotonous, but it is a healthy one for the trout, if not helpful to the fly fisherman. Certainly any general rise was a rarity in the four years I fished there, and it was obvious that the trout had adapted to being mainly bottom feeders. Despite stocking, the pressures of holiday and local angling have made big baskets hard to get, and fish of over a pound a good catch, one of two pounds a whopper. That is a sad change from pre-war days when the capture of large trout, particularly brownies, from the Chania and other rivers is well documented, especially in the fishing book at the Outspan Hotel at Nyeri. Another hotel of interest in my time was the Silverbeck, sited on the Equator so that you enjoy your beer with a foot in each hemisphere.

'The rivers around Nanyuki have magical sounding names. As you approach Nairobi from the south there are the Naro Moru, Burguret and Nanyuki rivers, and then the Liki, Ontulili and Sirimon to the north. They are all very similar in character, though the Liki is the largest. They flow through deep valleys, ravines almost in places, with tumbling rapids between deep holding pools. Vegetation tends to meet overhead so you frequently feel that you are fishing in a green tunnel. Where possible, upstream casting is far more effective than working the flies across the downstream current. The upstream cast sinks the fly more quickly and the fish are more securely hooked.

'During my tour of duty popular flies included Royal Coachman, Blue and Black Zulus, Matukas, Coch-y-Bondhu, Dunkeld, Watson's Fancy and the Kenya Bug, the last-named a rather fat and overdressed Black and Peacock spider, ribbed with silver. All waters are fly-only, one must have a local licence (obtainable from the District Commissioner's Office), and one is likely to be asked to produce a licence by the fishery wardens who will produce their game book for completion, and are frequently seen.

'Due to a process of rapid deforestation (the cedar trees on the upper slopes of the mountains are being cut for their timber), rainfall, usually heavy although short in duration, tends to run off quickly, and the rivers rise and fall, colour and clear quickly. It is quite possible to be fishing a pool when the rapidly rising water suddenly floods one's boots – I know, it happened to me, although more sensible footwear would include jungle or safari boots and the acceptance that one is unlikely to stay dry for long.

'I have mentioned poaching. This can be fairly serious on the quieter and infrequently patrolled reaches, as trout in Kenya, as in any other country, command a good retail price even in an illicit market. Another disadvantage about fishing on the Equator is that the transition from daylight to darkness is rapid. It was always tempting to try one more pool before returning home, and the last trout could frequently result in a stumble home in pitch darkness. Another "disadvantage" is that wild animals are occasionally encountered. Bush, reed and water buck are seen quite commonly, buffalo and rhino occasionally, and leopard are about but rarely seen. A dog is not only good company, but an early warning mechanism. Even ants can present problems. I was fishing a favourite pool when my wife and her dog jumped straight in – they had been standing on a safari ant trail and the little beasts had just started to get vicious! One might pick up the odd tick or jigger as well. Fishing on the Equator is rewarding, exciting and challenging, with the added interest that something different might always happen.'

Indeed it is likely to if you venture into some of the wilder places. For the best of the fishing in the Aberdare mountains you require strong nerves rather than strong casts. This is well illustrated by an entry in the gamebook of Mark Conroy: '21 Dec. 1985. *River Amboni*. With the indefatigable Mohamed and his companion I went through the forests of the Aberdares to the high moorlands where the rivers of the lower slopes have their source. Beset by buffalo and rogue lions these streams are rarely fished – even less since the wife of a Danish fisherman was taken by a lion a year ago. We fished in the rocky gorges, for safety, and only crossed open ground after a careful study. Still we came across wet lion pugmarks on the bridge we used, and the fresh prints and droppings of buffalo were everywhere. It adds an undoubted spice, which is missing in Hampshire ... We had 25 trout for our daring, and they ranged from ½ to 1¼ pounds. It was a modest bag by Mohamed's standards. He and two others once had 74 trout averaging a pound from a very open stretch – to which they never returned because of an oppressive feeling of danger.'

Mark Conroy adds that the waters of the Aberdare plateau are the most prolific he has ever fished in wide-ranging experience from Africa to the Falklands. Further down on the edge of the jungle there were larger pools and larger trout. A local expert guaranteed him trout of 3 or 4 pounds provided he could supply 'a sniper guaranteed to drop a lion within twenty yards of its leaving cover'. In practice the lion, buffalo, and elephant act as river wardens for large stretches that might otherwise be fished or poached nearly clean. These risky fishing waters indicate the potential of others in safer areas where he also caught reasonably well on the Sivimon, Nyamindi, and the Nanyuki. The Nanyuki was a different, but delightful experience. A week later he was enjoying himself catching wild rainbows in a little pool of the Nanyuki in the garden of the famous Kenyan angler, Sam Weller of 'The Ark'. The gamebook recorded: 'The stream is small and heavily bushed, but even without trout it would be a delight. Colobus monkeys rattle through the high branches disturbing the brown parrots; Hadada Ibis roost by the water, and sunbirds haunt the flowers. And the waters hold surprising numbers of fish. These are wild rainbows which breed in the icy and oxygen-rich waters which tumble from the snowfields of Mount Kenya, always visible through the lacework of branches. They are reputed to subsist largely on freshwater crabs, but they seized a Kingsmill with commendable enthusiasm.'

Nigel Montgomery, chairman of the Kenya Fly Fishers Club, has some advice to add:

'The season lasts all year, but fishing can be very uncomfortable in the monsoon periods from late April to mid-March and again in November. So give these times a miss. Club or syndicate water is generally the best, but restricted to members and guests. So get an invitation if you can.

'The newcomer should always get local advice with the two best sources being the Government Fisheries Department at the Nairobi Museum and the Kenya Fly Fishers Club. Olive-green and khaki predominate in fishing dress – informality and camouflage. Waders are not necessary even though the water can be very bracing in early morning. Heavy jerseys and jackets become a severe encumbrance as it warms up later. Short trousers and light bush jackets are the popular wear, with dark glasses also desirable.

'Not many people fish for trout in Kenya so those of us who do are able to get full enjoyment from the remoteness and the splendour of the surroundings. Vast stretches of river are virtually unfished and exciting to explore, which is half the fun. Only a few of the best stretches are patrolled by scouts as river watchers. The average weight is higher on the dams, where you usually need a boat. Traditional wet flies are the most consistently successful, but you can catch on nymphs and dry flies as well. My selection includes Coachman, Connemara Black, Kenya Bug, Invicta, Watson's Fancy, Mrs Simpson, Mallard and Claret, Peter Ross, Alexandra, March Brown, and Pheasant Tail Nymph. All the main patterns are cheaply available in Kenya, though other equipment should be brought in.

'Big trout are a rarity and a cause of much excitement when located. Recently a club member sighted a brown trout of about four pounds, hard to spot at first as it lay in ripply water behind a thick fallen branch. Again and again a Coachman was drifted past without effect. A change to a nymph soon led to a check on the line. The strike tightened it into the fish, with the member's heart racing in excitement. The trout immediately tangled the cast, apparently hiding under the branch. With one hope left the angler strode forward, pushed the net far below the branch and tried an "under and up". It worked, for the net came out well weighed down – but with a pile of sodden rags. As they waved gently in the current they had nearly deceived many other club members, but only the short-sighted one had spent so much time in pursuit of the inedible. Genuine four-pounders are as much of a rarity, but there is always entertaining fishing to enjoy amid scenery to lift the heart and in the solitude so dear to many fishermen.'

Wheat in the Fields, Trout in the Streams

Southern and Eastern Africa

South Africa

During the early stockings of Africa Lord Delamere wrote to a friend: 'What our settlers need is wheat in their fields and trout in their rivers.' He left his friend the difficult job of getting the trout there, but much of the continent still benefits from the widespread import of that fish.

Now that troubled country, South Africa, still has at least a quiet and peaceful resource in its excellent trout fishing in a wide variety of waters. 'Go a'Angling. Study to be quiet,' wrote Walton in the middle of England's Civil War, and in the time of strife many South Africans too seem to be concentrating on developing the fishing, particularly of small stocked still waters. There are increasing numbers of these up to 25 acres in size, with more than 100 in Natal alone. Often they have trout averaging over two pounds. This was the recent experience of George Westropp, when mixing pleasure with business on a trip from England:

'The accountant from Johannesburg took me fishing near Belfast – not the Ulster version but a rather smaller, warmer Belfast in the Eastern Transvaal.

'My South African Touche Ross partners had suggested that if I would come on a marketing lecture tour of the Republic they would fix a long weekend's dam fishing. The bribe worked a treat and in October 1984 I duly lugged reels, fly boxes, casts and green boots from London to Cape Town, Durban and finally Johannesburg in expectation of a day or two's outdoor relaxation. The four-hour drive east of Johannesburg took us to a landscape rather like dry and parched North York Moors. The big difference lay in the altitude, the strength of the sun and the rich red soil.

'The dams are strung down the farmland hills like strings of blue beads. Few are larger than a few acres but each one I covered that weekend at Dulstroom near Belfast – the self-styled "Rainbow trout capital of South

Africa" – was heavily stocked with rainbows of from one to three pounds. The rainbow trout species has travelled far wider than I, but it still came as a shock to hear of countless farm dams or reservoirs fin-deep in rainbows up in the red hills and plains of the high veldt.

'To say that Peter and Helen Hibbit and the other accountant partners in his syndicate were keen on fishing is an understatement. Hardy rods and reels, dozens of familiar and some unknown fly patterns were all on offer to the visitor and much local advice and hospitality. While I had brought a floating line and a selection of dry flies with me, none of my South African hosts appeared to own such things. Slow-sink and sink-tip lines seemed to be the then current favourites, and I was advised to take their lead.

'Over a drink on our arrival at the Dulstroom Inn, I asked Peter for his views on fishing dry with something big like a G & H Sedge. Some of the bugs flying round that little dorp looked as large as saucers and I reckoned that they had to be on the trout's menu. Well, first my chum had never heard of a G & H Sedge, nor had his partners and, second, he hinted that I should stick to a traditional wet-fly pattern or a lure. Knowing better than the locals has caused me more blank days than I care to remember, but this time I was convinced that I might just be right.

'A stocky and hairy professor from Witwatersrand University virtually fell over with mirth as I tied my biggest Deer-Hair Sedge onto my leader while tackling up at the back of the Hibbits' car. "It won't work, man," he called back, stumping off through the red dust towards the nearest dam with a size 8 Whisky Fly hooked through his top ring.

'The professor was wrong. My first cast resulted in what looked like a fishy underwater version of the Battle of Britain as trout fought to get at the Sedge. I had three fish of over two pounds on the bank within three casts and was wondering whether there was a limit when the Hibbits arrived by my shoulder. The surprise on their faces said everything. However, I had to slow down since the bag per rod on their syndicate dams was restricted to four fish. By lunch time I had been visited by every fisher on that flight of dams and my stock of G & H's had been exhausted.

'My growing number of friends that day found that the fly worked well immediately after casting but lost its efficacy shortly after that. The fast-sinking lines were dragging the Sedge under and negating more than half its attraction.

'Back in the Long Bar of the Dulstroom Inn that evening, I had been transformed from another visiting Brit to a celebrity. The Hibbits spent most of the evening introducing me to other fishers up from Johannesburg for the weekend who wanted to meet the Englishman with the revolutionary dry-line tactics.

'The next day – before and after the most dramatic thunderstorm I have ever witnessed – proved a repeat performance. Take it from me, the South African rainbows think very highly of a floating Sedge.'

John Beams's book *Introducing Fly Fishing in South Africa* is the first of a series of four covering the trout waters of southern Africa. These are Top Farmer publications, 13222 South Coast Road, Mobeni 4060. They all give useful general information. Information on a specific area can be had from pamphlets like *Fresh Water Fishing at the Cape*. This is produced by the Cape Piscatorial Society of Cape Town, founded in 1931. As provincial laws on fishing vary this is a necessary check. For instance, all principal trout fisheries there are designated trout areas and no species of fish may be caught in such areas without a trout licence. Except where special provision is made, as with the Steenbras Reservoir and some dams, trout can only be taken on a 'non-spinning artificial fly'. This is defined as 'a hook with one point and one barb to which is attached matter not edible to fish and which is used without any rotating blade, spinner, or spoon.'

The Steenbras Reservoir was formed when an upland valley above Gordon's Bay was dammed as a reservoir for the city of Cape Town. This created a lake of over 800 acres set amid magnificent scenery. The amber-coloured water, which has a plentiful supply of aquatic insects – notably 'glassworms', the larvae of a midge – aids rapid growth. The trout become two-pounders in their second year, with the brown trout doing best in this prolific fishery.

Trout were first introduced to Natal from Scotland in 1890 when a small hatchery was established in Balgowan. From there several rivers were soon stocked and it is the river fishing that is still the essence of the sport in South Africa, still Natal that is the main centre for trout fishing. The Drakensburg escarpment has many rivers full of trout from the Umzimvubu in the south to the Tugela in the north. Streams in south-west Natal also contain a good head of trout, which thrive above 5,000 feet. Drought is the only threat to fishing in a country where November to March is often too bright and hot for consistently good fishing. The best is in the cool September spring or the rainier autumn period of April and early May.

There are 22 streams in Natal stocked with rainbow trout. The best of the fishing is in the Umzimvubu near Matatiele and in the Ingwangwane, Umzimkulu and Polela in the Underberg-Himeville district. A further 16 rivers have brown trout, with the Umkomaas, Loteni, Moei and Bushman's outstanding. Seven have both rainbow and brown, notably the Inzinga, Mlambonjwa and the Mhlwazeni.

The National Parks, Game and Fish Preservation Board runs three hatcheries, of which the largest is in the Royal Natal National Park with some 300,000 fingerlings being annually sent out from there. The hatchery at Underberg is about a third the size, and the newest hatchery at Kamberg concentrates on bringing on larger fish to stock the dams. Rivers are open for fishing from 1 September to 15 May. Midsummer is the variable time for fly fishing but it can be good in rivers, particularly in the headwaters when they are clearing after rain. There is no closed season in the dams, where winter fishing is often productive.

On most rivers the fish average under a pound, though there are a fair number of that size or up to two pounds. In dams the average is much higher and in both the occasional large trout is landed. The western Cape area has many fast-flowing streams ideal for fly fishing, some in the suburbs of Cape Town itself. The best of the fishing there is in the mountain areas near Worcester and Wellington.

Michael G. Salomon's booklet, *Freshwater Fishing in South Africa: The Complete Guide to Freshwater Fishing*, gives full information about the fishing in the country. Salomon's advice is that dullish-coloured flies are usually best. His own selection includes Walker's Killer, Mrs Simpson, Black Widow, Invicta, March Brown, Hardy's Favourite, Dusty Miller, Gold-Ribbed Hare's Ear and Parson's Glory. He has also designed the Scampy, which has had much success. This is tied on a size 6 hook with black silk. The body is red and yellow chenille, the rib three lengths of peacock herl, the wing and tail yellow-pink bucktail with fur from his toy pom, Scampy (or any gingery fur). There is also a small bunch of toy pom fur at the throat and the head is yellow varnish with gold dust dabbed on. Other local flies recommended are the Vlei Kurper, the Machadodorp and Mike's Secret. Walker's Killer is rated the number-one fly.

As Salomon comments 'Walker's Killer is probably the fly with the best reputation in South Africa. It is principally a daytime fly, at its most effective during the summer months when the water is warm. When wet this fly simulates most of the brown/sepia dragonfly nymphs, which are very common and an important part of the trout's diet.'

Another popular fly is the Tadpole, and the Mickey Finn is rated an excellent cold-water fly with its yellow and scarlet making it an attractor fly and trout hit it hard. Also of this type is the Porringe with the rear half consisting of fluorescent orange and the front half of fluorescent pink floss over which is wound a layer of PVC film. A black silk head and the colourful body make this another successful attractor pattern.

Writing in *The Field* in 1985 Tom Sutcliffe gave this as his experience of South African trout fishing: 'I have fished in many countries and I doubt that trout are more beautifully located anywhere than in the foothills of the Drakensberg or among the granite peaks of the Cape.' Of the fishing itself he wrote:

'Whereas the Cape streams are swift, clean and wadable, the waters in the rest of the Republic, with odd exceptions, are not. Throughout, the water tends to be a greenish ginger-beer colour at best and the rivers are deep and slow. Sudden thunderstorms are inclined to discolour the water for days on end.

'Without doubt the area around the picturesque Eastern Cape village of Barkly East is the best for fly fishing. The colder temperatures are ideally suited to trout, which grow rapidly to trophy proportions in the fertile water of this mountainous district.

'Dozens of rivers provide some 150 miles of the most beautiful and the most underutilized fly fishing in the world. Last season anglers fishing less than a mile from the village took trout of 8lb 14oz and 8lb 3oz on two consecutive days from the same pool, and fish over 4 pounds are commonplace. But, like any other area in the Republic, quality fishing is always dependent on good rainfalls in the previous two or three years.

'In Natal the rivers are especially good in autumn, when fish of two to three pounds are not exceptional. While most of the water is in the hands of private owners, fishing is inexpensive and remarkably easy to come by for the visitor. These streams tend to be slower-flowing and most of the fishing is done from the bank because opportunities for wading are few.

'The techniques of the local anglers vary considerably, with a tendency to move away from the time-honoured use of large traditional wet flies like the Invicta, Connemara Black or Walker's Killer fished downstream on a sinking line. The more modern approach favours a light or medium floating line, fishing a variety of nymphs and Woolly-Worm patterns on a free drift. The technique is much the same here as anywhere else in the world of freestone streams: it is to fish up and across, let the fly drift until it is downstream, then lift to hope for an induced take and cast again.'

The greatest concentration of trout fishing is in the Underberg-Himeville area with facilities available through the Natal Parks Board, the Department of Forestry, the Underberg-Himeville Trout Fishing Club and the Kwa-Zulu Government Service. The same agencies and the Natal Fly Fishers' Club arrange facilities for the Mpendle, Lions River and Mooi River districts. There are some good rivers and a few dams in the Estcourt and Bergville disticts, with the local club the Natal Midlands Fly Fishing Club.

The main rules:

1   In the scheduled trout waters, details of which are available from the Natal Parks Board on request, only artificial, non-spinning flies (commonly known as trout flies) may be used, along with a rod and reel. Fixed spool reels are prohibited, and no more than three hooks may be employed on any one line.

2   The bag limit for trout in trout waters is ten fish of over 200 mm.

3   A licence, obtainable from most magistrates and sporting goods dealers, is essential for all freshwater fishing in Natal. In addition, the permission of the riparian owner must be obtained. A charge is levied for fishing in Natal Parks Board reserves and state forest waters, as well as those controlled by fishing clubs. The cost of a day's fishing seldom exceeds R2,00.

Some useful addresses are:

The Director
Natal Parks, Game and Fish Preservation Board,
PO Box 662,
Pietermaritzburg
3200
The Board is responsible for administering all inland fishing in Natal as well as offering anglers facilities in the game and nature reserves under its control.

Secretary,
Underberg-Himeville Trout Fishing Club, PO Underberg
4590

Secretary, Natal Fly Fishers' Club,
PO Box 1535,
Pietermaritzburg
3200

Secretary,
Midlands Fly Fishing Club,
c/o M. Moor Esq.,
'Avalon',
PO Estcourt
3310

Regional Director,
Department of Forestry,
Private Bag 9029,
Pietermaritzburg
3200

Department of Community Affairs,
Kwa Zulu Government Service,
Private Bag XO2,
Ulundi
3838

With helpful advice and information available from such sources the visitor can enjoy excellent trout fishing.

Zimbabwe

Zimbabwe has a great variety of fish and many keen anglers, including some seventy fishing clubs with more than ten thousand members. With clear waters and little pollution, the many thriving species include the ubiquitous tigerfish, carp, barbel, bream, black bass, hunyani salmon, and smallmouth yellowfish running up to twenty pounds. Only for trout are there close seasons, though the cool winter season from May to August is apt to put the others off their feed. In Chimanimani National Park the trout season runs from 1 October to 1 April, in other streams and rivers to 1 May, but Mare and Rhodes dams are open all year. Only in the above two dams can you fish through the winter for any of the three species of trout in Zimbabwe, which has brook trout as well as brown and rainbow. The charges for trout fishing are minimal and permits can most easily be obtained from local wardens' offices at Inyanga and Chimanimani.

For information there is a helpful pamphlet, *Zimbabwe Fishing*, prepared by the Tourist Board. More can be obtained from the central body, the Zimbabwe National Anglers Union, or the largest club, the Zimbabwe Angling Society in Bulawayo. As usual, the trout fishing is confined to the higher levels with the downlands and mountains of the Eastern Highlands providing high-quality trout fishing in wild and beautiful surroundings. This is on the border of Mozambique, which also benefits from trout in this area, though the sport remains undeveloped there. Rainbows are the dominant species with the record for this area one of eight pounds, while 6½ pounds is the largest recorded weight for a brown.

The most exciting and testing of the fishing is in the Chimanimani National Park high up in the Chimanimani mountains. There the spectacular views, the arresting scenery, the plentiful trout in fast streams are the reward for effort. There is no access road and you have to hike in to base yourself in mountain chalet accommodation. Remote and lonely, beautiful and absorbing, the Chimanimani fishing is worth the hard climb.

The Inyanga region provides the bulk of the good fishing in stream and a variety of manmade lakes such as Mare, Rhodes, and Purdon dams or Lake Gulliver in the Rhodes Inyanga National Park. There are also hotels which have their own fishing, as with Lake Troutbeck and Loch Moodie. The largest trout are to be found in the Purdon dam and Lake Gulliver. All the main lakes and rivers in the area are kept well stocked, particularly the Mare and Rhodes dams and the Pungwe, Inyamgombe, Marora, and Mare rivers. The main trout hatchery is just downstream of the Mare dam in the

Rhodes Inyanga National Park and is open to the public most days, with thousands of rainbows, browns, and brook trout in the large ponds. Fishery research and development has high priority for trout and is carried out by the Department of National Parks and Wild Life Management. In most of the trout-fishing areas there is good hotel accommodation as well as lodges, cottages, and caravan and camping sites.

In the Inyanga area there are several private lakes and streams where it may be possible to fish on payment of a fee. The Troutbeck Inn and the Montclair Hotel also own well-stocked private lakes available to hotel guests.

Fishing methods and flies are as elsewhere in Southern Africa, with Walker's Killer, Wilber, Wildcat, Coachman, Kemp's Favourite, Invicta and Coch-y-Bondhu among the favoured flies. All trout fishing is fly-only and for the fly fisherman there is a promise of excellent sport.

Malawi and Zambia

Malawi and Zambia both have trout fishing of interest, though not of the quality of South Africa or Kenya. In Malawi there is still trout fishing to be enjoyed today on Zomba plateau in the Mlungusi stream and a 3-acre dam, which in theory at least is controlled by the Forestry Department in Zomba. The season is from September to March, fly only with size limits for the stream and dam. The area is easy of access and tends to be overfished. The stream is a typical mountain one, fast, rocky and liable to floods or very low conditions. It holds plenty of trout but mostly small, up to about 8 inches long. Some good trout up to three pounds or so may be taken from the dam but they are well educated and not easy to tempt. Tickets can sometimes be obtained from the fish guard on duty.

There is also trout fishing to be had in streams in the game park on the Nyika plateau in the north. This is a most attractive part of Malawi, high grass-covered slopes reminiscent of a large, wild Salisbury Plain with an interesting selection of wild animals to be seen. But roads in the north are poor and frequently impassable in the rains. Here too the fishing is restricted, and controlled by the park warden. The trout are mostly small but not overfished, as tends to be the case on Zomba plateau.

As in other African countries, there is also good fishing to be had for indigenous fish, either in the Shire river or Lake Malawi (Nyasa). There is also a species of fish known as 'lake salmon' (*Barilus Microcephalus* and *B. Microlepis*) which run up some rivers to spawn. The local name is Sanjika, but they have been decimated by fish traps, nets and poison in several of their spawning rivers, particularly the Luega. They can be caught on large flies or spinners and fishing can still be obtained in the Bua river, which runs through a game park and is very strictly controlled. Tickets are expensive and fish caught must be returned.

On the Zambian side of the Nyika plateau, north of Chipata, there was an experimental stocking a few seasons ago. Rainbow trout were put into the headwaters of the Shire River, and such developments may improve the trout fishing. The Nyika is the best area for both Zambia and Malawi. Information about the fishing may be obtained from the Noirande Angling Society, PO Box 102, Blantyre, Malawi.

Tanzania

Jonathan Niblett enjoys the fishing in another African country. Tanzania is no exception to the changing conditions in Africa, where deforestation, poaching and population increase can affect rivers and the quality of fishing. Changing administrations also alter fishing regulations overnight. It is therefore useless to advise on permits, fees, licences, and so forth. The intending fisherman must ask around and find out for himself. The charges, however, are ridiculously cheap.

A knowledge of some basic Kiswahili is a great advantage, but generally you will find Europeans living in the highland areas where trout are to be found. Talk to every person you meet in likely country and soon you will find yourself on a river bank.

In Tanzania few seem to realize that trout are protected, and that the intending fisherman requires permission to fish and a trout licence, which can be purchased from the fisheries division of each district centre. One licence should cover all trout fishing in Tanzania, but you need to check in each district.

The biggest problem in a country as huge as Tanzania is transport. Public transport is rare and hitch-hiking is at best problematic, except along main roads. Once in a trout area, it is possible to walk, so travel light. The lucky ones will have the use of a four-wheel-drive vehicle.

As a country Tanzania has everything to delight the visitor from the highest mountain in Africa to the superb beaches along the Indian Ocean, from hundreds of square miles of fine rolling highlands to great areas of lowland wilderness with game reserves of every kind. There are cattle land, rivers and vast swamps for fisheries and rice growing, forests and deserts and very few people.

It is indeed a most beautiful land, full of contrast and history, and it is still young, waiting to be sensibly developed.

Development of trout fishing began long ago. Trout ova were first imported by sea in 1924 and hatched by the Forestry Department in the Usambara and Pare streams and two years later a further consignment of ova was successfully hatched and stocked on the rivers flowing off Kilimanjaro and Meru mountains. Ten years later, in 1934, a hatchery was built, again by the Forestry Department, in Mufindi and the resulting fry stocked in Mufindi and Njombe streams. By this time Imperial Airways were landing at Mbeya, the provincial capital of the Southern Highlands, and streams in Mbeya and Rungwe districts were stocked with ova from South Arica. Further importations of ova from Kenya, South Africa and England took place after the war. Only recently were brood fish at Mufindi stripped and a hatchery operated from scratch. Streams and dams were also stocked by catching wild fish and transporting them by head load, horse and Land-Rover to virgin streams.

All trout fishing is in the highland areas above 5,000 feet. The streams are therefore neither very large, nor very long. With few exceptions they are of the torrent type – fast and rocky with deep holes and pots and some fine waterfalls. In the north, trout streams drop down off the mountains through forest whilst in the south many flow through rolling moorlands before tumbling down through gorges.

When you approach trout country there will be more people around and the hot, dry and dusty bush will give way to maize fields and little patches of wheat and potatoes. Plum and peach blossom show white and pink in the small gardens and the cattle and sheep will be fatter because of better grazing. Tea and coffee estates will appear and plantations of pine and eucalyptus trees may be seen along the hillsides. In the south the pale yellow mimosa and the black wattle will be everywhere.

The rivers themselves, unless you have seen rain in the hills above, will be clear, as they run over rock and gravel. If the banks are covered with brambles and bracken, so much the better; if you notice pale, oval and pinnate fronds of osmunda – the royal fern – overhanging the water, trout should be there. A streamside path is a hopeful sign, as are trodden down stances by obvious lies. Any angler will be fishing for trout, because in these highland waters trout are the only fish, other than very small mountain cat-fish (*Clarias* spp) and a tiny golden minnow (*Barbus* sp). Look too for little scraps of muddy polythene. These are the worm bags of the local fisherman, who cuts his 5-foot rod from the bush on his way down to the water. He may have a home-made reel fashioned from a tin or cotton reel, but other than cheap hooks, fishing tackle is unobtainable in Tanzania. On the larger private farms and estates there may also be dams that have been recently stocked with trout. The information is easily found at the farm.

Rainbow trout in order to reach maturity at two years will eat anything that comes along. There are few ephemerids in these torrent streams and the main food supply is freshwater crabs, small fish, caddis and any terrestrials, such as beetles, flying ants and grasshoppers. In the dams dragonfly and damsel nymphs, pond olives, caddis and snail are generally abundant, along with small trout and *Barbus kerstenii*, a small minnow. After heavy rain flying ants falling on to the water provoke the trout into reckless feeding, but for a day or two afterwards they are dour and satiated. A big pale Partridge and Yellow or a white deer-hair Hedgehog Fly are good patterns to use during a fall of ant.

The best times for fishing are early in the morning, an hour or so either side of midday, and lastly during the final two hours of daylight. Remember that darkness falls quickly at around seven o'clock, so make sure you are back on a familiar path before nightfall. If you get 'bushed' in thick forest stay put until next morning: not a nice experience and you will get hungry, cold and wet and give your friends a heart attack.

In the north you may be confronted by dangerous game. Don't panic, withdraw quietly downwind, or stay still. Among such are elephant, rhino, hippopotamus, buffalo, lion and leopard. You will not find crocodiles in trout streams, but keep an eye open for snakes.

Trout fishing is possible all the year round in the north, since there is no definite breeding season. Trout will spawn as they become mature at any time of year, for water temperatures remain constant. The months of March, April and May are best avoided as the heavier rains occur at this season.

The local inhabitants do much damage by poisoning the bigger and slower pools using plants of the euphorbia family that contain rotenone. However, because of the swift flows, the poison is rapidly diluted and not all fish are killed and others drop down from upstream. The trout stock slowly recovers until the population is large enough for the poachers to try again in about two or three years. Any stream may therefore hold either many small fish, or a few pounders, or the odd whopper, or nothing at all. Just try fishing and find out.

The principal areas follow the road from Arusha to Tanga on the coast and are as follows:

MOUNT MERU. NEAREST TOWN: ARUSHA   A good base for fishing the streams that come off Mount Meru and also West Kilimanjaro. All the streams are small and heavily bushed. Trout-holding streams are the Teme river and the Nduruma.

USA RIVER. NEAREST TOWN: ARUSHA   The Abu Sero Rest-House operates a trout farm and has fishing in their dam. Roads good.

MOUNT KILIMANJARO. NEAREST TOWN: MOSHI   There are two hotels at Marangu, the Marangu and the Kibu, who will help you find fishing. These are the starting-points for the mountain climbers and are well organized for tourists. The rivers are medium-sized and were controlled by the Kilimanjaro Fishing Club. Most run through coffee country in steepish gorges. Roads are good to fair. Trout-holding streams are the Kikafu (the only brown-trout river in Tanzania), Mue, Ona, Mchili and the Ngare Nairobi in West Kilimanjaro.

PARE MOUNTAINS. NEAREST TOWN: MOSHI A few streams in wild country hold trout. Camping gear essential. Roads poor.

USUMBARA MOUNTAINS. NEAREST TOWN: LUSHOTO The Mgambo and Mkussi streams used to hold trout and may still do so. Roads fair.

In the south only four districts ever held trout, but one of them, Njombe District, probably boasted the most perfect trout fishing in any of the three East African territories. In the south there is a definite winter that provides ideal spawning conditions and the climate is similar to that found throughout Southern Africa. There are four seasons: December to March, warm and wet; April to May, cold and wet; June to August, cold and dry; September to November, warm and dry.

Fly fishing in the streams is impracticable between February and April because of heavy water, but dams can be fished at any time. From mid-May trout become gravid. Spawning reaches its peak in July and trout are back in condition again by mid-September. Although there are no legal close seasons trout fishing should not be attempted from mid-May until the beginning of September.

For streams the visitor's fishing tactics are simple. If no information is forthcoming, begin with a worm or a small silver Mepps just to find out if the trout are present. Once found, stick to the wet fly. Rainbow trout lie deep, so use a quick-sinking line. They are also greedy, so use big flies – size 6, 8 or 10 – except in the small moorland burns. Fish up or down as conditions demand, but always try to fish deep and slow. Don't fish finer than 5 pounds BS.

The dams are fly-only. Normal stillwater tactics and flies work well. Unlike fishing in the UK, the stiller and calmer the water the better the fishing. Floating line and long rods help to solve the water-lily problems. Use 7-pound leaders in normal water and anything up to 12 pounds in heavily weeded ones. Many trout can be hand-lined out of weedbeds if strong casts are used.

Whether fishing in stream or dam, wading is essential, but only in Mufindi are waders useful. Everywhere else just use good rough-soled boots or shoes. Ignore landing nets – they are a nuisance along bushy streams.

Trout fishing in Tanzania is not sufficiently organized to merit a holiday for that purpose alone, but the country has so much else to offer and the fishing can provide a fascinating sideline, as the following story written for

the Journal of the Mufindi Rod and Gun Club by a traveller who found
himself stranded there for a few days illustrates:

'Mufindi came to mind. I had been there on business some six months ago
and had enjoyed a very fine evening rise on a trout pond with Jonathan
Niblett. Some quick phone calls to EAA and Iringa to arrange for a hire car
and flight and to warn John and Mary that they were shortly to be invaded
and off I went.

'Mufindi is a tea-growing area with a population of forty, addicted to
coffee and Scotch. Other prevalent diseases in the area are golf, rugby,
tennis, a very keen sense of hospitality and, of course, the fishing bug.
How the people there manage, with so many vices, to grow the best tea in
the land, to maintain such beautiful gardens and factories and roads and
dams is a subject of permanent wonder to me. The dams, of course, were
my main concern.

'I had hardly arrived before John was driving me along a maze of roads
to a little pond named Lulanje. He apologized about the season not being
right as we are only emerging from the Mufindi winter and the trout are
not yet very active. On arriving at the pond, John made me tie on a fly of
his own making which is an imitation of the dragonfly nymph. Very soon
after that he had a trout dancing on the water. He landed it and it was a
good pound in weight. I did not start connecting until he called me over to
where he discovered the trout had concentrated in some weed. Very
gallantly, John made me fish that spot and moved on down to where I had
not been having luck. Suddenly the action became frantic. Six casts
bagged me four fish, two of which were well over the two-pound mark.

'It was a strange fight these fish gave you. They took the fly with the
casual greed of large trout and immediately headed for the sky in four-foot
leaps. The next thing you knew they were boring into the weeds and
creating a fabulous tangle. Only strong nylon, which fortunately I had,
could coax them out to the waiting net.

'The next day I tried Lake Ngwazi for bass. They were not very active,
at least not the large ones, and I only managed four one-pounders on a
floating Rapala. The African kids were hauling out stringers of smaller
bass yet. Nothing much really, but fun, as I had never caught a bass before
and, besides, I had returned to the Lulanje dam just before and caught two
more trout, one of which was 2 lb 5 oz.

'The third and last day was the best trout-size-wise. Lulanje gave me
two big ones before lunch, weighing 2 lb 5 oz and 2 lb 7 oz. The pond also
gave me a dunking when I tried to wade out and stepped into a hole. The
farewell flick came from the tail of a third large fish, who made the most
beautiful jump ever and escaped with the point of my hook.

'That evening I tried for the evening rise in Luisenga, a large body of water with the fishing lodge set beside it amongst the pines. There were no risers until late and then again too small to be much worth trying for. But it did not matter because as evening drew close frogs began to call to each other, an ape laughed at me from somewhere nearby and, for the first time in many months, I heard a hyrax. His rattle was soon answered by others, many many others. For ten minutes they kept the concert going and then went off. Some time later one of them gave the tone again; he tried three times, but none of the others would have it. "Time up" their silence seemed to say. I strolled into the lodge when it was already quite dark. I sipped a beer John had brought down as a great big fire crackled at me. I began to feel really warm. Still do.'

13

Faraway Places

Sri Lanka, Kashmir, India, Pakistan, and Japan

There are many distant lands into which keen anglers introduced their favourite trout, despite impossible obstacles. There are others in which they were fortunate to find the wild variety already established, the sport of fly fishing ready for development. In two such faraway places the effort to introduce trout was rewarded with fishing in surroundings of remarkable beauty as the British stocked browns into the highland streams and lakes of old Ceylon in 1882, and surmounted even greater difficulties to introduce them into Kashmir.

Ceylon

Graham Swanson has enjoyed fishing in modern Sri Lanka and gives this account of how it has developed more than a hundred years later:

'After that original stocking the trout grew big and gave good sport, fish to fourteen pounds being taken, but temperature was too high for them to spawn successfully. Initially ova were imported privately, later with government support; but with the failure to breed they withdrew their aid. So in 1896 the famous Ceylon Fishing Club was formed. With no indigenous fish of commercial importance in waters above 4,000 feet, the government was happy to lease these to the club and legislated to protect the introduced trout. In 1899 rainbow ova were introduced; these stream-dwelling shastas from California found the waters to their liking and they were soon breeding freely, especially in the stream on Horton Plains. This *was* the premier trout stream, especially for rods up from the low country and visitors, though many other streams were stocked and fished mainly by the planters of local estates, who ensured that the streams were well watched – fish being the main meat ingredient of the local population's curry!

'The club thrived, with prodigious catches of trout from what old fishing club reports claimed were some of the finest and cheapest waters in the world. Independence came in 1948 and the Republic of Sri Lanka was proclaimed in 1973. Inevitably the European community dwindled and few Sri Lankans, with notable exceptions, were interested in the sport. Club finances suffered, the fishing deteriorated. Village expansion, timber felling, agriculture and illegal gem digging all contributed to the silting of the streams. Then in 1958 the Government Wild Life Department declared the Horton Plains a game sanctuary and nature reserve, which it is to this day. So rainbow trout can still wax large to breed in the stream. Although we have lived in Sri Lanka for four and a half years, I have only visited the Horton Plains five times – twice to fish, but mainly to research this and other writings. The only way to be sure of anything is to see for oneself, such is the nature of the locals to please by telling you what you want to hear. But the peace and beauty of these plains is well worth the logistics of making the expedition to the little Belihul Oya (stream) which meanders and tumbles through five miles of the deserted Horton Plains. There is a rest-house right next the stream, called the Farr Inn after the famous planter, angler and conservationist Thomas Farr. Now run by the Ceylon Hotels Corporation, who manage most of the best situated rest-houses, it is great fun and the only place for the serious stream angler to stay. By all means visit also the Hill Club in Nuwera Eliya, admire the great trout in glass cases, dine (do not forget your tie), sit by a roaring log fire and find a hot-water bottle in your bed – it may well be frosty outside.

'The Horton Plains are a large area of fairly level patna grass, surrounded by jungle-clad hills rising a further 1,800 feet above the 7,000-foot plateau, or plunging almost vertically to tea estates 3,000 feet below. The grass has formed a 3-foot spongy layer over the reddish-brown laterite clay and gravels, and as on Britain's Exmoor this layer absorbs the heaviest rainfall and releases it to the stream as very clear water. Fishing was said to be best during heavy monsoon rain, when the water rises several feet and yet stays spring clear. Numerous rhododendrons blaze red in May, amidst orchids, gentians, harebells, buttercups and yellow-flowered potentilla-like shrubs. For company there is very rarely another angler, just teal and snipe and other birds, particularly raptors. From the jungle you will hear the bark of sambhur and the growl of bear-monkeys. Elephants no longer roam the hill country and the leopard is said to be harmless to humans. There is no midge problem, though a bottle of locally available Tik will ward off nocturnal mosquitoes as well as grassland ticks.

'The fishing water available to tourists starts about 25 minutes' hike below the inn, though a vehicle can be taken half this distance. From here the water extends another three miles to finally plunge over falls to the low country. Given time, I strongly suggest a day spent walking the whole stream; it takes two hours down and somewhat longer back as the altitude takes its toll. Besides savouring the beauty, one can also spot fish. To catch one of the bigger trout of 2–3 pounds is a stalking game, as they do not rise. Apart from wading the shallow lakes of the western highlands of Tasmania, the only time I use polaroids for angling is during this initial recce. The stream, which alternates between rocky runs and slower reaches above the numerous huge pools, lies well below as one follows the old planters' tracks along its course. Sit and watch a likely pool and eventually a monster will betray his presence by a swirl. The reddish bottom makes fish difficult to see, but once spotted his beat or lie can be noted. In May 1986, after an unsuccessful friend was told "all fish poisoned, Master" (to console him no doubt), I spent a whole morning walking the stream, and besides seeing numerous smaller fish rising – probably taking snail – there is no worthwhile daytime fly life – I marked down at least six good fish. Alas, I could not fish the following day, and the usual peal of distant thunder was heard at 1 p.m. Descending mists and rain chased me all the way back to the rest-house, certain that the stream was still well stocked.

'These afternoon storms are the reason for staying at the rest-house. Be up at six to see the mists burn off to reveal countless sambhur grazing at the jungle's edge whilst your breakfast and packed lunch is prepared. Your obligatory game guard will call for you at 8 a.m. For just a morning's fishing, go down to Sunken Rock Pool, just above Baker's Falls, where the redoubtable Sir Samuel Baker once killed his hunted sambhur, at bay on a ledge in the falls. This will take about 50 minutes from the rest-house, and give you four really large pools to fish, numerous smaller ones, and several runs which look ideal for dry fly but are not except during the short dusk when the proverbial white moth ventures forth. But there are also superb pools below Baker's Falls – Governor's, Old Gem Pit, Tiger, Hunter's Crossing, to name but a few, if you are prepared for a possible soaking in the afternoon. You fish essentially upstream, but cast in any direction which suits. The idea is to work towards shelter, should the rains come down, which is usually about midday during the best season from May to October. Fish spawn during the coolest months of November and December, but there is no close season, nor any rule as to bait, method or limit. I find a largish wet fly, such as a Peter Ross, retrieved fairly quickly in likely spots will have fish darting out to grab it, but this has no appeal for me. Numerous 10-inch fish do rise during late morning and I find a black gnat good, though hard to connect with. This makes me suspect the fish are taking snails hanging on the surface. That they will take a Pheasant Tail Nymph as it hits the surface substantiates this. But I prefer to stalk my previously marked fish, and again find a well presented PTN is good medicine. My best fish was a 2½-pound rainbow, spotted on a previous photographic mission, cruising as one of a pair in the aptly named Leg of Mutton Pool. This is made shallow by a dense layer of "asparagus weed", a form of curly-leaved pond weed, I think. At 9 a.m. two dorsal fins showed their cruising circuits and at this time the next day I was in position. Twice she passed me within feet on her 50-yard-diameter circuit. On her second pass my cast was just too short, but twenty minutes later my second seemed just right, but to my dismay it produced a terrific swirl under my line tip. Then seconds later my leader drew under – I must have spooked her unseen mate. Her recent diet consisted of one dragonfly larva, a grasshopper, two grubs and 96 per cent little black beetles. The PTN is a fly of many parts.

'The visitor has two ways of getting to the plains. Hire a car (cheaper with driver, and he will be a great help and worth his eventual tip – he will find his own quarters and victuals). Insist that he take you by the scenic, but tortuous, A7, built to serve the rubber and tea estates, via the valley of the Kelani Gunga (river) and the tea-growing townships of Hatton and Nanu Oya. From Nanu Oya you can either drive another 20 minutes to the Hill Club, or make the one-hour and 1,500-foot climb to the plains, passing the Kande Ele dam and following the once famous Ambawela stream. You can return to Colombo by the popular road and visit Kandy, but the traffic and driving may well scare the wits out of you. The alternative is to take the early morning "express" from Colombo. The first-class (bookable) observation coach gives splendid views of paddy, rubber, mountain, tea and river. If you care to hike for 1½ hours, ascending 1,200 feet, alight at Ohiya, otherwise continue to Nanu Oya, where bus or taxi will take you to Nuwera Eliya. There, having stayed at the Hill Club, a suitable vehicle can be hired (the roads may be impassable by car) and advice is available on where to obtain permits. For these visit the trout hatchery and ask for Francis Cruze, a Christian Tamil who is in charge and does all the breeding and stocking. He will also be your expert angling companion if you can transport him.

'In 1982 the Government were only interested in growing food fish for the nation, not luxury sport fish. But since then they have imported rainbow ova from New Zealand, to be hatched in Fowkes's original hatchery and grown on in cages in Kende Ele Dam for the hotel trade. Some have been released for boat (outrigger canoe) fishing, and the lake at the near New Zealand Cattle Farm, made by damming the Ambawela stream, has also been stocked, and can be fished at the stream entrance from the bank or from a canoe. The famous Portswood Dam, near Nuwera Eliya, which was *the* big-fish still water, delightfully set amid the tea, has recently been restocked. Unfortunately it is also full of carp, and I could only hook these when I tried it with fly. Permission is required here; the two dams are free for all. For the Horton Plains the Wild Life Department's ranger, whose office is on the right just before the Farr Inn, issues permits to enter the reserve and fish – 250 rupees a day for tourists (9 US dollars) and 100 for residents. The latter can also fish the famous beats above and nearer the rest-house.

'All you require are a trout rod with a suitable floating line, some largish traditional wet flies, some nymphs and dry flies, and perhaps a grass-hopper imitation. A net is useful and a rush bass can be bought to keep the catch in. The guard will carry your lunch, cameras and liquid refreshment. Leave the beer to later; it is very good but potent, and you will probably be drying yourself out in front of a log fire by mid-afternoon anyway. I use a Kelly kettle (an Irish device which will boil a kettle of stream water – quite pure – in minutes, using twigs) to make tea. Beware of sunstroke – wear a shady hat and protect your arms. Light slacks and trainers are ideal for walking, scrambling and wading, and try and get one of the colourful plastic capes worn by the pretty tea-plucking girls. It is only a plastic sack slit down one side, but tied under the chin with coir twine it will keep you drier on the way back to base camp.'

Kashmir

For my brother Philip the thought of fishing for trout in Kashmir was so attractive that recently he arranged a rewarding visit there with his family, undeterred by the difficulties of planning from afar. This was his experience:

'When we had to leave the Sudan prior to Independence in 1956, a friend of mine joined the Foreign Service and was posted to Lahore in India. I joined an oil company operating in the Middle East. In 1970 we met up in Abu Dhabi where he told me that in 1958 he and his wife had gone trout fishing in Kashmir. During the previous four years, no fishing had been permitted. Neither of them were experienced anglers but they caught a large number of trout, averaging some two pounds with fish up to six pounds. I decided then that, when opportunity arose, I must go there, too. In 1974, when I was in Baghdad, I read an article recently published in *Country Life* about trout fishing in Kashmir. The author and his three companions, in ten days' fishing, had "killed 86 trout averaging a pound and a half, and returned at least 150 of a pound. The three best fish averaged 3¼ pounds." With this additional spur, I started to plan a trip to Kashmir for the spring of 1975.

'Making arrangements from Baghdad was no simple matter and, as events were to prove, not everything went according to plan. I made the bookings through travel agents in Delhi, obtained some helpful infor-mation about trout fishing from the Government of India Tourist Office, and also wrote to H. Goffara & Sons, merchants of Srinagar who sell fishing tackle and generally cater for visiting anglers. Our plan was to drive to Kuwait, fly Kuwaiti Airways to Delhi, thence by local flight to Srinagar, where we would spend the night on a deluxe houseboat on the Dal Lake. We would then have four nights at Yanyar Lodge in the Lidder valley, fishing the Lidder and the Kotus, followed by six nights at Kokernag Lodge in the Bringhi valley, fishing the Bringhi, Kokernag and Verinag rivers. Then back to Srinagar and the houseboat for a couple of nights, before returning to Delhi for visits to the Taj Mahal and other places.

'There were four of us in the party, myself, my wife and two daughters, Carol and Julia. Much of my time in Iraq was spent in Basrah and it was from there that we drove to Kuwait. Aware that imported alcohol was unobtainable in India, and local substitutes not highly recommended, we each took the one bottle of spirits allowed through Indian customs, but as we approached the Kuwait border I remembered that Kuwait was dry and all alcoholic imports strictly prohibited. I hoped my explanation would satisfy the Kuwaiti customs officials. But my company car and driver were well known to them and no questions were asked. Before catching our plane we dined at one of the luxury hotels in Kuwait town. Dinner, of course, was unaccompanied by wine but it was possible, at a price, to obtain a pot of "cold tea" to which could be added water or soda according to taste!

'On arrival at Delhi airport in the early morning of 1 May, we were met by a helpful representative from the agents who collected our luggage. It was soon evident that something had gone wrong with one of Carol's cases. Her bottle of gin had broken, so all her underwear had to be hung up to dry around the airport lounge while we waited for our flight to Srinagar, where we duly arrived in time for lunch on our houseboat.

'Kashmir is a popular tourist centre and has much to offer apart from trout fishing. The scenery, with the Himalayas in the background, is unsurpassed; guided climbs or treks through the mountains and valleys or sightseeing drives to places such as Gulmarg (which boasts the highest golfcourse in the world) or Sonamarg ("Meadow of Gold") offer much variety; wintersports, watersports, shooting or viewing big and small game are all available according to season; and a few days of comparative idleness on a deluxe houseboat on the Dal or Naga lakes, looked after by a bearer with his turban, white uniform, cummerbund and white gloves, exactly as in the days of the British Raj, is an unusual and memorable experience. It is said that in the distant past, when Kashmir was ruled by a maharajah, he decreed that no foreigner should build on his land; and that was why the British who wanted to spend their local leaves up in the hills conceived the idea of building houseboats on the water. But this does not protect their occupants from the local traders, who do the rounds of the houseboats in "shikaras" (rather like gondolas), peddling their wares with much persistence – flowers, fruit, vegetables and assorted stores – or inviting you to be peacefully punted round the lake, resting on cushions under an awning. Others come to offer cloth and materials for suits and dresses to be cut to measure, fitted and tailored within two days in Srinagar's "Saville Row". The town itself offers a wide variety of articles to purchase – carpets woven in the local factory, embroidery, silk, papier mâché and much besides.

'It was in about 1900 that brown trout were first introduced into Kashmir. The ova were brought from England, without benefit of refrigeration in those days, followed by a difficult overland journey to Kashmir – a remarkable feat. But the ova survived and hatched, and the fry they produced have thrived and multiplied in many of the rivers and lakes of Kashmir. The rivers are of two types, the snow-fed streams such as the Lidder, Bringhi, Sindh and Kishenganga, on which the season is from 15 March to 30 September; and the smaller spring-fed streams such as Kotus, Verinag and Kokernag, where the season runs from 15 April to 15 October. Most of these streams flow into the Jhelum, the main river of Kashmir, in which there is said to be good Mahseer fishing. The lakes lie high up in the mountains, twelve to thirteen thousand feet, and can only be reached by driving to the end of the motorable roads and "then by Pack Pony March with own-camping equipment, or can be hired", as my guide book described it. According to one account I read, "the trout average four pounds", and the lake-sides are carpeted in wild flowers in spring and wild duck congregate there in autumn.

'The best fishing in the snow-fed streams is in April and then in August and September. The rivers run steeply down the valleys, the pools are mostly short and rocky, and when the snows are melting between mid-May and mid-July the rivers, particularly in late afternoon, tend to become a rushing torrent, and are also subject to timber-floating. The rivers are divided into beats, for which bookings can be made from 2 January each year. The number of rods per beat is restricted, usually to two, and a watcher is always on duty to ensure that regulations are observed and the catches recorded at the end of the day in his troutbook. Licensed Shikaris (gillies) are also available for individual rods at a small daily fee. Under regulations made in 1961, each beat, or stretch of river, had a size limit laid down, usually 25 or 30 centimetres, more on a few beats. There was a limit of six fish per rod per day and all fish over the size limit had to be kept and count against the limit, smaller fish being returned. Spinning is permitted in certain specified rivers or beats, but in most places it is strictly fly only, and notices, composed by some Kashmiri poet, abound: "Spinning is Sinning" or "To Spin is to Sin".

'Having lunched on the houseboat, I set off to find Mr Goffara, obtain our fishing licences, stock up on tackle and check the arrangements. There had been a problem. Although the lodges at Yanyar and Kokernag had been booked, and my programme listed the rivers we were to fish, the beats themselves had not been booked by the agents. Fortunately, Mr Goffara had discovered this and had taken it upon himself to make some bookings. It had been too late by then to get a beat on any of the spring-fed streams, but beats were booked on the Lidder round Yanyar Lodge, and subsequently on the Bringhi. As the beats on the upper Bringhi were some distance from Kokernag Lodge, Mr Goffara had arranged that, after two days at Kokernag, we would transfer to Dandipura Lodge, higher up the valley, for the last four days, and this was to prove a fortunate arrangement. Then there was another problem. The agents had said they would book a driver and car to stay with us throughout our time in Kashmir, and a cook "to look after all your gastronomic requirements". The driver and car were there, but no cook, so Mr Goffara arranged one and supplied the necessary provisions, including live hens and ducks.

'Next morning our driver turned up in good time and we embarked with all our luggage and fishing gear. There was of course no room for the cook and his livestock, and he was left to follow later by bus. Like most Kashmiris, our driver's name was Gul and an admirable fellow he was, courteous, friendly, willing and most helpful. His driving was no more nerve-wracking than that of all the other Kashmiri drivers with whom we nearly collided, and we soon accepted the probability that he had an instinct for survival on the roads. Yanyar Lodge is some 80 kilometres from Srinagar, sparsely furnished and with very primitive cooking facilities, but these did not upset the cook when he arrived later in the day.

'When my friend from the Sudan had fished in Kashmir in 1958, he also had stayed at Yanyar Lodge and told us about a shikari known as Balu, the Bear-man. Balu in his younger days had been attacked by a Himalayan bear and, in the ensuing fight, had been badly scarred about the face and arms. We wondered if he would still be there. Not long after our arrival the watcher came to check our licences, explain the beats and offer us the service of shikaris. Among them, unmistakably, was Balu, a powerful, imposing man who proved to be an excellent gillie.

'Next day we set off early with our shikaris, two to a beat. The river was beginning to run fast with snow-water and a well-sunk fly was needed. We soon caught trout but many were small. If a trout was landed that appeared to be near the size limit, the shikari, trying to be helpful, would immediately pronounce "Good-size fish", and we felt obliged to kill it. So we caught our limits early, several of them of questionable size, and had to stop. That afternoon I cut four measuring-sticks to a generous length and next morning handed them to our shikaris to measure any doubtful capture before it was pronounced "Good-size fish". Thereafter the average size of the fish we kept improved! The days in early May were warm and bright, under clear skies, but the nights were cold and chilly. So too were the river waters and we had no waders but waded where necessary in our sand-shoes. While we were fishing our driver collected wood and chopped it up for the cook's stove and lit a fire to keep us warm in the evenings. There was no electricity and after supper we either read or played cards by the light of candles, or pressure-lamps when we could get them to work. We made no memorable catches. Our best fish was a little over two pounds, and a few were over one pound, but most were around three-quarters.

'In view of what my friend from the Sudan had caught, and what had been written in the magazine article I read in Baghdad, it would be dishonest to say I was not disappointed at the size of fish we caught. But in every other way – climate, scenery, type of river and fishing – the days were so enjoyable that it did not matter. Like many things in life, weights of fish are relative only to what you hope to catch.

'The trout books for the neighbouring beats were kept in Yanyar Lodge; their daily records went back for several years and I looked through them in the evenings. The average catch over the years on all beats was very much in line with ours. But every year, on every beat, some big fish were caught. The best I saw recorded was seven pounds and a half. The lodges did not provide weighing-scales and I do not suppose the weight of fish was underestimated by those who had not brought their own. It was perhaps with this thought in mind that the proud captor of a 5½ pound trout (struggling with the peculiarities of English spelling) had written beside his entry, "wheyed by the wheying-machine". But bigger trout than these can certainly be caught: "the biggest trout supplied for the Viceroy's camp near Harwan weighed 12½ lb." A by-pass of the Lower Lidder is the Trikker, a quiet-flowing stream not unlike an English chalk stream, "where the record fish stands at 14 lb".

'From Yanyar, the route to Kokernag Lodge took us down the Lidder valley on the road towards Srinagar, then left up the Bringhi valley. The cook had caught the early bus to Srinagar, where he needed to stock up with more livestock and provisions and obtain a few other essential items from Mr Goffara – more of his peacock flies, torch batteries, toilet rolls and the like. There was no doubt that the trout preferred Mr Goffara's flies to those I brought from England, particularly the peacock lures. These were crudely tied with two hooks in tandem, joined by a short length of gut, which not infrequently parted company when a trout was hooked only on the end one. Perhaps that was why they liked them.

'It was when we got to Kokernag that our next problem arose. No one could tell us where the lodge was. Eventually we were directed along a track up a hill but soon the car could go no further. The driver and I walked on and eventually came to the lodge – half-built, no roof, deserted and uninhabitable. Some miles further up the valley was Dandipura Lodge, so our driver telephoned a message back to Mr Goffara, hoping to catch the cook, and then we drove on, hoping to find Dandipura Lodge habitable and untenanted. The fates were kind to us, the previous occupants had left that morning and no one else was due before our own booking started. Miraculously, the cook arrived the same evening, with peacock flies, more livestock and assorted stores. But the chickens were small and tough, and it was mostly on trout that we dined by candlelight in the evenings at both Yanyar and Dandipura Lodges.

'The fishing on the Bringhi was similar to that on the Lidder, a fast-flowing stream with brief pools, or eddies round the large granite boulders, interspersed with a few longer pools where a dry fly was possible but at that time of year mostly unproductive. The ubiquitous watcher had located us soon after arrival and brought shikaris whom we engaged. They were well worth the small fee we paid them, not only as guides to the fishing but they were also companionable, amusing, and helpful in many ways. Although we always declined their offer to carry us pick-a-back over the river when we needed to cross, a helpful hand was often very welcome, and they were great experts at climbing the trees which so often ensnared my daughters' flies. On one occasion, as Carol's shikari – another Gul – peered out of the top of about the fifth tree she had hooked up in that morning, she called up to him, "I'm sorry, Gul, I'm a very poor fisher", and he called back, "No, Memsahib, you a very good fishing Madam." And he was right. She had not much experience of fly fishing and certainly caught more trees than I did, but she also (by a short head at the final count) caught more trout, including our best of 2½ pounds.

'At Dandipura too I looked through the watchers' trout books for all the surrounding beats, which gave very much the same pattern as at Yanyar. But there was one beat, not often fished, where the average size of fish caught over the years was very much larger than on any other beat, sometimes well over 2½ pounds for a limit catch. On the day we had that beat, Julia and I fished it with much optimism. It was an attractive stretch of river, with excellent pools and the prospects looked good. But we caught no "good-size fish" (38 centimetres for that beat), the only blank day that any of us had. I do not know why, and I do not disbelieve the records. It surely holds a lot of good trout and I would have liked to try again, had that been possible.

'We had eight days' fishing in all and killed 140 "good-size" trout between the four of us, with an average weight of three-quarters of a pound. Back in Srinagar I met up with two fishermen who had been fishing the spring-fed streams of Kokernag and Verinag. Their catches had been much the same as ours, similar average size and similar maximum. We had a day at leisure before returning to Delhi. Gul drove us up to Sonnamarg, a beautiful drive along the valley of the River Sindh, then through a narrow pass, where the river ran under extensive bridges of snow, to an open valley high up in the mountains where the early spring flowers were showing through. The Sindh river itself seemed less inviting than the Lidder or Bringhi, too fast, and broken, without the large granite boulders which create deep eddies and pools.'

Keith Howman was weaned on from his father of fabulous trout fishing in Kashmir in the 1930s. Hardy's in Pall Mall in London then stocked special 'Himalayan Trout Flies' and when stationed in India his father caught many trout up to seven pounds on visits to Kashmir. Keith's own recent experience confirms the fishing is still very good in rivers like the Lidder and Bringhi, and the Bringhi's tributaries, the Ahlan, Naubug and Diusu. With the majestic Himalyas as backdrop to the fishing, his party averaged over forty trout each in five days. Indeed, on one morning on a beat of the upper Bringhi, Keith and Jean Howman caught and returned over eighty. But now fish over two pounds prove rare as one change from 'the good old days'. But they are still there in quantity, still providing fascinating sport.

The Director Games and Fisheries, J & K Government, Srinagar, can give full information on fishing, departmental fishing lodges, and the main laws laid down in the Fishery Act of Samvar 1960. Their pamphlet *Rod & Line in Kashmir* gives comprehensive information, including such details as that small trout taken on fly must be gently returned, but all those taken on spinner must be kept and count towards the limit – even if taken on the single-hook spinners which are advised rather than trebles. The pamphlet lists waters where floating timber may be a nuisance at times and includes this summary of the fishing:

'There are three main types of trout waters. The large rivers like Sindh, Lidder, Kishenganga are foaming torrents in the afternoon during the months of May, June, and July, with occasional gentle current behind boulders. Spinning is allowed in these rivers, except the Lidder, but wet-fly fishing using weighted casts produces better sport. These rivers are at their best in April, August, and September when the water is relatively clear and the climate pleasing.

'The second type includes Bringhi, Erin, Madmati, Kulgam, Ferozpore and other similar streams where fly fishing is generally the rule and wet fly works well for the best part of the season. The third type includes small spring-fed streams, Verinag, Kokernag, Kotsu and Isthal, which provide excellent sport throughout the season and are suitable for both dry and wet fly.'

John Stewart, the British High Commissioner to Sri Lanka, enjoys the Kashmir fishing and records this unusual experience:

'In 1980 I was fishing the Lidder at Pahalgam and one morning I was allocated a shikari different from the one who had been with me during previous days. This shikari looked at my fly box and decided that the (wet) Coachman and Greenwell's Glory that I had been using successfully previously were no good at all and picked out a Bluebottle which I had made up based on an article by Neil Patterson in the *International Fly Fisher*. The Bluebottle was indeed very successful and in the course of two hours I caught 18 trout varying from ½ to 1 pound, returning all but two of them, to his outspoken horror. Around lunch time I announced that I was going to stop for half an hour for a glass of beer and a sandwich. The shikari said that if I stopped now I would not catch any more fish. Assuming that he was just keen for me to catch as many as possible to improve his tip, I paid no attention and sat down for half an hour. After lunch I fished solidly for four hours on that same stretch of water and did not get a touch. I questioned him intensively about the reason for this but our only common language was a very basic Urdu and he volubly failed to explain what had happened.'

John Stewart's own experience also confirms that Kashmir offers by far the best and best organized of Indian trout fishing. My father-in-law, a Madras sapper, used to show me pictures of the delightful small trout streams in the Nilgris, and recount successful fishing there. My wife was born in the Nilgris and was sad to read John Stewart's recent experience there:

'In January 1986 I made elaborate arrangements to fish in the Nilgris around Octacamund, but found that since the time of the Raj there has been very little attention paid to the fishing there. My wife and I spent many frustrating hours driving to recommended spots only to find that no trout had been seen or caught in recent memory.

'Still in South India, however, I can recommend the Cauvery fishing camp run by Jungle Lodges and Reserves Limited of Bangalore. They have a tent camp on the Cauvery and from early January to the end of March can and do guarantee mahseer of between twenty and eighty pounds. It is expensive at around 100 US dollars a day, but very comfortable and the fishing is very good with two or three large mahseer a day regarded as poor fishing.'

Jagdip Inder Singh is primarily a tour operator involved with adventure camps. He takes a rosier view of Indian trout fishing possibilities and gives this helpful summary of the available trout waters:

'Popular and effective wet flies in Kashmir and in all Indian rivers are Zulu

23 Dermot Wilson prepares to release a trout hooked on the broad Henry's Fork at the Snake river in Idaho.

24 Charles Jardine absorbed in experimenting with a successful variant of the American 'outrigger' nymph technique as he works the fast runs of Colorado's Frying Pan.

25   A promising stretch of Argentina's River Limay thirty miles from Barilouche in the Andes.

26   Mark Conroy fly fishes the Swan Inlet river in high water as it flows through the bleak
Falklands landscape.

27 Is this the record Orontes brown trout? Philip Pawson with his six pounder caught in wartime, in a then more peaceful Lebanon.

28 (*Left*) The River Blyde flows quietly, close to Pilgrim's Rest in Eastern Transvaal.

29 (*Right*) When the angler may himself be bait. Mark Conroy's rod beside the wet pug marks of a rogue lion which had just padded across the bridge over the Upper Amboni in Kenya.

30   Rafael de Madriaga Giraldo fishing dry fly in the fast runs of an outstanding Spanish trout stream, the Pisuerga.

31   'The Temple' revered by generations of anglers, but rarely seen. This is the fishing house Charles Cotton built in 1673 for Izaak Walton, the master. The initials 'CC' and 'IW' are intertwined above the door and it stands beside a bend of the River Dove unchanged after more than three hundred years.

and Blue Zulu, Butcher, Jungle Alexandra and Black Gnat. The best dry flies are Alder, Brown Moth, Mayflies, Coachman and Sedges, with nymphs also very useful. Apart from Kashmir, the best trout fishing in India is in the north. In Himachal Pradesh the Kulu valley offers many attractions to the angler as well as being famed for its beautiful girls. The rivers Larji, Ool, and Beas have rainbow and brown trout, with the Larji also having stocks of golden trout. Permits are issued by the divisional forest officers of Banjar and Kulu. Spinning is permitted as well as fly, and the Mepps Trout Killer kits are very popular. Light spin-casting rods and trout spinners are standard fishing technique in most Indian rivers, rather than fly fishing.

'The Larji flows down to join the Beas, which is a large river with plenty of fish. From Aut to Manali you can catch good bags of trout and also fish for the famous mahseer. The trout run as large as eight pounds, though the average is much smaller with a two-pounder a big fish. Like the Larji, the Ool is a tributary of the Beas and the fishing there is also similar, though the Ool is in a more remote and less accessible area. The whole Kulu valley is very beautiful and a great attraction for hikers and mountaineers. At the junction of the Beas and Larji there is a forest rest-house which is fully furnished, and rations are available at Aut and Banjar, both only some 10 kilometres distant. There is also said to be a lake with golden trout close by, but as it is up in the mountains at 9,000 feet I have not visited it personally.

'In the area around the Sutlej river there is good trout fishing, though the Sutlej itself has no trout. Browns and rainbows up to four pounds can be taken in the River Pabbar, a tributary of the Jamma. Spinning is also permitted here and the permits are issued by the Divisional Forestry Officer, Rohru, H.P. You can stay in forest bungalows at Rohru or Jubbal. The River Baspa is very close to the Tibetan border and in this very remote area foreigners are at present banned. That is a pity as this river is teeming with very large brown and rainbow trout. Further information on this area may be had from Himachal Tourism, Chandralek Building, 36 Janpath, New Delhi 110 001.

'In the Garhwal Hills of Uttar Pradesh there are some trout in the upper reaches of the rivers Pindar and eastern Ramganga. More important, the only really good and approachable trout lake in India is the Dodital. Like the Baspa this is full of trout, but they are rather small since it is overstocked and underfished. It is in a lovely setting at 10,000 feet and is also the home of the near-extinct musk deer. Lake Roopkund, too, is at similar height and fishes much the same, but you need to be a mountaineer as well as an angler to reach it. Information can be had from myself at Haldua Farm, PORTC, Hempur 244716, Dis. Nainital, UP, or from UP Tourism at the Kanishka Hotel, New Delhi 110 001.

'Bhutan (which, of course, is a nation by itself) is full of trout, but fishing is banned unless with the King's permission, which is not everyone's cup of tea. There are trout in West Bengal, but the waters are so badly poached that it is of no importance to anglers. I am not aware of any very good trout fishing in eastern India, but have not researched it myself.

'Any mention of trout fishing in India must include mention of three species other than normal "trout". The so-called Indian trout (*Barilus bola*) is found in all the waters mentioned and most of the Himalayan spring-fed rivers. This fish resembles the brown trout, but rarely grows above four pounds, though specimens of ten pounds were caught in the days of the Raj. This game fish is a superb fighter and delicious to eat, and it is a shame to classify it as anything but a trout. Then there is the snow trout, very similar to *Barilus bola* and found in the landlocked lakes of the inner Himalayas. Finally there is the "tiger of the Indian rivers", the mahseer. This fish (*Barbus tor*) is found in all major rivers of India and grows up to 100 pounds, though the average fish is from ten to fifteen pounds. There are three subspecies, the blue mahseer of southern India, the largest variety; the black mahseer of eastern and northern India, the gamest of them all; and the golden mahseer of north India and Nepal, the handsomest of the three. The fighting qualities of these fish are widely renowned. To be hooked into one is like being hooked into a submarine.

'You need to bring or tie your own flies as none can be bought locally. The book *Fly Dressing and some tackle making* by W. E. Davies gives good comparisons of the type of flies mentioned above as best in our waters. The fishing itself is very cheap if you are prepared to rough it a little and are not fussy about only eating "Western" food or the like. Alcohol is prohibitively expensive, and good guides will also cost you a lot. Outfitters like our company cost about £60 a day, including transport to fishing within 300 kilometres of Delhi in our case, as well as board and lodging. This is a sample of 1986 prices to give an approximate idea of cost. It is best to treat fishing in India as an adventure in which the fishing complements the unique and beautiful surroundings.'

Pakistan

Jean Howman, Secretary of the English Association of Stillwater Game Fishery Managers, with her own Ashmere Fishery near London, has this up-to-date knowledge:

'In Pakistan trout fishing is being developed to the point where it may become as interesting as that in Kashmir. The trout fishing is still mainly for locals, with few facilities yet organised for tourists. But happily there are many good trout streams with indigenous stocks being supplemented by further stocking with both browns and rainbows. That was fortunate for me since for the only time in my life I had to fish well to survive. With the chief conservator of wildlife I went to the Swat river area, only to find when we reached the forest rest-house that there were no provisions. The message that we were coming had not got through to this truly remote and beautiful area, so for four exciting and entrancing days we lived on what we caught.

'The Pakistan Fisheries Departments are investing a great deal of money with the help of the Asian Development Bank in a programme to build hatcheries on the main river system. Many thousands of fingerlings are being stocked annually and trout for the table market are just being developed. The three provinces with trout fishing are naturally all in the north of the country. The rivers run fast in the Himalayan foothills, or in the main mountain chain itself, in the Hindu Kush, or in the Karakorams. The main Karakoram Highway, built jointly by the governments of Pakistan and China along the silk route, is now open to foreigners right through into China, opening up a vast area of mountains and streams for the fit and enthusiastic.

'The easiest area for the foreigner to fish is the North West Frontier Province. This covers north-central Pakistan across the whole country. Fishing is obtainable in the most westerly section called Chitral on the Chitral river and its tributaries, with permits obtainable from the chief fisheries officer in Chitral town. The same applies in the town of Dir in Dir State. The next area with beautiful rivers and a trout hatchery in existence for many years is Swat, with fishing on the Swat river system, permits available from the chief fisheries officer in Saidu Sharif.

'Moving east you come to Hazara and the mighty Kunhar river in the Kaghan valley. All the mountains here are 18,000 feet upwards. The original trout hatchery, the first in Pakistan, is still in existence here. Eggs came originally from the Srinagar hatchery in Kashmir, from trout sent out around 1900 from the Surrey Trout Farm. This is a big river to fish and lower down becomes a mahseer river. There is also some lake fishing here, including Lake Saiful Maluk, where there are reputedly large trout. There is a long walk to this lake surrounded by superstition. Permits are obtainable at Abbotabad on the way to Kaghan, or at the village of Balakot at the entrance to the valley.

'The cost of fishing is extremely cheap – at the time of writing (1986) around 15 rupees a day for four fish taken. The minimum takable size is supposed to be 9 inches but this is around the size of the average trout, although some run to a pound or over. There are local variations in price and number of fish allowed, but these are small. The season varies too, running mainly from the beginning of April to the end of September, but it is wise to check from the fisheries officer as they do suddenly decide to vary this, and one river closed on 15 September this year.

'The second province, moving east, is Azad Kashmir, which is well organized in its fishery department. Unfortunately at present it is a sensitive area for foreigners and special permission would have to be requested, and not necessarily granted. The Neelum valley runs due north up the cease-fire line between India and Pakistan. There are three hatcheries in this area feeding the Neelum river system and the Jagran stream and also the Leepa valley. About 200,000 fingerlings are stocked annually and trout for the table are sent to Lahore at the very good price of 40 rupees per pound (about £1.50). In Azad Kashmir fishing is only allowed with a rod as opposed to handlines, sticks and other means. The cost throughout the province is 10 rupees per day, 30 rupees per week, with a limit of five fish taken away, size limit again 9 inches. The fishing season now starts in March and ends in October annually. This is a difficult area for travel as one road is frequently washed away with melting winter snow or during the monsoon. The rivers are quite beautiful and absolutely gin-clear. As with all trout fishing in Pakistan, most rivers are snow-fed, as opposed to being spring-fed, and the snow melt will ruin the fishing for part of the afternoon as the snow melts in the mountains. This usually clears in the evening so it is sensible to fish early and late in the day. Permits are available from the fisheries department in the main town of Muzzafarabad.

'The final area for fishing should really not be missed. It is the Northern Territories, including Gilgit, Hunza and Skardu. The rivers are fast and crystal-clear, and I defy anyone to find more stupendous scenery and surroundings anywhere. The mountains rise to over 10,000 feet, with numerous glaciers and spring-fed streams besides. To drive from Islamabad to Gilgit takes some 18 hours. Flying in Pakistan is extremely cheap and the flight to Gilgit costs only about £6.50. It must be the world's most sensational flight, curling around Nanga Parbat at around 25,000 feet. At some stages I felt that I could reach out and scrape the lichens off the rocks. Because this is a hazardous flight it only runs in good weather conditions and is only for those with strong nerves. Permits to fish here in the Northern Territories are obtainable from the fisheries department in Gilgit town. When you are fishing in Pakistan you will have to hire a jeep and probably a driver. Distances and times are misleading – for instance, it once took us 14 hours to cover 160 miles. Accommodation must be booked in advance through the forest department, which is ultimately responsible for forests, fishing and wildlife; or through the tourist board. Accommodation will be in a rest-house unchanged since the British times. You should take everything with you for safety, although there will probably be a resident chokidar or caretaker. He may not, however, be prepared to cook. Take sleepings bags, towels, lavatory paper, and all food and cooking gear. All fishing tackle should be taken with you as it will not be provided. Rods and reels are exactly those you would require for a small Scottish stream, with the usual selection of wet flies. We found that we had enormous success with nymphs, caddis, chironomids and the like and in the evenings, when the water was low, huge fun with dry flies. Most of the locals do not fish now with fly, but use small spoons. Needless to say, very few women fish and I, over the years, have got very used to being the main attraction and am followed by large numbers of locals who will stand right behind me, until someone gets hooked. My husband, on the other hand, is left to get quietly on with his fishing in the traditional way. Conclusion – a super country to fish if you don't mind doing without your creature comforts and are prepared to take things as you find them and get on and organize things yourself. You will incidentally in many areas be accompanied on your fishing trip compulsorily by either the local hunter or shikari, or by the local range or forest officer.'

Japan

No country is keener on fishing than Japan, where there are estimated to be 20 million active anglers. A relatively small proportion of these fish for trout; fewer still fly-fish for them. But the sport is growing in popularity all the time and it is indicative of its importance that this is one of the areas in which the House of Hardy has a casting school. Jim Hardy was kind enough to assist in the inclusion of information in this book by organizing Anglers Research Ltd of Chiba in Japan to prepare a summary of the available trout fishing.

Trout were first introduced into Japan from America in 1892 with a stocking into Chuzenjiko Lake, and many interesting species of trout are now available to anglers there. There are four normal varieties: the buraun, or brown trout; the nijimasu, or rainbow trout; the burukku, or brook trout; and the lake trout of Chuzenjiko. An unusual species very widespread in Japan is the yamame, with markings along its body not dissimilar from the thumb-print markings on salmon parr. The amago is a kind of yamame but with red spots on the body; and the sakuramasu is also a yamame-type trout which goes to sea and back over a 3- to 4-year cycle. The iwana is more char than trout, with a strong jaw and great fighting qualities. The ito is similar to the iwana, but grows up to 150 centimetres.

Local fishing associations control many areas and permits can usually be obtained at their office on a daily basis. There are also many private stocked fisheries where the charge is higher. Throughout Japan there are many tackle shops, which are a useful source of information and can often arrange guides as well as give advice. Not many will speak other languages so bring an interpreter or ask your hotel to phone for you.

For Japanese anglers the most popular 'trout' is the yamame, which only averages about 20 or 30 centimetres. So it is fished for with light tackle with a short river rod and AFTM 3–5 lines. For lakes AFTM 5–7 lines are recommended, with rods to match. Western fly fishing has become very popular in recent years so many tackle shops are well stocked with suitable equipment, with the Japanese themselves having pioneered much of the cheaper – but good-quality – tackle which has helped widen the numbers in Europe who can afford to fly-fish. But the vast majority of Japanese anglers are pole fishermen for ayu and the like, so the hiring of fly-fishing equipment for short periods is not easy and it is best to come equipped.

Some of the best trout fishing is located within easy reach of Tokyo – 70 kilometres away there is the Ashinoko Lake administered by the Hakone Fishery Association. There is a great range of accommodation in the area and more than ten tackle shops. The 1986 permit cost was 500 yen per day. Apart from yamame, brown and rainbow trout, bass are there in quantity as a major sport fish for the Japanese. One and a half hours by car from Tokyo's western area you can enjoy fishing the narrow river valleys in the Akikawa Keikoku district, with stocked brown and rainbows as well as the wild yamame and iwana. There are local private fishing areas where permits may be had. Particularly at weekends, all public waters are liable to be so crowded that it is worth arranging and paying for such fishing if you want to enjoy your trouting to the full.

One specially recommended fishing area is the Mount Fuji district not far from Hakone. Here there are five major lakes in an area noted for its remarkable scenery, and all types of trout. There is also a special fishing hotel to cater for an angler's needs and arrange his trout fishing, as well as excellent accommodation. This is the Shishidome Holiday Lodge, which provides an ideal base from which to explore the possibilities of Japanese trout fishing.

Finally there is the Chuzenjiko mountain lake in the Nikko city area. In a country famous for its remarkable views this is rated the best sightseeing place of all. Lake Chuzenjiko is also the fishery where brown and rainbow trout were first successfully imported and western-style fly fishing pioneered. In its waters fish grow large and it is reported that trout of over 100 centimetres have been caught here, presumably challenging the Argentine record had they been officially listed. It is also an area with several good trout rivers, a western-style hotel, and much use of the Hardy 'Smuggler' rod.

Below is a summary of possible fishing areas to interest the trout angler:

District	Water	
Hokkaido	Sarobetsu river	ito, yamame
	Nemuro ponds	ito, yamame, iwana
	Shiribetsu river	yamame, ito, iwana
	Dohnan area	ito, amemasu
	Shikotsu Lake	illmemasu
	Sapporo area	yamame, ito
Northern Mainland	Towada Lake	himemaru
	Tazawa Lake	yamame, iwana
	Sendai area	yamame, iwana
	Murakami area	yamame, sakuramash
Central Mainland	Chuzenjiko Lake	lake trout, iwana
		yamame, brown, rainbow
	Northern river/lake	yamame, amago
	Southern river/lake	yamame
	Ashinoko lake	yamame, brown rainbow
	Akikawa river	yamame, rainbow
	Private area near Tokyo	rainbow, brown, yamame
	Shishidome area	yamame, brown
	Mount Fuji lake area	yamame, iwana, brown, rainbow also brook.
	Lake area, private	
	Tokai and Nagoya area	amago iwana
Western Mainland	Kyoto, Osaka district	yamame, amago
Kyushuu Island		yamame, amago
Shikoku Island		yamame, amago

Brook or stream fishing for trout is growing in popularity in Japan influenced by the numerous casting schools. There is considerable stocking of rivers with brown and rainbow trout. The development of fish farming has also lead to an increase in stocked still waters. Elaborate artificial lakes have been created, as in the Anglers' Park in Yokohama.

In many of the lakes there are landlocked salmon, or himemasu, and most of the lakes with trout have other species as well. With Japanese tackle now widely available, there is no problem over equipment or flies and as always local advice on flies is the best initial guide. Additional information can be readily obtained through the travel agent contacting the local fishery department or through the hotel in which you stay in fishing areas.

14

Best of British

Wales, Scotland, Ireland and England

Anglers in the British Isles are fortunate to have such a wealth of trout waters so fully documented. Detailed guides such as Dick Orton's regularly updated and very comprehensive *Where to Fish* are complemented by more descriptive books such as *The Haig Guide to Trout Fishing in Britain*. The British Tourist Authority, Thames Tower, Black's Road, London W6 9ET, also publishes a pamphlet entitled *Salmon & Trout Fishing Holidays in Britain*, which contains much useful information about fishing hotels as well as details of fishing seasons, licences, and permits. The authority has as general agent and information office in America: Frontiers International, Box 161, Wexford PA 15090, USA, who specialize in arranging fishing trips to Britain.

Britain can also offer much of historical interest to the visiting angler, not least in the Winchester area, where Izaak Walton's tomb is in the Silkstede chapel of the cathedral and his figure on the Great Screen. The outstanding angling writer of the nineteenth century, Francis Francis, also has a commemorative bust in the cathedral. In the border area between England and Scotland the Ellem Fishing Club is the oldest such club in the world, having been founded in 1831. Many of its fishermen were experts on Loch Leven, which lies close to Edinburgh. Leven trout with their yellow bellies are a strain famous throughout the world, having been sent to stock many far-off waters. The first ever national fly-fishing competition was staged on Loch Leven in 1880, and the first international there in 1928, with the late King George VI as England's captain elect. Back in England Dovedale is forever associated with Charles Cotton and Izaak Walton. Though no trace remains of Cotton's stately Beresford Hall home, the fishing hut he built on a bend of the Dove is still intact, still inscribed with their linked initials.

There is no shortage of advice on where to fish in Britain, no lack of choice. Organizations like the Rod Box, Fishing to Let, St George's Street, Winchester, can book on the outstanding dry-fly rivers of the area, or point you to the best of the still waters, or to distant fishing, whether in Scotland or Alaska. In Britain there is the option of the clear chalk streams like the Test with its dry-fly fishing, or of Welsh rivers in which wet fly is more effective. You can fish on a mountain burn, a highland loch, a Northern Irish lough, a large reservoir, or a small still water. Trout seasons vary, but in most places run from the middle of March to the end of September. More and more now there are trout fisheries open all year round and stocked with sterile rainbows which stay in good condition. So there is no time of the year that you cannot fish for trout, unless such lakes are iced over. Most water in Britain is private and you need a permit to fish. In England and Wales you also need a licence from the water authority of the area.

Wales

For me the most notable feature of Welsh fishing is in the run of big sea trout up rivers such as the Dee or the Towy and its tributary the Cothi. Received wisdom is, of course, that you wait until it is quite dark before starting to fish at night. But if the sea trout are moving at dusk that is the best time to catch them. Then you can move on to a different place where you can settle to fish the night through and on into the dawn. The biggest sea trout are likely to take after midnight, so there is no thought of going back to bed.

But it was in Wales too that I learnt how to catch brown trout, fishing wet fly down, up, or across as occasion demanded, fishing quietly on the flats or bobbing the dropper on the edge of fast currents. In high summer on the Wye below Builth Wells my brother and I caught grayling and dace on the dry fly. In the heat of the afternoon we would spot trout cruising under overhanging trees, climb along the branches, and dap the fly in front of them as they passed. There were prolific catches of trout from half to two pounds in the Wye's upper reaches, with March Browns deadly in April. The tributaries such as the Irfon also provided excellent sport, especially for early-season wet-fly fishing, though big bags are less common now.

Yet it was the Usk that particularly caught my imagination and gave me the best early lessons in both wet- and dry-fly fishing. Below Brecon you could search out the trout in the long quiet pools, or fish with hope in the fast streams even when nothing was showing. Once a rise started the water would boil with fish, often choosy, sometimes easy. Then dry fly or nymph fished upstream did best. The Usk is Wales' main trout river, and has reasonable runs of salmon and some sea trout as well. In its early course the river, like many of its tributaries, flows over red sandstone, which colours it in times of flood. Lower down, the bed is limestone, the feed richer, the trouts' growth quicker. The trout fishing is at its best between Brecon and

Abergavenny. The spring is the best fishing time, with most trout taken on the wet fly in March and April. There are a number of hotels which have fishing on the Usk, with the Gliffaes near Abergavenny having a delightful stretch of the river. The town of Usk was the base for Lionel Sweet, the most knowledgeable of Usk fishermen and a man who could cast six rods at a time as his party piece. The Sweet tackle shop in Usk is the place to get information about Usk fishing and Usk flies, including the Dogsbody, Harry Powell's successful creation.

Apart from its wealth of smaller trout rivers and streams, Wales has some fine lakes and reservoirs. The most unusual is Llyn Trawsfynydd, with the power station brooding over it, the heated water channelling in, the large trout stocked into it caught by every means from maggot to fly. There is also the beautiful and productive Llyn Brenig with its browns and stocked rainbows. The most famous is Lake Vyrnwy. The Vyrnwy Hotel is ideal for anglers and the lake has some fine trout fishing. Set amid a forest it can be a forbidding place on a dark day, enchanting in the sun. The hotel also manages the River Vyrnwy, which is part of the Severn system and has in the Banwy and Tanant tributaries excellent trout fishing.

There is such variety of trout fishing that everyone has his own personal favourite water. Moc Morgan, Secretary of the Welsh Salmon and Trout Association, feels that way about the Teifi:

'Fishing for wild brown trout in rain-fed rivers is to me the cream of angling. That is how I started my angling career over fifty years ago and it is the type of fishing that I aim to practise to my dying day. The upper section of the River Teifi is just such a challenging fishery. There the angler is denied the luxury of a constant flow and of the clear water which is the feature of the chalk streams, but the dramatic fluctuations of river levels and climatic conditions add uncertainty as a spice to the sport.

'The River Teifi near its source does not hold big trout, but it would be wrong to think that the modest half-pounders provide easy conquest. What they lack in stature they make up for in guile and cunning. Having hooked one in a fast stream, trying to keep it out of the weeds soon makes the angler realize that he's got a tiger by the tail.

'In the early days of the season the wet fly is the normal offering. Many anglers today tend to regard the wet-fly down-river technique as something of a "chuck and chance" method. What a pity these anglers have not been privileged to glance over the shoulders of the giants of yesteryear, who were masters of this method. Watching anglers like Dai Lewis, Dai George and Dan Jones was an education. They seemed to be able to charm the trout from their watery hides by skilful use of this technique.

'I quickly found that this method demands good control of the line and a careful approach to the fishing position. The art is in getting the line, leader and flies to sweep across the river, moving smoothly from the far side like a windscreen wiper. All your concentration is on the line and any unnatural movement or pull must be answered by an instantaneous tightening. The hooking of brown trout on the upper Teifi when using this technique is the pinnacle of the art of wet-fly fishing. On some occasions when I have suffered a severe failure I realize how difficult it is to graduate from the beginners' class with these quick-reacting trout.

'Come the grannom to the upper Teifi in the third week of April I take to the dry fly. Now the main skill is in casting and in keeping in control and contact with the dry fly. The upper Teifi was the playground and classroom to such renowned anglers as Oliver Kite and Vicar Powell. Here Kite devised his famed Imperial, although it must be said that a fly dressed with heron herl and honey dun hackle was being used by the locals a long time before the birth of the Imperial. Both Kite and Powell were gifted creators of effective fly patterns. The reverend gentleman was responsible for patterns like the Paragon, Ermine Moth and Sun Fly, which have served anglers well through the decades.

'To me, going down on a May evening around eight-thirty to the Teifi is a little bit of piscatorial heaven. I generally choose a stretch of water flowing westward as it gives me some fifteen minutes more with light enough to see the dry fly. This extra time is really important if the evening rise is delayed for some reason.

'By now my casting is accurate enough to present the dry fly just off the main flow and let it bob down with the running water. The thrill is either seeing a fish break the surface, or watching the fly disappear into the water as it is sucked down.

'Most of us anglers love to go back to where we started. Is it that we are seeking to regain youthful happiness, or even youth itself? Whatever it is, there we go when we return from supposedly greener pastures. After taking 92 trout in one day on Loch Leven, spending four memorable days on the Slaney in Ireland, having a bumper catch on the Tweed and some unforgettable fishing on the Itchen, back I went to the Teifi. There I was able to equal the pleasure experienced on the more famous locations.

'It is not surprising that the late Cynan, one of the famous Welsh poets who was also a great angler, said that after he had died and gone on to fish the celestial rivers, his younger fishing companion should not be afraid if he saw him again one evening:

> Fear not if I steal to your side as of yore
> From Paradise to fish Teifi once more.'

For those wanting details of Welsh trout flies there is Moc Morgan's book *Fly patterns for the Rivers and Lakes of Wales*.

Scotland

Scotland for Fishing is the title of a Pastime Publication constantly up-dated and produced in conjunction with the Scottish Tourist Board. This is a comprehensive guide to fishing available and is given world-wide distribution by the British Tourist Authority. Apart from details and descriptions of Scotland's trout and sea-trout fishing, and every other type of fishing, it advertises a wide variety of tackle shops and fishing accommodation. Such accommodation ranges from Lady Janet's caravan and camping site at Thurso to chalets in Bonnie Galloway, to self-catering cottages in Blairgowrie's Craighall Sawmill, or Sutherland's Loch Shin, to prestigious hotels like The Boat Hotel, Boat of Garten, Speyside, where the internationally famous angler, Hugh Falkus, is based to teach sea-trout and salmon fishing. There are luxury log cabins at Croft-Na-Caber on Loch Tay or Butterstone's at Dunkeld. Many such fishing hotels or sites can offer free fishing and all the necessary advice. Other publications such as *Fishing in Scotland* by Charles McLaren and Rob Wilson or Bruce Sandison's *The Trout Lochs of Scotland* complete the picture.

The Tourist Board's *Scotland for Fishing* also outlines the fishing waters, lochs and rivers, of each of the Scottish regions and lists all the local tourist boards where further advice is freely given. In addition, it gives details of the relevant laws and of the safety and other standards to be observed to keep waters clean and anglers healthy. The close season for brown trout is from 7 October to 14 March, but private fisheries may extend this. There is no close season for rainbow or brook trout. Sunday fishing for trout is legal, but not all fisheries allow it. Except when enclosed in 'stanks', brown trout are regarded as wild creatures belonging to no one except the captor. Only in tidal waters, however, is there any public right to fish for trout. Elsewhere permission must be obtained from the landowner or the tenant of the fishing, preferably in writing. Legering for trout is only permitted if the rod is at all times held in the hand. If the rod is supported by stones or in a rest it is deemed to be an illegal 'fixed engine'. Salmon parr and smolts are protected under salmon legislation and care must be taken in returning them, if caught while trout fishing.

Scotland for Fishing 1986 includes a review by Ian Muckle of that 'desirable alien' the rainbow trout and of the best rainbow-trout fisheries. These include the 22-acre Coldingham Loch near St Abbs Head, one of the oldest and best regarded rainbow fisheries; Clubbiedean, near Collington on the outskirts of Edinburgh; Morton Fisheries near Mid Calder; and the specimen water of the Inverawe Fisheries near Taynuilt in Argyll. The Inverawe rainbows are bred in the salt waters of Loch Etive, red-fleshed and excellent to eat. The commercial smokery there adds an encouraging aroma and there is the chance of double-figure trout. As Muckle comments: 'It is quite feasible to contact a rainbow in the 10 to 14 lb range, but landing it is a different matter!'

There are special pamphlets to cover individual areas, including Orkney, where all the fishing is free thanks to ancient Norse law and *Udal* tradition. Boats can be cheaply hired on many fine lochs, including the 3,000-acre Loch Harray, where Scotland staged the recent home internationals. June, July and August are usually the best months, as it is also in Lochs Boardhouse and Hundland and Orkney's only 'highland' water, Loch Kirbister. There is also Loch Stenness, an extension of the sea where sea trout and wild brownies are equally plentiful and where great trout have been taken in the past.

Typical of other areas is the pamphlet *Trout & Salmon Fishing in Caithness, the Game Fisherman's Paradise*. Among the lochs detailed, Bruce Sandison has this to say of Watten, 10 miles from Wick on the way to Thurso: 'Watten contains some of the finest brown trout in Scotland, as silvery as sea trout, pink-fleshed and fighting fit. Their average weight is 1 lb 2 oz, though fish of 3 lb and over are taken. Watten is a shallow loch and trout are caught throughout its three-mile length.'

While most waters can only be fished with permission and on payment, no licences are needed for fishing in Scotland, which is perhaps indication enough of the wide choice. There are many fine trout rivers, or salmon rivers with excellent trout fishing like the Aberdeenshire Dee. There are many small burns like the Tullich and Coulags, flowing into the Carron river, where at the age of four I caught my first trout on a worm. There was the excitement also of catching the occasional sea trout in these little streams, as is so often the case when they run down into a sea-trout and salmon river like the Carron. Then it was my father who fished the Carron, my brother and I who explored the burns, usually with my mother in charge and the fear of the day ending early. If we hooked an eel it would twist itself around the cast and as my mother hated the snakelike eels that was on occasion the finish of our fishing. Some forty years later I fished the Carron myself and was amused to find one pool signed as Pawson's Pool. No one could tell me why, but I needed no telling. It was a small pool with snags above, overhanging trees below, certain disaster if a salmon ran out of it. There my father one day caught two salmon of close on twenty pounds with my tweed-skirted mother urged into the water to throw stones to turn them back whenever they looked like heading into danger.

But for me the essence of Scottish trout fishing is in its remote hill lochs, or the large well-ordered ones, like Leven, with fishing from a drifting boat the traditional method, dropper fishing the supreme art. Many such lochs have been noted for large trout. A 39 pound trout from Loch Awe was long accepted as a world record fish and as authenticated before the cased fish was lost in a hotel fire. P. D. Malloch recorded mounting a Loch

Stenness slob trout caught on night line of well over twenty pounds and trout close to that size come now from lochs like Rannoch. The current authenticated UK record is a Loch Quoich trout of 19½ pounds caught in 1978. Bruce Sandison's *The Trout Lochs of Scotland* lists over 800 lochs in its second edition and is a splendid guide for visiting anglers. For instance, he rightly qualifies the above statement on Rannoch in order to ensure that the reader is not misled. After listing trout of over twenty pounds caught in the past, he comments that those were taken trolling and that the heaviest taken in a recent season was 5½ pounds, the average around ¾ pound.

For me fishing Loch Leven – with its historic connections, its island where Mary Queen of Scots was imprisoned, its ordered boat fishing – was a real experience. Of late it has had its poor seasons, but has come back to form in the last year or two. The trout run large and are of unrivalled beauty. Leven is almost round, 3,400 acres of water set amid pleasant farmland. It is only 85 feet above sea level, has many small islands as well as the 80-acre St Serfs. It is generally shallow with the golden sands area an intriguing one to fish. On the pierhead bar there is a 1912 photograph of part of a catch of 2,200 trout in two days of fishing by the boats. Leven trout are not quite as prolific as that today, nor is the fly life as pervasive as of old. Malloch spoke of the bloodworm as the trout's main diet and the extraordinary hatches in April. 'One who has not seen them can have little idea of the immense swarms which appear on Loch Leven. As the season advances more appear in the evening, and on warm nights the surface of the water is almost covered with them and the trout suck them down everywhere.'

An old Scottish angler told me of a time that six trout rose at once to his four flies, three of them being caught. No such hectic activity now, even at the best times of the evening rise, but the average size then was around ¾ pound and has risen to almost double that. No question now of boatmen having as part of the job the sweeping of the piles of dead flies off the pier, but it is still a lovely loch with unrivalled trout and the most stable of motor-driven boats from which to practise the traditional loch-style fishing on the drift. You need to update your information on the best of flies and methods. For a long time 'wee doubles' were the popular choice, short-lining the most effective method. Then larger flies and longer casting had a vogue. What is unlikely to change is the trouts' reaction to weather conditions. A bright sun and cloudless sky has them diving deep and proving uncooperative.

This is a sophisticated fishery, well ordered, dominating the locality, with excellent hotel accommodation close to the water's edge at Kinross. It is managed in the traditions of the legendary P. D. Malloch, perhaps the most outstanding Scottish trout angler of all time. It is another favourite area of Malloch's that appeals to me even more. 'The famous Altnacealgach lochs', as he called them, are contrast indeed. Wild, remote, natural, they have only a few boats on them, just enough fishing pressure to keep the teeming trout stocks averaging three to the pound, rather than the six or seven when Malloch began to fish them hard, to get a proper balance. Urigill is the ideal beginner's lake, where you will soon learn how to catch fish. It appeals as much to the experienced trout angler because there are many good fish among the small, vast differences in catch rate between those who can fish the dropper well and the average loch-style fisherman. There are great weedbeds too where the skilful can enjoy the best fishing, conjuring the trout up by bobbing the flies across the surface or in the clear gaps. Fighting the larger trout is then a matter of being bold and resolute before they either break you or leave you anchored to the weed. With forests being planted round its shores Urigill has lost some of the isolation, the freedom of spirit which enhanced its beauty. In this mountainous area, however, it is hard to spoil the setting of any loch – Urigill, or the dog-legged Cama, the deep, narrow Veyatie, or the surprisingly neglected Boralan, the loch beside the road with more char than the others and a fine head of trout. Size 8 flies you must use here for there are great hatches of mayflies drifting off the heather and even the small trout get used to large offerings. Late June and early July are the best weeks for fly fishing, but if you want to troll spinners you can take trout up to eight pounds or so more easily in early spring, with Veyatie and Cama both holding a number of large browns, as do nearby Shin and Merkland. The Altnacealgach lochs are best fished from the comfort of the Oykel Bridge Hotel – if you are lucky enough to be able to book into this ideal fishermen's hotel, which caters primarily for the salmon anglers of the Oykel, and also has boats on fascinating Loch Ailsh, with its runs of sea trout and salmon to add to good stocks of browns averaging ¾ pound. This is an area that calls me back every year and where my children have so enjoyed their fishing.

But everyone has his own choice. Brian Peterson is one of Scotland's better trout anglers and he takes as his favourite fishery the only water in Scotland called a lake, rather than a loch – the Lake of Menteith:

'I have chosen this water as my favourite commercial fishery in Scotland as it in no way appears as such, either in looks or in catch returns. The Lake of Menteith is one of the most picturesque waters in our country and the fishing on it can be so erratic that I never look upon it as a commercial water. It has, however, always been kind to me and I have never returned home from it without a fish.

'Over the years the sport at Menteith has been very patchy, but the angler cannot complain about this as the good days make up for the bad. As on all other waters, we rely on the weather conditions to help us have a good day's fishing. The shallow depths at Menteith contribute to the inconsistency of the fishing, and maximize the influence of the weather.

'The stocking policy at Menteith has varied over the years, with the manager, Bill Martindale, trying hard to hit on the right one, remembering that it is very hard to please everyone all of the time. His latest policy of stocking with large numbers of smaller fish seems to have got it right. In the best conditions the angler can now expect to catch his ten-fish limit fairly easily. The lake contains not only rainbows but browns and a scattering of old stock brook trout. It also contains its fair share of big fish up to double-figure weight as the result of stocking with large fish a few years ago. Thanks to the large shoals of perch and roach fry, the stock fish do not waste any time in putting on weight.

'Everyone has his own favourite drifts in the lake. My own will be the same as many others, since they are the best known – Gateside Bay, Heronry Bay and Road Shore drifts. The rules at Menteith are few, but sensible: fly-only, no anchors, with a drogue being very important sometimes. Bank fishing is not allowed. Stick to these rules and all will be fine. Break them and you can expect to see a large white boat downing on you at great speed. Talking of speed, there are no engines on the boats, but you can bring your own if you dislike rowing.

'Catching the fish from this water can be either by traditional fly fishing, or by the now very popular method of lure fishing. I myself prefer the traditional method, but if conditions make for lure fishing then I am not slow in changing. Fortunately, I have not found many situations when I have had to put on a sinking line. The floating line has proved successful enough when coupled up with 10- or 11-foot cast of 6-pound nylon.

'Traditional patterns in order of preference are Woodcock and Yellow, Red Palmer, Wickham's Fancy, Mallard and Claret and the Dunkeld. My choice of lures would be the Killer, Ace of Spades, Honey Bear, Texas Rose Muddler and the Cat's Whisker. The list could go on and on, but if you are armed with these few I am sure you will have some fun. Even if you cannot persuade one of the trout on to your hook, I am sure you will enjoy the magnificent scenery. If you decide that the Lake of Menteith is for you than you can book a boat by telephoning (087) 75664. By car head for the Port of Menteith, which is situated just off the A873. From Glasgow take the A81, and from Edinburgh the M8 on to the M9.'

Ulster

The Northern Ireland Tourist Board at River House, Belfast (0232 235906), can pass on advice about trout fishing there. The best of it is in the vast Lough Erne or the remarkable Lough Melvin. The boundary between north and south runs through the middle of Melvin, which has some of the cleanest, clearest water of any big lake in Europe. It also has an unusual variety of trout – four distinct species. There are the ordinary wild browns, the beautifully marked gillaroos, the torpedo-shaped sonaghans of the wild fighting strain, and the ferox, which in this case are a distinct species, not just big cannibal trout in poor condition.

The cleanness of the loch was confirmed in a survey by Dr Ferguson of Queen's University who made a detailed study of a loch, 'which has interested scientists for over 150 years, since it is unique in Europe in holding these four strains of trout. The large deep-water ferox feed on char, which only come into the shallows at spawning time. If the water was to become polluted the char would be the first species to succumb and their presence in large shoals indicates the cleanness of the loch.' The gillaroo are beautiful vividly coloured trout, redder than any others and with as golden a belly as Leven trout. Their thick stomach walls, like a fowl's gizzard, earned then the name of 'gizzard' trout, but to the Irish it is their striking colour that is most significant – 'gillaroo' is derived from *giola ruaidh*, 'the red servants'.

These trout you will catch in numbers in shallow rocky areas, where they feed on snails and molluscs. The Gosling, bobbed as a dropper, is very effective in the early months of the season, for every type of trout. The sonaghans shoal in deeper water and are spectacular fighters, leaping as soon as hooked. Dark of hue, the sonaghan's slim shape and large tail make it a powerful opponent. In Melvin there is also a good run of grilse, which adds to the variety and attraction of this very special water.

Loch Erne is at its best in mayfly time, with every opportunity to catch large trout on fly. Even larger ones may be taken trolling, with brown trout up to nineteen pounds caught in recent years. Fishing author and lough Melvin aficionado Larry Nixon wrote the pamphlet *Game Fishing in Northern Ireland* for the Tourist Board. Apart from giving all the addresses and fishing clubs to help a visiting angler, he has this to add about the waters: 'The lakes of Tyrone and Armagh are special. They hold stocks of the largest rainbows you are likely to see in Ireland, with the trout being reared in the Department of Agriculture's fish farm in County Londonderry. One of the lakes to which they are transferred, Roughan, tucked away among the rolling Tyrone hills near Coalisland, produced an 8 lb 14 oz beauty.'

Ulster waters hold several varieties of trout. Apart from those in Melvin, where there are also Arctic char, there is the dollaghan which frequents the Lough Neagh system, with large specimens caught in August and September. One lough not regularly fished, Lough Macnean, holds very big trout with one of twenty pounds reputed to have been caught there by an Enniskillen blacksmith. Lower Lough Erne, however, is the most likely water in which a new record might be set, overtaking the 19¼-pound brown trout caught there on a copper spoon on a famous drift from Eagle Point to Lusty Beg in Kesh Bay. Big wild trout can be taken on the surface there in the mayfly season which usually lasts from around 20 May to 15 June. Trout fishing in Northern Ireland is cheap and prolific and is overlooked by the Fisheries Conservancy Board for Northern Ireland, 21 Church Street, Portadown.

Eire

Belleek is one of the best places to stay when fishing Melvin and there is the added attraction of the famous black china produced there. But Melvin is a shared lough, just as easily fished from Eire's side. Trout fishing in Southern Ireland also centres on large loughs, often as wild and beautiful as the trout in them. Corrib is perhaps the most famous of them, especially for the dapping for big trout at mayfly time. Late in the year those trout run up the streams, and the happiest of my boyhood memories is of catching brown trout up to four pounds in the Glenloss, and in Joyce's river close to Leenane in Connemara. The Leenane Hotel, much changed now, was then a delightful one for anglers, with the day's catches displayed in the hall, and with advice and gillies readily available. The man who looked after my brother and myself was a remarkable fisherman, despite having only one arm. In a case in the dining room was a morning's catch of his from the nearby Finney river. Of the four trout the largest was 9 pounds, the smallest 3 pounds. James had stopped then, as it was a problem to cycle home one-handed with such a weight of fish.

There are many fine trout waters in Southern Ireland, with the dry fly fishing on the Suir outstanding. Full details of the options can be obtained from Bord Failte, Baggot Street Bridge, Dublin 2 (Tel. Dublin 765871). But for me Eire's great loughs are the special feature.

There are waters full of sea trout like the Screebe loughs, which can be fished from the hotel Screebe House, Camus-Connemara, Co Galway. There are other fine sea trout loughs in the area with the dapping especially productive in late September on those like Doo Lough. One of Ireland's best anglers, Brian Geraghty gave me this general advice on the way they fish:

'The very early fishing from late March depends a lot on the water levels, the temperature, and the wind. In early April the Duck Fly is often the most successful pattern. Then comes the season for traditional wet flies, and wet-fly nymphs, until the Mayfly brings even more satisfying returns. It heralds also some very good fishing for those who dap on Lough Corrib.

'Spent Gnat in early to mid-June can be marvellous, especially on Lough Arrow. In July, with the trout feeding on perch fry, lure-type fishing can be most effective. August is sedge time, with the Peter and the Murrough the most effective flies. Terrestrials and daddy-long-legs also attract the trout when fished dry on the bob or dapped. In the midland lakes in particular chironomids are prevalent for most of the season.'

Favourite patterns for me in Ireland are the Black Pennell, the Connemara Black, and the Green Peter.

Corrib, Mask, and Conn are difficult to get to know because of their great size, but you can be sure of a good chance of trout everywhere if you fish the rocky shallows. You can be sure too that the trout rise swiftly and reject the fly even faster. The strike has to be instantaneous. Or as some Irish gillies put it: 'You should strike ten seconds before you see or feel the fish!' Both Mask and Conn stage major competitions annually, open to entrants from anywhere in the world, with an entertaining and hospitable experience guaranteed. Patrick Langan, who has organized many matches on Conn, has a slightly different preference for that water: 'We fish mainly wet fly and sunk line with three flies. The most effective patterns are Golden Olive, Black Pennell, Mallard and Claret, Hackle Mayfly when the hatch is on, Green Peter, Cinnamon Sedge, Alder, and Black and Peacock Spider. Another all-round fly is the Invicta.'

Peter O'Reilly of the Central Fisheries Board gave me the following advice on fishing Lough Sheelin, which applies also to most of Ireland's large loughs:

'Sheelin is a large alkaline lough with some 4,500 acres of relatively shallow water which supports an abundance of fly life once noted for its profuse mayfly and Green Peter (large trichoptera) hatches. The onset of eutrophication in the lough has left chironomids as the main organisms of interest to the angler.

'When the season opens at the beginning of March, the trout congregate in the shallows feeding on freshwater shrimps and lice. April's warmer weather starts the first hatches of duck fly, mostly along the northern shore. The best fishing then is around midday and in the evening until after sunset. In May there are fine hatches of buzzers, with a free rise of trout, particularly in Bog Bay and Gore Port Bay. Dry Murroughs can be used from dusk until midnight with good effect. Olives, mayfly, stonefly, alders and the black curse (*Simulium damnosum*) also hatch in numbers.

'This continues until early June, when there is a pause until the trout discover perch fry. That brings much excitement for the angler if he finds feeding fish, which will then take a variety of flies from a Dunkeld to dry Sedges. Caenis hatches also make for good sport in calm sheltered bays in the early morning. On bright sunny days July fishing is very difficult, but at dusk and early morning buzzer hatches can bring good sport.

'Traditional flies will bring good catches on overcast, windy August days, particularly Invictas, representing a hatching sedge. Dapping a natural grasshopper or a big sedge takes some big fish, as does a dry sedge in the evenings. But it is in September that the bigger trout really move. You can catch them in shallower water with a team of wet flies such as a Green Peter on the bob, an Invicta, and a Connemara Black up to size 8.'

Peter O'Reilly has now written a very comprehensive book on the Irish loughs entitled *The Trout and Salmon Loughs of Ireland*. There is also an excellent Tourist Board Guide costing £1 and entitled *Ireland – Freshwater Game Angling*. This booklet gives details of addresses of all Regional Fisheries Boards, as well as the two main information sources: Department of Tourism, Fisheries, and Forestry, Fisheries Administration, Leeson Lane, Dublin 2; and Central Fisheries Board, Balnagowan House, Mobhi Boreen, Glasnevin, Dublin 9.

Isle of Man

The Isle of Man has a number of small lakes and reservoirs stocked with rainbows. There are also some pleasant little streams with wild brown trout as I found during my wartime training there. There is also the chance of some big sea trout and some salmon. While not worth a visit for trout fishing alone, it is sensible to take a rod if you go there as there is reasonable trout fishing within easy range of Douglas.

England

Turangi on Lake Taupo in New Zealand may boast the sign 'Trout Capital of the World'. More reticent Anglo-Saxons claim the city of Winchester as trout capital of England. Here Izaak Walton spent his last years, his little fishing hut in the Dean's garden having only recently fallen into decay and the house where he died, 7 The Close, having only recently been renovated. He rated Hampshire above all other counties of England for its 'clear, pleasant, fast, shallow streams and store of trouts'. The stained-glass window in the Walton Chapel shows him fishing the Itchen below St Catherine's Hill, and not far away at Droxford he would fish the similar-type Meon River, when living there earlier with his son-in-law, Prebendary Hawkins. The Meon, too, is a fine trout stream for dry-fly fishermen and has a run of large sea trout, like the Stour in

Kent, which also figures in the *Compleat Angler* for its unusually large trout.

Neither of these rivers, however, has quite the compelling attraction of Test or Itchen. The Itchen, which flows through Winchester, exercised, as it still does, a fascination for great names in angling. C. E. M. Skues, who developed nymph fishing, had his ashes scattered on its banks. Lord Grey of Fallodon, that delightful writer, had a 'Cabinet room' in the Fishing Lodge at Itchen Abbas, since Cabinet members had to come there to get much sense out of him if the fishing was at its peak. As the Prime Minister said of his Foreign Secretary, 'Lord Grey could have been anything he liked in public life, but preferred to waste his time fishing'. A very popular sense of priorities for a trout fisherman too!

Only nine miles from Winchester the prestigious Houghton Club has its base at the Grosvenor Hotel, with a wealth of old records in its club room there. The club controls miles of the Test, now so well stocked to maintain that 'great store of trouts' despite the fishing pressure. Not too much pressure for the Houghton Club, as it is limited to 23 members. The only American to have been a full member of the club was Ambassador Douglas, whose injudicious cast cost him the sight of an eye when fishing the Test for salmon.

Hampshire also abounds in small stillwater fisheries which take their water from chalk streams or springs and hold large stocked trout. The UK rainbow trout record was for a long time a 19-pound Avington trout, caught by Alan Pearson (who also took from one of its three lakes the record brook trout of close on 6 pounds). In 1986 Peter Cockwill pushed the record up to 20 pounds 7 ounces.

There are many other areas of England where trout fishing abounds: the Devon rivers, the Cotswolds, or that other area beloved of Walton, Dovedale. The Izaak Walton Hotel there is a good base for sampling some of that fishing even if you do not want to go as far as American, Robert G. Deindorfer, who followed Walton's footsteps and methods in recently writing *The Incompleat Angler, Fishing Izaak Walton's Favourite Rivers*. Deindorfer reminded us that, though under Charles Cotton's influence in Dovedale, Walton was a fine angler for 'trout and grayling in clear streams', he was also a 'celebrated old wormslinger' for whom all anglers were brothers. As Deindorfer sensibly added, 'If the old boy stretched the truth occasionally it strikes me that makes him an even more appropriate father figure for a cult whose members are often given to hyberbole'.

Trout fishing in England had been concentrated in localized areas, and often been priced at a figure which made it the preserve of the privileged. This has changed dramatically in the last fifty years with the explosion of reservoir trout fishing. Blagdon was the first to start the revolution. With their large trout and beautiful setting in the Mendips, Blagdon and the neighbouring Chew Valley Lake are still prominent. But there are now so many fine midland reservoirs like the compact Grafham and the formidable Rutland Water. In the north is another large stocked reservoir, Kielder, and the many natural waters of the Lake District hold good fish. In the south an ideal fishery for those who want to hop across from Europe for a couple of days' fishing is Bewl Water near Lamberhurst in Kent, a lake of character in a silvan setting. It is best fished with floating line and nymphs, or small traditional wet flies, but it will be equally kind to the sunk-line lure fisherman, particularly in early season. From bank or anchored boat black and green nymphs fished deep often do well.

With so much choice it would be invidious to select, but there are a few special places for me, apart from the Test and Itchen. The Wharfe from Grassington down is a Yorkshire river with a special appeal, not least in the remarkable variation of fishing there at weekends, with half the population appearing to be out walking the banks or camped in the dales, and the peaceful seclusion of midweek. Then you can pursue the plentiful trout and grayling with small lightly hackled flies, free from disturbance. Finally there is Avington Trout Fishery close to my Winchester home. Every angler needs a familiar water where he feels completely confident, completely at ease, at one with his surroundings. Avington is just that type of happy place for me. Some of the stock fish are easy early in the season. But thereafter it can be challenging fishing in the clearest of water where you can stalk individual fish or chuck and hope as you will. To stalk the big fish requires a special ability to spot them and present leaded flies at the right depth and the right speed and angle. They will not move for anything that is not in their cruising circle, and are usually larger and deeper than you think. I am pleased to have caught the occasional double-figure fish – a red-letter day once or twice a season. Others are more dedicated and expert at this specialist kind of fishing for big trout. Peter Cockwill, a fishing companion, who has just completed a book on how to catch trophy fish, is one such. In 1986 he went to Avington after a report that there were several big fish there which no-one could catch. That day his bag was a record four-fish limit of 51½ pounds.

A few days later he was looking for more large fish. 'Caught anything?' asked a fellow angler. 'Just one' drew the smug retort that the chance acquaintance had three already. How was he to know that Peter's 'one' was a new rainbow UK record of 20½ pounds. This was how he described the capture to me:

'As usual I was using a leaded Hare's Ear size 8. When I spotted the fish it was clear there would be a problem playing it as it was in a weedy area and close to trees on the bank. So first I had to get it to follow the fly and take just below me. Hooked under my rod tip I was able to hold it close in. Only that way could I put on enough strain to keep it from running for the weeds and breaking me.'

Within three weeks an even larger rainbow had been caught. One of 21¼ pounds was taken from Scotland's Loch Awe. Avington will no doubt be looking to better that, as will Peter Cockwill.

Most Englishmen have some such fishery which is enchanted for them, perhaps ordinary for others of different outlook, different temperament. For Donald Downs it is a different lake:

'Lullingstone and I first met in 1948, when I was a callow ex-soldier not long 'de-mobbed' and with the interest in fly fishing not yet blossomed into the great mellow tree in the garden of my life.... and she was a little lakelet threaded on the river Darent like a jewel, that lay along the valley at the front of the castle.

We next met early in the '60s. By this time gravel workings had extended her shores up the valley to the estate boundary, and kindly Nature had grassed and bushed the banks until it looked as if she had been clasped in the embrace of the hills since time began.

She had been taken over by an Angling Society, and stocked, tended and cherished. She seemed to revel in this treatment and attention, yet often behaved like a capricious jade towards those of us who endeavoured to take her trout.

In my book there is no greater joy in angling than to read the water, choose the right fly, outwit the fish and bring him to the net. But oh how that joy is magnified tenfold if all this is done in rolling pastoral surroundings – with great sleepy trees suckling along the flanks of the downland and smiling Lullingstone with all her giggling ripples dimpling along in the breeze.

In the last twenty-three years, I have fished Lullingstone in April's sleet and snow, Summer's balmy days and sudden showers and Autumn's golden glow, when leaves go scurrying in a last frolic, and Earth draws them as a shawl about her, ready to sleep away the dour days of Winter. Seldom, despite excellent stocking, has she given her fish to me easily.

Occasionally she plays impish tricks; sometimes my fishing companion Joe and I have fished a drift in our cockleshell of a boat, using the same tactics, identical tackle and the same flies. I blank, he has a brace. On other occasions, the reverse will happen.

Many a long evening have we spent trying to unravel this over our pewter tankards – while Lullingstone and the stars exchange winks.

For some years, in the pile of hats on my shelf, there lay a friendly old cloth cap that sprouted a great collection of flies. It is sadly now long consigned to the dustbin after an over-enthusiastic drying in front of the fire. It served as a reminder of a particular evening at Lullingstone.

Usually flies after drying out are replaced in boxes – but not this lot! I took the cap, flyless, one evening to fish. A gentle benign evening in late Summer, when Lullingstone smiled enticingly at me and the whole fly world and their wives seemed to be abroad. Fish humped, jumped, sucked, swirled, hoovered, bopped and clopped in a great excitement of supping.

After trying combinations of floating and sinktip lines together with various lengths of variously greased leaders, the tried and discarded flies slowly spread over the hat. Assorted dry sedges and pupae in several sizes sat cheek by jowl with a collection of buzzers and a couple of gnats. My pet aversions of caenis marched with an Invicta, a Wickham's Fancy and a small Dunkeld, while a couple of Pheasant Tails and a Pheasant Tail nymph conferred gravely with two Rough Olives and a Greenwell's Glory. A Deer Hair Moth kept its own council, while furtively under the fold by the peak there lurked a great black hairwing, with bulging ball-chain eyes. . . .

Oh Lullingstone, my greatest wish is that I may have a further twenty-three years to try and understand you.'

In Britain the available trout fishing is varied enough to suit all tastes and the many guidebooks are sufficiently comprehensive to allow informed selection.

Fly fishing is my own chief interest, so that has been the main concentration in this book. But trout may be taken by many legitimate methods and each angler has to choose what suits him best.

That is the right Waltonian sentiment shared by myself and certainly by Donald Downs. The last words should go to this President of the Fly Dressers Guild, who is the happiest of anglers. These are the verses he wrote after a recent re-reading of *The Compleat Angler*:

> I cast my angle where I might
> The season being permitting,
> A bag of fish is my delight
> With any bait that's fitting.
>
> A juicy lob or cheese for some
> A fly betimes for others
> Where'er the fishers' pleasures come
> All anglers should be brothers.

The brotherhood of trout fishermen is world-wide, their opportunities of pleasure limitless.

Index

82, 83, 84, 87, 93, 94, 101, 102, 103,
108, 109, 111, 119, 120, 122, 125, 133,
143, 152, 154, 157, 159, 178, 204, 209,
213, 226
black 226
damsel 189
Dormouse 92
dragonfly 7, 172, 182, 189, 191
Flashback 30
Gacka 94
green 8, 18, 226
Jig 25
Pheasant Tail 55
Prince 134
red and black 8
Ritz-D 55
Skues 105
stonefly 133, 134, 136
Teeny 132
wet 12
wet-fly 222
Yellow 172

Oliver, Mike 20, 21, 22, 29–30
olives 72, 76, 104, 108, 135, 157, 189,
223
Orkney 217
Osterreichische Fischereigesellschaft 81
Owaka 20

Pakistan 206–8
palmers 47, 220
Papua New Guinea 13–15
Paragon 215
Parson's Glory 21, 29, 182
Partridge fly 189
Paul Bunyon's '66' jig 146
Pavel, Janicek 111
Pawson, John 57, 81–7 *passim*
Pawson, Philip 197–203
Pawson, Tony 57, 80–7 *passim*
peacock flies 201, 202
Pêcheur Belge, Le 51
perch, red-fin 13
Peru 160
Peter Ross fly 178, 195
Peterson, Brian 219–20
Peverel of the Peak 20
Pheasant Tail Nymph 178, 195, 196
Pheasant Tail Spinner 105, 109
picket fence 24, 25, 26
Piggott, Terry 7, 13, 16
pike 68, 77, 82, 148
Plaisirs de la Pêche 58, 86
Platinum Blonde 151, 152
Poland 105–11
polaroids 4, 5, 13, 67, 194

Polish Angling Association 106, 110
Popper Bug 151
Porringe 182
Portugal 77–8
Price, Taff 89–94
Professional Guides Association of New
Zealand 18
Pyrenees, The 61–2, 75–7

'Queen's Chair' 17

Rabbit Fur Fly 5
Rainbow King Lodge, Alaska 148–9
rainbow trout (*salmo gairdneri*) xvii, xviii,
xix, 1, 7, 8, 10, 14, 21–30 *passim*,
43–58 *passim*, 65, 76, 77, 82, 84, 85,
91, 93, 94, 98, 99, 102, 103, 104,
107–13 *passim*, 118, 119, 131–8 *passim*,
142–6 *passim*, 149–59 *passim*, 169–73
passim, 177, 180, 181, 185–90 *passim*,
194, 205, 206, 209, 210, 211, 214, 216,
217
wild 147, 150
Reckinger, Mark 52
Red Eye spoons 145
Red Palmer 220
Red Setter 21, 24, 29
Red Tag 49, 51, 107
Red-Tipped Governer 20
releasing fish 141–2
Resch, Reinhard 81–8
Rio Grande 152–5
Ritz, Charles 104
Robin Fly (black and red) 9
Romania 112–14
Ministry of Forestry 113
National Tourism Office 114
Rotorua Trout Fishing Guide 17
Royal Coachman 92
Royal Wulff 20, 21
Russia 114

Sakuramasu trout 209
Salmo platycephalus xviii
salmon 2, 33, 34, 37, 38, 39, 43, 44, 47, 48,
63, 110, 131, 146, 150, 213, 216, 217,
219
Atlantic 150, 151, 152
Danubian (*Hucho hucho*) 93, 108
hunyani 185
lake (*barilus microcephalus* or *barilus
microlepsis*) 186
Pacific 138, 140, 144, 147
silver 149
*Salmon and Trout Fishing Holidays in
Britain* 212
Salmon Ponds of Plenty 3